An Introduction to Aesthetics

Introducing Philosophy

Introducing Philosophy is a series of textbooks designed to introduce the basic topics of philosophy for any student approaching the subject for the first time. Each volume presents a central subject of philosophy by considering the key issues and outlooks associated with the area. With the emphasis firmly on the arguments for and against a philosophical position, the reader is encouraged to think philosophically about the subject.

An Introduction to Aesthetics

Dabney Townsend

First published 1997
Reprinted 1998

Blackwell Publishers Inc.
350 Main Street
Malden , Massachusetts 02148
USA

Blackwell Publishers Ltd
108 Cowley Road
Oxford OX4 1JF
UK

Library of Congress Cataloging-in-Publication Data

Townsend, Dabney, 1941–
        An introduction to aesthetics / Dabney Townsend.
        p.   cm. — (Introducing philosophy)
        Includes bibliographical references and index.
        ISBN 1–55786–730–5 (alk. paper). — ISBN 1–55786–731–3 (alk.
    paper)
        1.   Aesthetics.   I. Title.   II. Series.
    BH39.T635   1997
    111'85—dc20
                                                                96–38819
                                                                CIP
British Library Cataloguing in Publication Data

A CIP catalogue record for this book is available from the British Library.

Typeset in 10 on 12pt Bembo
by Graphicraft Typesetters Ltd, Hong Kong
Printed in Great Britain by MPG Books, Bodmin, Cornwall.

This book is printed on acid-free paper

Contents

List of Acknowledgements

The Author and Publisher are grateful for permission to reproduce the following copyright material.

William Shakespeare, extract from *Hamlet* Act 2, Scene 2 from *Hamlet: A Norton Critical Edition*, by William Shakespeare, second edition, edited by Cyrus Hoy. Copyright 1992, 1963 by W.W. Norton & Company, Inc. Reprinted by permission of W.W. Norton & Company, Inc.

Sir Thomas Wyatt, 'Who so List to Hunt' in *Collected Poems of Sir Thomas Wyatt*, edited by Kenneth Muir, Mass: Harvard University Press, 1963. Reprinted by permission of Routledge and Kegan Paul, Ltd., UK.

Introduction

This book is an introduction to aesthetics and the philosophy of art. Philosophers did not begin to use the word 'aesthetics' until the eighteenth century.[1] Then, it began to appear as a term to describe the whole area of feeling, as opposed to reason.[2] A conflict between feeling or emotion and reason is one of the oldest problems in philosophy. Usually, philosophy defends reasoned argument and rejects emotion. In the renaissance and seventeenth century, however, individual minds tended to replace a universal reason as the authority for knowing. But individuals are not simply reasoning machines. Philosophical rationalists thought that pure reason made up of clear and distinct ideas linked by the mind

1 In philosophy there is an important distinction between using a word and mentioning it. For example, in the preceding sentence 'philosophy' is used, but in this sentence it is mentioned. Conventional practice is to enclose a word that is mentioned in single quotation marks unless the context is so clear that they are not required. Double quotation marks are used for all other occurrences, including calling attention to a special meaning of a word, except for a quotation within a quotation, where single quotation marks are used for the internal quotation to avoid confusion.

2 No book that claims to be an introduction to its subject can or should be wholly original. It must present a variety of positions that are well known in the area to be introduced. At the same time, it is awkward to burden an introductory text with footnotes to attribute each position to its proper sources or to try to trace the history of a philosophical argument through its variations. Moreover, by now many of the positions referred to have achieved considerable circulation. They have been discussed and modified any number of times. The positions outlined in this text are often composites. Where a distinct version of a theory is referred to, it is still presented in a condensed, summary fashion. I will adopt the expedient of relegating attributions to the end of each chapter, therefore, where the reader will find reference material combined with suggestions for further reading. Notes at the foot of pages will be limited to brief clarifications or cross-references. For the origin of the term 'aesthetic,' therefore, see the "References and Suggestions for Further Reading" section at the end of this introduction.

into logical chains was the true form of knowledge. Even rationalists had to admit that human beings had another side to them, however. Aesthetics arose as an attempt to provide a positive account of the role played by feelings and emotions in human thinking.

At about the same time, our modern concepts of fine arts – the arts of music, painting, poetry, dance, etc. – began to be more clearly distinguished from crafts and the decorative and useful arts. The idea that some arts should be regarded as fine arts, that they are basic to culture, and that they represent finer feelings is a relatively recent idea. The arts themselves existed in classical cultures, of course, but they were treated either as adjuncts to some other institution – the state, religion, the court – or as ornaments and decorative embellishments. Craftsmen and artists were not sharply distinguished, except in poetry, which sometimes had a special function as the voice of the gods. The changing conception of the individual that began in the renaissance and continued through the seventeenth and eighteenth centuries gave individual artists and their art a status that they could not achieve as long as artists were basically craftsmen and their art was a means to some other cultural or institutional end.

Once the fine arts were promoted to a special place in culture, a particular kind of feeling was especially associated with art, so that gradually we have come to use 'aesthetic' as a generic term not only for certain special feelings but for all of our relations to art as well. In that sense, aesthetics is not restricted to post-eighteenth-century philosophy. The term itself is anachronistic before the eighteenth century, but we need a term to cover both the philosophy of the arts and our responses to art and nature. In this book I will use 'aesthetic' in the broadest possible sense to indicate all of the underlying concepts and feelings that form our experience of art and nature in its art-like appearances.

Philosophers use 'aesthetics' to refer to a discipline of reasoned discourse like ethics or epistemology (knowing). The subject of aesthetics may be an intuition, feeling, or emotion, but aesthetics itself is a part of philosophy and is subject to the same demands for evidence and logically controlled argumentation that characterize all philosophy. In that sense, aesthetics should be able to account for all of the phenomena of its field, though there may be many different theories that compete within the discipline. If two theories both claim to explain the same facts, and they are not reducible to each other, then at some point they must be inconsistent. They cannot both be true. In principle, only one correct theory is possible, though no practical arrogance is implied by that claim. Possibly neither is true, of course, and perhaps theories themselves should not be considered true or false but only more or less adequate to some task. Nevertheless, the theories of philosophical aesthetics are in competition with each other.

We should say a word about how philosophers use the term 'theory' to be sure that there are no misunderstandings. In some common ways of speaking, 'theory' refers to something that is yet to be established. Holmes might have a theory about how the crime was committed, but he then must prove who did it. Once the culprit is identified, his theory is no longer a theory. It has become fact. Philosophers and scientists use 'theory' in a different sense, however. A theory is a high-level explanation that ties together many facts and guides our investigations toward further, as yet unobserved, phenomena. Newton's theory of gravitational attraction accounts for all of the cases of falling bodies and also explains weightlessness in space, something that Newton could not observe. Theories are judged by how much they explain correctly without any incorrect assertions and how far they can be extended. Individual observation sentences are true or false. "This book has a red cover" is true if (and only if) this book does in fact have a red cover. Theories cannot conflict with observation sentences and be acceptable theories. If a theory requires that some observation is one way and it is not in fact that way, the theory is wrong. So we can say that theories are true or false depending on the truth or falsity of the observations that they include and that they predict. It might be better to say that a theory is adequate or inadequate, however. True and false do not have degrees; a sentence is either true or false. But theories are better or worse, good or bad. While two theories may be incompatible, a more comprehensive theory can take account of several more limited theories.

When we speak of an aesthetic theory in philosophy, we are trying to give an explanatory account of the fine arts and natural beauty. One theory, for example, claims that all art is a form of imitation. That theory has then to go on to make clear what 'imitation' means, how it applies to individual arts like poetry and architecture, and how it accounts for what artists, critics, and art appreciators experience. If it can do all of that, it is a good theory. Yet it still might give way to a better theory that can explain more. In philosophy and science, what we want is the best theory that we can construct. So a theory is our goal. Unlike Holmes, we will never replace theory with something else that is not theoretical but factual, because our theories are just ways of arranging and accounting for all of the facts that we know of. Aesthetic theory can exist without the concept of aesthetic experience or feeling as long as feelings are not considered part of the phenomena that need to be explained. When, in the renaissance and afterward, feeling is recognized as something closely related to art, new theories must be formed to account for the wider scope of what must be explained. Our task, as philosophers, is to construct such theories and evaluate their success or failure. Or, as some have argued, if art and aesthetic feeling are not the kind of thing that theory can ever explain, we must construct a philosophical theory that explains why aesthetic feeling cannot be explained. (Skeptics do the same thing when they try to explain why certainty is impossible in knowing.) Either way, philosophical aesthetics is about reasons and evidence that apply to aesthetic theories.

Artists and art historians, on the other hand, tend to speak of many different aesthetics depending on the kind of art and style that is being exhibited. So, for example, they think of a new aesthetic as arising with each revolution in art. The idea is that new art forms require new approaches and produce new feelings. In that case, there could be many compatible aesthetics. For example, a medieval aesthetic promotes feelings of awe and clarity. It requires recognizable symbols such as haloes, but it is not concerned that things look in the painting as they appear to the eye. By way of contrast, an impressionist aesthetic seeks to match perception with painting. As the light changes, so does the painting. Thus Claude Monet (1840–1926) paints repeated views of the cathedral at Rouen. The subject of his paintings is as much the light itself as the building. Different responses to these styles can be characterized as different aesthetic visions. One might have a taste for one or the other (or both), and be said to include or exclude that aesthetic from one's own perception.

This is a book on philosophical aesthetics, so we will follow the philosophical practice and speak as if a single aesthetic theory is our goal. Modesty will prohibit our making too strong a claim to have actually supplied it. The more diverse usage common to artists is not wrong, however. We can say the same things that are meant by multiple aesthetics by using words like 'style' and 'way of seeing.' Instead of saying that Monet produced a new aesthetic, therefore, we would say that he was part of a revolution in style based on a new way of seeing in art. The point is that as philosophers we want to operate at a higher level of generality than is common for artists and art historians, but we are talking about the same things.

Aesthetics must be based on observations about art, about the feelings and ideas that art produces, and about the specific interpretations and kinds of interpretations that art elicits. Thus aesthetics depends on facts from art history, on observations about perception and how we know through our senses, and on reflections on the language that we use to talk about both art and our responses to it. Inevitably, aesthetics must refer to examples, therefore. Yet aesthetics is not the same thing as art history or criticism. They supply its data, but aesthetics goes on to try to understand what possibilities are implied by the facts about art and criticism and what judgments in the realm of the arts are. Aesthetics also reaches beyond art to nature and perhaps to a larger picture of perception and sensory awareness. In some of its theories, aesthetics is indistinguishable from theories about what there is and how we know it more generally (metaphysics and epistemology). In the following pages, we will range freely over examples from many arts. We must always try to keep focused on the theoretical task, however, even if what we are doing is to challenge the existence of theory in its traditional forms as applicable to aesthetics.

Our first task will be to get clear about what the basic forms of aesthetic questions and aesthetic language involve. Then we will see what kinds of evidence we can assemble. Some of this analysis will take us very close to specific works of art. On that basis, we will then examine three relations: the relation of an artist to a work of art; the relation of a work of art to its audience; and finally, the way that an artist and an audience are mutually constitutive of each other. A certain amount of repetition is inevitable as we approach many of the same facts from different perspectives and with different questions in mind.

Roughly, we will distinguish three kinds of aesthetic theories that have been successful at one time or another and that still compete for our philosophical attention. The first we will call participatory aesthetics. Its central theoretical term is 'beauty,' and it holds that the ultimate aesthetic goal is to participate in or be united with that which is beautiful. It has taken many forms, but its strongest influence was in classical theories based on imitation and form. It is most successful in dealing with nature and the larger, cosmic significance claimed for art.

The second we can call a theory of aesthetic experience. It holds that aesthetics is marked off by some unique kind of experience that is felt directly. The evidence is to be found in our individual senses. Those senses are understood either as additional ways of perceiving or as modifications of our basic sensory awareness. So the theory depends on concepts such as an aesthetic attitude, aesthetic perception, and aesthetic intuitions. As a theory, it is most successful in dealing with the kind of feelings and personal significance that we associate with fine art. Its central theoretical term is usually 'expression.'

Finally, an alternative form of theory altogether also claims to be empirical, but in a different, more historical sense. It looks not to purely individual experience but to the relations produced within what is called the art world – the complex of artists, their audience, and the various institutions like museums and art schools that support the arts. It is strongest in accounting for the shifting historical forms of art and response. It looks to the relations of artist and audience and emphasizes the importance of reception or aesthetic response over imitation or expression.

Our task is not to make a final choice among these theories, though inevitably any philosophical discussion involves taking positions that favor one theory over another. Philosophy works by a kind of trial by combat. Each theory must be defended and attacked to see how it will hold up. A complete refutation comes only when the field changes to such an extent that a theory no longer has any defenders. For example, no one in physics any longer believes in a subtle ether that transmits energy because too many phenomena are left out by that theory. A crucial experiment is one that shows finally that a theory cannot explain something or that its explanation is incorrect. A complete triumph for a theory is much less likely, however. Instead, theories grow to a certain point and then are surpassed by others that supersede them. We should not expect any contest between aesthetic theories to be finally settled by the kind of arguments and examples that are available to us, but that does not mean that we cannot argue for or against a theory. The process of argumentation is philosophy's version of the experimental method in science.

The position of this book is oriented toward postmodern theories of response and institutional activity. But more important than choosing one theory is understanding what aesthetic theory is, whether and to what extent it is possible, and, finally, what the alternatives are. The position of this book will be that that can be done only by keeping firmly in contact with the actual history of art, criticism, and the developments of culture, including our own popular culture. Beyond that, any conclusions will be strictly provisional. There are good arguments and bad arguments. Facts matter. To lose sight of the difference between a good argument and a bad argument, between sound and unsound arguments, and between what is and what is not the case in the art world is to cease to be a philosopher. But neither arguments nor facts should be expected to settle once and for all philosophical disputes that have continued throughout the history of our discipline. The only true failure would be to miss the possibility of understanding by not trying to understand. In that respect, alone, what follows is intended as a guide.

References and Suggestions for Further Reading

One of the joys of aesthetics is the scope of work that it includes. Philosophy, criticism, literary history, art history, and cultural analysis are all grist for its mills. Problems in aesthetics overlap problems of the philosophy of language and philosophical logic (e.g. fictions, metaphor, definitions), metaphysics and ontology (e.g. the ontological status of the work of art, of beauty), and epistemology (e.g. authorial intent, truth in literature). One can be overwhelmed with such riches, however. In these sections of "References and Suggestions for Further Reading," I make no attempt to provide a complete bibliography. Instead, I include those works that I most clearly had in mind in writing the relevant section of the text, including especially work to which specific reference is made. Then I also include some suggestions for further reading, both background and contemporary.

Philosophy is a discipline that operates first of all through professional journals. Books tend to come later and to sum up much work that has gone before. For the beginning student, however, the journal literature is intimidating. Therefore I have tried, as much as possible, to limit citations of journals to those required by academic honesty and those that are readily available in one or more introductory anthologies. Given a choice, I have tended to favor older articles because they lay down the foundation that later discussion presumes. I have tried to provide a selection of recent books that seem relevant, however. Those interested in pursuing the matter need only follow the trail of footnotes and references to fill in the gaps.

A number of useful anthologies that provide easy access to important historical and contemporary sources are available. They include H. Gene Blocker and John Bender, *Contemporary Philosophies of Art* (Englewood Cliffs, NJ: Prentice-Hall, 1992); George Dickie, Richard J. Sclafani, and Ronald Roblin, *Aesthetics: A Critical Anthology* (New York: St Martin's Press, 1989); Albert Hofstadter and Richard Kuhn, *Philosophy of Art and Beauty* (Chicago: University of Chicago Press, 1976); John Hospers, *Introductory Readings in Aesthetics* (New York: Free Press, 1969); Joseph Margolis, *Philosophy Looks at the Arts* (Philadelphia: Temple University Press, 1987); Alex Neill and Aaron Ridley, *The Philosophy of Art: Readings Ancient and Modern* (New York: McGraw-Hill, 1995); Melvin Rader, *A Modern Book of Esthetics* (New York: Harcourt, Brace, 1979); Stephen David Ross, *Art and its Significance* (Albany, NY: State University of New York Press, 1984); and Dabney Townsend, *Aesthetics: Classic Readings from the Western Tradition* (Boston: Jones & Bartlett, 1996).

The word 'aesthetics' is first used philosophically to refer to feelings as opposed to clear and distinct ideas by A. G. Baumgarten, *Reflections on Poetry* (first publ. 1735; Berkeley: University of California Press, 1954). The thesis that the fine arts emerge in their modern form in the eighteenth century can be traced to Paul Oskar Kristeller, "The Modern System of the Arts," repr. in Peter Kivy, ed., *Essays on the History of Aesthetics* (Rochester: University of Rochester Press, 1992) and elsewhere. The triangular arrangement of artist, work of art, and audience adopted in chapters 3–5 below is found in M. H. Abrams, *The Mirror and the Lamp* (Oxford: Oxford University Press, 1953).

1

Language About Art and the Aesthetic

Getting Started

Beauty

What is beauty? By asking such a question, we enter the area of aesthetics and the philosophy of art. But why ask such an odd question? If beauty is something, it is not the kind of thing that we normally think of as an object. It is more like a property – like redness or heaviness. But properties of objects have two characteristics that beauty seems to lack. First, we can say what makes an object red or heavy. It is red because it reflects light of a certain wavelength. It is heavy because it has a certain mass. Its reflectivity and mass are, in turn, caused by what it is made of – its physical construction. Chemistry and physics can teach us about such properties, and we can predict how any object will look and feel to a normal observer as a result. Second, virtually everyone agrees when an object is red and heavy. Disagreement is easily resolved by examining the observer or conditions of observation. John is color blind, so he does not see normally. Mary is uncommonly strong, so she does not find the same objects heavy as others do. Or the light is peculiar. Gravity on the moon is not so strong. Our observations of common properties are founded on the way the objects are and the conditions under which we observe them. We have no need to ask "What is redness?" because when it is present we see just see it. Its presence is obvious. Talk of redness is just a shorthand for our common ways of referring to objects that we see as red.

Beauty seems to be a property as well. It appears in the same place in sentences as more ordinary properties. "The sky is red, and it is beautiful," we say. But we cannot account for beauty in the same way that we account for other properties. There is no physics or chemistry of beauty; and, even more disturbingly, normal observers disagree about beauty. Yet we continue to say that some objects are beautiful and that others are not. So the question "What is beauty?" seems to need an answer in a way that "What is redness?" does not.

It remains an odd question, however. If we call some things beautiful and deny that others are, we should be able to give an account of what we mean. We seem to know. Some sunsets are beautiful. Others are merely ordinary. Some poems are beautiful. Others are downright bad. Some things, such as bleeding, mangled bodies in an accident, seem to be impossible to call beautiful. Many others are matters of individual preference. (We will have occasion to question all of these judgments later in this book.)

We usually feel no need to give reasons for what we say when the reasons would be more obscure than what we have already said. "What is redness?" is that way. If pressed, we can give reasons for saying that "the car is red," but we feel no need to, and the question "What do you mean by calling it red?" seems unnecessary as a result. If pressed about beauty, we have difficulty giving reasons at all (or good ones, at least), yet we feel no discomfort in our judgments. Now the question seems doubly odd – because it seems needless, and because it should not seem that way.

One solution is to try to make the question go away. We might admit that our talk about beauty is only a manner of speaking. It just seems to be about some property. On this view, what we are really doing when we say that something is beautiful is praising it. We are saying something like "I like this object because of the way it appears to me." Many of our sentences that use 'beauty' and 'beautiful' do seem paraphrasable in that way. "The sunset is beautiful" would just be a way of saying that I like the appearance of the sunset. If someone seems to disagree, then they are not really disagreeing with me but expressing their different feeling about the appearance. The two sentences, "the sunset is beautiful" and "the sunset is not beautiful," would not really contradict each other (i.e. they can in fact both be true)[1] because they are about different speakers. "I feel positive about the sunset" contradicts "I do not feel positive about the sunset" only if 'I' refers to the same person at the same

---

1 Contradictions are best thought of as the incompatibility of sentences. Two sentences are contradictory when the truth of one implies the falsity of the other. We have a great tolerance for incompatibility in our ordinary lives. We believe and assert all sorts of contradictory things, both by accident and because it is easier to live with. ("Why, sometimes I've believed as many as six impossible things before breakfast," the White Queen tells Alice in *Alice Through the Looking Glass*.) But knowingly to assert a contradiction is to give up rational thinking. It can be done, but the price we pay is irrationality.

time. That would make giving reasons a very different task. The reasons why I like or dislike something are more about me than they are about the object. The appropriate reasons would respond to the question "Why do you like that?" instead of "What makes that beautiful?" It is often enough to answer the 'why' question by saying "I just do." In many cases, preferences are just matters of individual psychology.

There are a couple of reasons for thinking that this solution will not do in all cases. First, some of our seeming disagreements do not go away so easily. I do not just like the painting reproduced on the cover of this book. I think it is beautiful. If you do not consider it beautiful, I think that we disagree about more than our likes and dislikes. We disagree about what kinds of things are beautiful. Such disagreements may not be earth-shaking. I can still find you a normal, admirable human being even though you do not agree with me about what is beautiful. But I would not trust your judgments about beauty the way I might trust someone else's. And I think that in this area, you lack some ability or insight that others have.

Second, if 'beauty' is only an expression of preference, it is hard to see why we should continue to speak about beauty at all. The language of beauty would have to have arisen as a kind of linguistic mistake. At one time, people believed there was something called beauty or some property of things that made them beautiful. When those people said "The sunset is beautiful" they were trying to refer to something. But they failed to do more than express their feelings of approval. Once a mistake is pointed out, it seems foolish to go on making it. Once upon a time, people believed in ghosts. They referred to ghosts. But there are no ghosts, and what people were really doing was expressing their fear in some situations. When we cease to believe in ghosts, we stop talking about them (except in fictional situations where we pretend to believe). But I feel no need to give up talking about beauty. So presumably I still believe that there is more to beauty than just my approval. I may be mistaken, but I am not yet ready to admit my mistake.

Possibly, we should restrict the use of the word 'beauty,' however. Words presume a whole complex of associated ideas. When we speak of gravity, for example, the word, 'gravity,' assumes the complex of physical theories that explain the attractions between bodies. Expecting to find some object called gravity is a linguistic mistake. There is no such *thing* as gravity. But gravity is an ordinary enough phenomenon nevertheless. Physics tells us how to fit the concept into our other language. Even when we use 'gravity' in a metaphorical way – when we say "Her sense of humor interfered with her gravity" – the metaphor is built on ideas of attraction of bodies and weightiness. We mean something like

"She does not show enough seriousness about important subjects." Some uses of 'beauty' are like that. They were supported by theories, and if we no longer accept the theories we would have to give up the literal use of the word as well.

Some evidence that that is what has taken place can be found. We are much less likely now than were earlier audiences to presume that all art should be beautiful. Are abstract paintings beautiful? Somehow that seems the wrong description. Is Hamlet's speech "What a piece of work is man" beautiful?[2] I would say that it is important, challenging, thought-provoking, disturbing. But beautiful? Not in any simple sense. So perhaps the idea that beauty is what artists create when they make works of art was only part of one theory of art. As we come to think of art differently, we do not use the word 'beauty' so often. Some works of art, like the one reproduced on the cover of this book, would still be properly described as beautiful, but other words would be used for other works of art. 'Beauty' becomes one descriptive word among others, and it is by no means the most important one today. We are less tempted in that case to think of beauty as some property, like redness, that some objects have and others lack.

Historically, beauty has played a central role in some theories. As an exercise, let's see how a theory that makes beauty central might look. This is a kind of thought experiment. We want to think up a theory, even though we may not accept it, that might account for the aesthetic use of the word 'beauty.' Since we are only experimenting, not writing history, we will use elements from a number of classical theories of beauty without trying to follow one philosopher's theory exactly. When we have finished we will have an example, though not necessarily one we find convincing.

Think of the universe not as a kind of machine but as an organism whose parts are controlled by a single soul. Such an organic universe is one great whole. All of its parts are related and combined in a harmonious relation. When that relation is disturbed, the whole is disordered and chaotic. We might say that it is ugly. When the whole is harmoniously related and every part is in its place, we might say that the whole is beautiful. Beauty is then a cosmological or metaphysical principle of order and relation. "God is in his heaven and all's right with the world." Beauty can be thought of in such theories as a property not just of individual objects but of the greater whole as well. Beauty is something in the sense that only one order is complete and best. The little beauties of individual objects are miniature orders reflecting the one great beauty.

2 See the appendix at the end of the book for Hamlet's speech.

We can call this a metaphysical theory of beauty. 'Metaphysical' here means that the theory tries to place something in the larger context of everything that there is. A metaphysical theory gives an account not just of individual things (this flower) and of individual kinds of things (daffodils), but also of what individual things and individual kinds of things are in relation to all of the kinds of things that there are or even could be. The particular metaphysical theory we are now describing includes beauty as one of the important properties of the whole. 'Beauty' is not just one descriptive term among others; it is a description of the final level of what there is. Beauty, truth, and virtue or goodness are intrinsic properties of an ordered reality. Without them, the whole disintegrates.

Let's see how this is supposed to work for beauty. Music may be the most important art form on this view. Music is formed from the harmony and rhythm of sounds. Without harmony, sound lacks order.[3] The ordered harmony of sound is found in precise mathematical relations of particular sounds. Those relations are believed to exist not just for the physical sounds we hear but for the same mathematical relations between all of the bodies that make up the universe. Classical philosophers assigned great importance to knowing and understanding these mathematical relations. So 'harmony' describes individual musical works, but it also describes in the same way the properties of anything that can be described by orderly mathematical relationships. That is virtually everything. We might speak quite literally of the music of the spheres. Harmony is then a fundamental property of beauty. Harmonious things are beautiful. Things lacking harmony are experienced as ugly. 'Beauty' is the generic term for the exhibition of the order and harmony in the universe.

Having begun with music, we can include other forms of art. Stories and poems also rely on rhythm and harmony. This was particularly true when stories were primarily told and poems recited. Oral literature depends very heavily on the sounds and repetitions of formulas and patterns. Painting too depends on ordered relations. Some colors go together; others clash. A painting of a thing is related to what it is a painting of by reproducing the order of the parts. Dance is ordered movement. Architecture is ordered building. Once again, mathematics describes the proper relation of the parts so that a building will be both structurally sound and beautiful to the eye. We can bring all art forms under the basic paradigm of music by relating harmony to mathematical order and beauty to the possession of harmonious structure.

A movement from beautiful art to beauty in nature is easy on this

---

3 This is not strictly true, of course. Contemporary music may get its order from other sources than harmony and rhythm. I am thinking here of classical forms of music.

theory because fundamentally the universe as a whole is beautiful. Natural beauty is just that harmonious order that exists as a result of the way nature is ordered rather than as the result of artificially imposed construction. For this theory to work, nature must be orderly. If we think of the universe as a random arrangement with no underlying order, then even if some order is imposed, it will not be able to survive. But if nature is itself harmonious, then it is enough for art to follow nature.

This is only an example. The metaphysics that makes beauty an intrinsic part of the order of the universe and thinks of abstract entities like beauty and goodness as real forms has its origins in the works of Plato (427–347 BCE). Socrates (469–399 BCE) may be regarded as the first philosopher in the western, rational sense of philosophy, but Socrates wrote nothing. The dialogues in which Socrates figures are the work of his disciples, particularly Plato, and they form the first significant foundation of western philosophy. For Plato, the highest forms, beauty, truth, and goodness, are the reality in which all other things participate. Whatever there is in the universe is connected to its forms, and ultimately to the highest forms. The parts of Plato's philosophy having to do with beauty are adopted and expanded later, particularly by Plotinus (204–70 CE), who argues that unity or oneness is the organizing principle of reality, and beauty is a product of that oneness as it appears in the world. Classical theories of art and beauty expand and develop the basic principles of Plato and Plotinus, so that 'beauty' is the central descriptive term for most theories of art prior to the renaissance.

Elements of a theory of beauty derived from Plato and Plotinus can be found in many classical philosophers, and it still has great appeal. It explains why 'beauty' is a generic term within those theories of art. But it solves our problems about beauty only if we are able to believe in the metaphysical implications of mathematical relations and the organic, holistic nature of the universe. The success of science in the seventeenth and eighteenth centuries gave plausibility to the continued use of mathematical relations, but it located them in different paradigms. It suggested that the universe is a kind of machine. A machine only works if it accomplishes something. Order just for the sake of order is subordinate to the ends to be accomplished, and those ends require different explanations. The term 'beauty' recedes in importance as the metaphor of a machine replaces that of a body in describing what there is. If there is no end at all, the machine seems useless, not beautiful. But that is another story.

The thought experiment we have just tried illustrates how beauty can be a part of a metaphysical system and get its use and support from belief in that system. This experiment teaches us that our uses of aesthetic language depend on the larger network of beliefs and theories that we accept. When those theories and beliefs change, our language must change with them. When it does not, the continued use of words like 'beauty' becomes odd in some contexts. So the oddness of the question "What is beauty?" arises from its continued use after our beliefs about the world have changed. We must be careful about what our words imply if we are not to confuse ourselves by our own language.

Taste

Let's begin again and examine a different approach to our talk about art and the aesthetic. Our problems with beauty arise because we find it difficult to believe in the kind of world in which 'beauty' is the primary theoretical term. Why, we might ask, is that? What limits our use of 'beauty'? Part of the problem, clearly, is our belief that each of us is a competent judge of what should be called beautiful. On many matters, we are prepared to defer to others who are more expert. We expect matters to be settled by facts attested to by knowledgable people. If a jeweler tells me that my ring is zirconium and not a diamond, I may think, "It looks like a diamond to me," but I will defer to the jeweler's expertise. If critics tell me that something is beautiful, I am much less likely to defer to their judgment. If it looks beautiful to me, that is an end of the matter. I am satisfied with my own judgment. Some judgments are based on our own feelings. Others are based on what we take to be the facts about the world. Factual judgments cannot depend solely on one person's perception. How I feel depends only on my perception. Whether I have cancer or not is a matter of fact; whether I hurt or not is a matter of how I feel.

When beauty ceases to regarded as a matter of fact about the world, its usefulness decreases. We have a different aesthetic language that more accurately describes our feelings. This is the language of taste. We use 'taste' in a number of different ways. It is used to express value-judgments. To say that someone has good or bad taste is to characterize their aesthetic abilities. To say that a work is in good or bad taste is to characterize that work's appeal. So 'taste' tends to imply goodness or badness as well. This is a natural enough usage. Ordinary taste also tends to include values. Things taste good or bad. We are seldom neutral about what we taste. Just because something has little taste does not mean that it does not taste good. Neutrality is a good taste in water, for example. However, the associations with goodness and badness are subordinate to a more basic sense of taste.

Taste is a sense. Like smell, sight, hearing, and touch, taste is a primary form of input into our mental systems. We encounter the world through our senses. Though we may be more or less acute in perceiving through our senses, we do not control that input. I cannot voluntarily choose how something tastes or smells. I may want a red car, but if it looks black, my desires do not change its looks. At the same time, no one else can experience my senses for me. Something may actually be green, but if I am red–green color blind, it will look red to me. Someone else can tell me that it is really green, but they cannot convince me that it looks green to me if it does not. So we cannot control our senses by our desires (except in abnormal cases of hallucination), and we cannot be corrected in our senses by others. These are the properties that make 'taste' seem a useful term for aesthetics.

The more fundamental sense of an aesthetic taste arises when we rely on our own judgment but also acknowledge that the object of our perception is beyond our control. Aesthetic taste is like ordinary taste to that extent. My aesthetic taste tells me that I respond to some object in a certain way; the object produces the taste in me, but it is uniquely my taste. To have a taste for something usually implies a close relation between the person whose taste is involved and the object. Both perception and attraction are involved. If I have a taste for peas, I will select them from among other vegetables, and I will be aware of their properties. If I lack a taste for jazz, I will neither listen to it nor be particularly aware of its nuances. I will not hear much of what is going on aesthetically. It is not just that I like or dislike it. I could have a taste for something that is not pleasant. I can have a taste for bitter greens. (Whether all preferences are reducible to some form of pleasure is an interesting question to which we will return later. For now, we note only that "finding pleasant" is not the same as "having a taste for.") I can have a taste for abstract art or tragedy that challenges me and makes me think without feeling any need to characterize them as pleasant. 'Taste' means that I respond to something in a way that is controlled by the object but is specific to me. If I have no taste for comedy, I miss the jokes. If I have no taste for music, I hear only noise. But when I do have a taste for something, denying its effects is pointless. I just hear the B flat or see the coherence of pictorial forms.

'Taste' tended to replace 'beauty' as the central aesthetic term because aesthetic taste was thought of literally as an additional sense. The word 'taste' was asked to do double duty. It applied to the sense arising from direct contact with the tongue, and it also applied to the additional sense that responded to the aesthetic properties of objects. The shift from beauty to taste may be regarded as part of a larger historical shift. In the seventeenth and eighteenth centuries, individual sense replaced the authority of a universal intelligence as the basis for our ability to know facts about ourselves and the world. The philosophical and scientific movement called empiricism limited knowledge to what our senses could supply and verify. Science developed rapidly as a result of this new way of thinking about the world, and philosophy followed and emulated the successful natural sciences. John Locke (1632–1704) laid down the foundations for philosophical empiricism at the end of the seventeenth century. According to Locke, all knowledge is ideas raised in us by experience. In aesthetics, Locke's new way of relying on experience was developed by Francis Hutcheson (1694–1746), who adopted an older idea of an internal sense and treated it as the basis for our knowledge in art and morality. Hutcheson's appeal to an aesthetic sense was rapidly adopted by other philosophers, and theories of taste and judgment appeared in many different forms. Artists from the renaissance onward had already been relying more heavily on their own senses and experience. Perspective and individuality in the visual arts and the presence of a narrator in literature show the increased empiricist influence. If we limit ourselves to what is given in our own experience, we have to learn about beauty by our senses. Taste was, in effect, the sense that accounted for beauty and any other aesthetic effects. That is why some writers could speak of a sense of beauty and mean literally what they said.

The reasons for making taste into an aesthetic sense are complex historically. Sight might seem a more appropriate sense. We tend to think of sight as the most important sense, for example. But sight gives a priority to visual forms. Aesthetic experience is not limited to scenery and painting. Hearing would give a similar priority to music and oral literature. Taste involves us in no such priorities, though it must be distinguished from merely physical taste. The art of cooking and eating was not included among the fine arts when that concept developed. The fine arts – music, painting, sculpture, literature – were distinguished theoretically from the practical arts and crafts such as weaving and metalwork as part of the cultural change that began with the renaissance. The metaphorical sense of taste helps distinguish the fine arts from the useful and decorative arts. At the same time, taste appeals directly to a sense. Sight is associated with understanding. We say "I see" when we mean that we understand something. Aesthetic experience is more a matter of direct experience than that. I want to understand a poem or a painting or a piece of music, of course. But my experience of them and my feeling about them is not limited to an intellectual understanding. Taste has the kind of sensory immediacy that is required. Taste occurs without thought. It depends on direct contact with its object. The feeling it produces in us is not a matter of debate. But taste comes from the object. Salt does not taste like sugar, and no amount of thinking will make them taste the same. It therefore became natural to speak of taste as a kind of aesthetic perception and judgment.

The advantages of 'taste' as our primary aesthetic term come from its immediacy and its likeness to sense. It works best in a system that accepts that we have more than the five ordinary senses. Then taste needs no further explanation. Whatever theory of perception we have will apply to aesthetic perception as well. Taste also incorporates the element of judgment into our aesthetic language. We are seldom neutral about tastes, and we are seldom neutral about our aesthetic perceptions. Taste allows us to include our judgments because we can easily speak of good and bad taste. By the middle of the eighteenth century, 'taste' had largely replaced 'beauty' as the most important aesthetic concept.

Taste is not without its difficulties, however. Senses operate by reasonably well understood physiological means. We know the parts of the eye and ear and how they work. The tongue has different taste buds that control chemical reactions that stimulate nerves that operate on centers in the brain. Nothing like this physiology is available for aesthetic taste. Without it, the idea that we have a direct aesthetic sense becomes mysterious. A few people still try to match physiology and aesthetics, but for the most part this is recognized as a dead end. So 'taste' is only one more metaphor. Metaphors are useful in constructing theories, but relying solely on them is misleading. Physics made use of a metaphor of the atom as a small solar system. Electrons circle around a nucleus like planets around the sun. But the mathematics of quantum mechanics allowed physics to advance. The model of the atom had to be recognized as only a model. So it is with taste. If we do not have a real sense, then aesthetic sense is only a model.

Taste also raised problems about judgment virtually from the moment that the metaphor appeared. The very advantage of taste as a concept – its immediacy and invulnerability to questions – also makes it problematic as a form of judgment. We act as if some of the things that we say about aesthetic matters are either true or false. If taste is a sense-type judgment, then it should produce sentences that are true or false like other sense-judgments. One of the most basic things we know about true/false sentences is that they must be capable of taking both values. Some sentences, like "That is either red or it is not red," are always true. But we could also say of those sentences that they are never false. Both 'true' and 'false' apply. Moreover, if the sentence is about something in the world (an empirical sentence), then it must be possible in some thinkable way for it to be false as well as true. Normal sense-judgments obey those rules. "The sky is blue" is either true or false, and if it is true, it could, under some other weather conditions, be false. No matter how sure we are of our sense-judgments, we could be mistaken. A class of sense-judgments like "I am in pain now" or "I see a red patch now" do not really violate these conditions. Such judgments are reports of immediate perceptions, and they are recognized as reports about the perceiver, not about some other object. They are true just in case the perceiver has the reported perception and false otherwise.

If we try to assimilate judgments about taste to the category of immediate perceptions, we remove them from saying anything about their objects. They become reports about the perceiver. If we treat judgments of taste as normal sense-judgments about objects, then they should obey the same rules of evidence. Neither alternative seems to work very well. As reports about the perceiver, they lose the element of judgment. But, as was frequently observed, we act as if our aesthetic judgments are real judgments about the goodness or badness of something. As David Hume (1711–76) remarked, to say that Ogilby (a very minor poet) is as good as Milton (one of the great poets of the English language) is as absurd as to say that a molehill is the same as a mountain. So at least some of the time, we want our judgments of taste to operate like other sense-judgments.

When we try to make judgments of taste operate like other sense-judgments we run into problems about evidence, however. The problem is not that our sense-judgments cannot be mistaken. Often they are. I look at a page and misread it. I look at a book on my shelf and make a mistake about what color it is. That is just the point. I can be mistaken, and I know how to correct my mistakes. I look again in better light, or I pay more careful attention. Sometimes I may have to make use of measurements or other kinds of evidence to correct my mistakes. Some optical illusions do not go away even if I know that they are illusions. But I can correct for the appearances by appealing to other evidence. What evidence corrects my judgments of taste? Assume that the illustration on the cover of this book is badly done; the colors are wrong. Then I might correct for that by looking at the original. But my taste is about whatever I perceived. What I have corrected is not my judgment of aesthetic taste but my visual perception. Moreover, two individuals may agree on all of the correctable kinds of things and still have very different judgments of taste. If their judgments are sense-type judgments, there must be something that counts as evidence directly about taste. But nothing does. They may agree about every fact and as nearly as possible agree that they are seeing the same thing and still have different tastes. So aesthetic taste does not seem to operate like a regular sense-judgment.

The problems with 'taste' as our central aesthetic concept do not invalidate the usefulness of the concept. We continue to speak of a taste for the music of Bach or someone who has good taste in music. However, the centrality of taste as a concept upon which to build aesthetic theory was limited to an earlier form of philosophy that believed in a simple relation between experience, ideas, and knowledge. As our views about experience have become more complex, the difficulties in holding a simple theory of aesthetic taste have become more important. We no longer think of experience as a simple compounding of individual ideas. We know, for example, that what we experience is a function of what we are prepared to see and of the concepts and paradigms that form our perceptions. That is why it is so important to be sensitive to the nuances of language. If I always say "he" when I mean persons in general, I subtly suggest that male persons are the paradigm for being a person. If I think of taste as a simple sense, then I look for simple ideas that are perceived by that sense. But people are not all male, and no simple ideas may correspond to a work of art. Awareness of the implications of a word like 'taste' leads us to further examine our aesthetic concepts.

Aesthetic feeling

A simple solution to the problems raised by the duality of taste concepts is to give up the idea that aesthetic concepts ought to be like sense-concepts and focus on only the felt part of the aesthetic experience. In the course of the nineteenth and twentieth centuries, the idea of internal senses for which there were no sense organs came to seem improbable. The psychology of individual perception offered a different approach to aesthetic experience. The important thing then is the feeling itself. Everything else can be left to other ways of speaking. The first move in this direction was to single out a special kind of experience. The idea is this: When I respond to something, part of my experience is sufficiently different to merit separate treatment. That part is the feeling I have. It is a pleasant feeling, and it is self-sufficient. That is, it is not satisfying some other desire. Ice cream is pleasant, but it satisfies my hunger. If I am full, I do not want ice cream, even though I may remember how pleasant its taste is. I never get full in the same way aesthetically because there is no other desire that my aesthetic pleasure fulfills. I may have had enough opera or have read enough novels so that I do not want any more. But then the experience of opera or novels itself has filled me. Such experience is its own end, and if I no longer want it, I no longer want aesthetic experience.

This does not imply that opera cannot fulfill other desires at the same time. When I go to an opera, I probably have a number of different reasons for going. I may want to learn about Puccini, to impress my friends, to get away from my family, and any number of other reasons. And the experience I have of the opera may satisfy all of those desires. I am instructed, elevated socially, entertained, etc. 'Experience' is a complex concept that can include many elements simultaneously. When philosophers speak of aesthetic experience, therefore, they should not be criticized for ignoring other aspects of experience. There need be no conflict. What is required is that one aspect – the self-contained feeling evoked by some situations and objects – can be identified and found pleasant for its own sake. That, the claim goes, is what constitutes aesthetic experience.

Such experiences have the immediacy that taste has. Whatever feelings I have about a particular opera are indubitably mine. Someone else may feel differently. A critic may dislike the tenor. But if I enjoyed the opera and got pleasure from it, then the critic's dislike is not about my aesthetic experience. The pleasure is mine; the cause is the opera. Thus far, aesthetic feeling and taste coincide. The difference is that aesthetic feeling does not claim to need any kind of special sensory apparatus or evidence because it does not involve any critical judgment. The feeling just is what it is, and feeling it is enough. 'Good' and 'bad' in their judgmental senses do not apply to aesthetic feeling. Someone may have bad taste if his or her judgment does not conform to a standard of taste, but aesthetic feeling is just the emotion itself. If one has an aesthetic feeling, it is by definition pleasant (one of the criteria for aesthetic feeling is that it delights or pleases), and no one can convince me that I am not pleased when I am. There is no bad aesthetic feeling in the way that there can be bad taste.

Aesthetic feeling must be distinguished from other feeling. After all, I have feelings of pleasure from ice cream and sex, from my team winning and from my brother getting a promotion. Not all pleasant feelings in experience are aesthetic. A number of different ways have been suggested to distinguish aesthetic feeling from other feelings. We have already mentioned one: the feeling is an end in itself; it does not satisfy some other desire. Immanuel Kant (1724–1804) described an intrinsic aesthetic intuition that was neither practical nor theoretical in his *Critique of Judgment* (1790). Another way is to distinguish aesthetic feeling qualitatively; it just feels different. In the nineteenth century, romantic poets and critics claimed that such elevated feelings were what made art different from the practical world. Then the problem is to say how aesthetic feeling feels. That may be difficult because it is difficult to describe feelings to others. Our language is public, and it does not cope very well with private feelings. But just because it is difficult to describe does not mean it cannot be done. A. E. Housman defined poetry by the feeling of the hair standing up on the back of his neck when he read some verse. That might be enough to distinguish poetry from mere verse. Perhaps aesthetic feeling provokes similar descriptions.

The most widespread attempt to describe aesthetic feeling characterizes it as a kind of intuition. The followers of Kant took this route. What is meant by aesthetic intuition can be a bit hard to grasp. Most of the time, our expressions of feeling and our language about our feelings clearly belong to some larger conceptual way of putting things. For example, if I am afraid, my fear corresponds to a class of frightening things – things that are, or are thought to be, dangerous, destructive, and threatening. I fear something because it is a frightening kind of thing, and it is frightening because it belongs to some class of experiences that I and other human beings have learned about. So we can infer what our reactions will be from the concepts and accumulated experiences that we and others like us have built up. When I look at a crashing wave, I do not just see just a wall of water. I see a wall of water whose weight and momentum can be known to me and can be calculated by hydrodynamics. Most perceptions and experiences have that kind of conceptual and theoretical underpinning. But, it is claimed, the direct visual experience is an immediate intuition that does not depend on theory and concepts. They come later (logically, if not temporally). Intuition is a kind of experiential first impression. It is normally lost in the simultaneous placing of the experience within our accepted, subconsciously organized world view. But, the argument goes, in some cases it need not be. Then we have an aesthetic feeling. The crashing wave is not a wall of water threatening to overwhelm me but a sublime (frightening but fascinating) experience of nature with no other implications. The pure experience is independent of what I believe about water. Such experiences can be produced by our encounters with nature, and they are captured by artists in their paintings, novels, and music. The works of art may or may not represent the wall of water. What they must capture is the feeling itself, by whatever means.

We began with the language that we use about aesthetic kinds of experiences. Beauty offered an objective kind of language, and taste introduced a more subjective element. Neither was completely satisfactory. A problem with the claims for aesthetic feeling is that it seems to escape language altogether. We are left with descriptions that try to evoke the feeling. Those descriptions have to do what they describe. That may not be wrong. Some language does perform what it says. An umpire who shouts "Out!" has not only described a situation; he has brought it about. But our aesthetic descriptions do not seem to be performing actions in that way. Perhaps works of art do, but then the only philosophy of art would be art itself. We are examining our talk about art, and if we have to become artists to talk about art, we will be no better off than when we began.

Aesthetic feeling is an enticing solution to our problem because it appeals to our sense that our experiences of art and beauty are somehow different from other kinds of experience. We resist examining those experiences because we want to preserve them from the rigors of analysis. In fact, many have felt that the ability to have aesthetic feelings would be destroyed by analysis. Thinking too much about what we feel would, it was feared, interfere with our feeling it. However, that fear must be based on a confusion. Analysis and feeling are not competitors for a limited amount of mental space in our lives. We have plenty of capacity for both. We can probably both feel and analyze at the same time, and it may even be, as some philosophers have argued, that feeling is a part of any analysis. Perhaps. Our problem is to make it clear what aesthetic feeling amounts to and to see whether the claims for its uniqueness can be supported.

Unfortunately, it appears that strong claims for aesthetic uniqueness cannot be supported. The problem is not just that aesthetic feeling is difficult to describe. Difficulty is not an argument against something. Quantum equations in physics are difficult to solve. That does not make them wrong. All feelings are difficult to describe. That does not mean that we do not love and hate, admire and fear, etc. The problem goes deeper. Aesthetic feeling is supposed to be unique in some way. Its descriptions must mark it off in some way from other feeling. Otherwise, 'aesthetic feeling' will not be useful as a theoretical term. The term will not help me to understand why opera evokes aesthetic feeling and is art but French cooking, which I also like, does not. But all attempts to say where the uniqueness of aesthetic feeling lies run into the claim that one must just feel the difference. That is a non-answer. It is never much help to refer a question back to the questioner. If I ask why I hurt, it does little good to ask me to examine my own pain to see what it feels like. In the case of aesthetic feeling, it is clearly illegitimate to turn the question back because the question itself is whether there is such a thing as a unique aesthetic feeling. To assume a positive answer to a question about existence or identity is never legitimate. If I ask whether Superman really exists, it won't do to reply that he exists because I just referred to him. If I ask whether there is such a thing as a unique aesthetic experience, it won't do to tell me that it is just whatever I experience as uniquely aesthetic.

Few philosophers who have defended a form of aesthetic feeling would find this blanket dismissal convincing. In the later nineteenth century and the beginning of the twentieth century, philosopher–psychologists such as Edward Bullough attempted to identify aesthetic feeling by telling us how to arrive at it. One should "put out of gear" one's ordinary, practical feelings to experience things aesthetically. The conviction of Bullough and his predecessors and followers rests on subjective grounds, and it cannot be moved by argument alone. But our problem was and remains one of language. Private conviction that remains private is unchallengable. It is like religious or mystical experience – something to which some defenders of aesthetic feeling compare their experience. We demand more because we are seeking a public language that will be adequate for our talk about art and the aesthetic. For aesthetic feeling to replace the older language of beauty and taste, it must be a language capable of withstanding analysis. That does not mean that it must conform to pre-established logical or theoretical criteria. For example, it need not be like scientific language. But it must be more than just an evocation of feeling. So far, all attempts to move the claims for aesthetic feeling into a more adequate linguistic realm have failed.

Why then, we might ask, did it happen that for much of the nineteenth and twentieth centuries 'aesthetic feeling' was the dominant aesthetic term? The answer to that question would require a much more detailed historical investigation than this book warrants. Aesthetic feeling captures some important elements of both beauty and taste. Beauty was understood to be metaphysically important. It was part of the harmony of the universe, the rightness of the ultimate order of things. As such, the proper response to beauty was a feeling of near-religious awe. Aesthetic feeling retains that sense of importance and emotional involvement. 'Beauty' gave way to 'taste' in part because taste was closer to the reliance on the senses that modern thought required. Taste was first a real sense, then a quasi-sense that incorporated immediacy of feeling and judgment. Taste proved unable to retain the union of those two elements, however. Aesthetic feeling holds on to the immediacy and surrenders the judgment. Thus aesthetic feeling has a powerful hold on the history of aesthetics.

Conclusions

In subsequent chapters, we will explore further alternatives that retain important elements of theories of beauty, taste, and aesthetic feeling. For now, it is important to see that the arguments against these theories do not lead to our completely discarding the language. It remains the essential language of aesthetics. Beauty points us toward objects. Two sorts of objects occupy aesthetics: natural objects and made objects (works of art). In both cases, beauty is a first step toward accounting for the inclusion or exclusion of some specific object in the field. Beauty also opens the field of theory to aesthetics. The language of beauty must be located in a larger theoretical context. How, and whether, beauty continues to play a central role in aesthetics depends to a large measure on the other theories about the world and what is in it that we hold.

Taste points us toward the perceiver and toward aesthetic judgments. Aesthetics depends on perception, and perception implies a perceiver. Aesthetic judgments are different from other judgments because they depend on the perceiver to an extent that most other judgments do not. For all of the problems with taste as a way of accounting for the perceiver's involvement in aesthetics, some comparable concept is needed.

Finally, aesthetic feeling has been for much of its modern history the focus of aesthetics. Aesthetics began because the dominant philosophies in the seventeenth and eighteenth centuries conceived of knowledge as a certain, perfect science independent of individual human control. That left out too much of human feeling, and aesthetics arose to fill the gap. Its task was to account for the subjective elements of experience with which science could not deal. Aesthetic feeling remained unsystematic, but it continues to be a part of human experience.

Aesthetic Predicates

Since we are concerned with our talk about art and aesthetic experience, we will now look more directly at aesthetic language itself. Terms and concepts like 'beauty,' 'taste,' and 'aesthetic feeling' include a lot of theory. The criticisms aimed at them also include a lot of theory. It is possible to take a more practical, limited approach. Instead of asking about the whole concept of aesthetic feeling, for example, we may examine specific uses of aesthetic language. This approach finds favor with those philosophers who are suspicious of any theoretical approaches to aesthetics. By the middle of the twentieth century, the analysis of language was considered the most direct way into the analysis of concepts and philosophical problems. Some of the results of that movement are very important for aesthetics.

Aesthetic descriptions and metaphors

The most influential direct approach to aesthetic language has been through its descriptive words. We seldom say simply that X is beautiful.

If we want to offer a critical or aesthetic description, we are much more likely to say that X is elegant, well composed, balanced, fascinating, graceful, or any one of an endless list of adjectives that either are primarily used in aesthetic contexts or can be adapted to aesthetic contexts easily. When I look out over a field of new green grass in the spring and say that it is fresh-looking, I am not thinking primarily of cattle feed. I am using 'fresh-looking' as an aesthetic predicate to describe my response to what I see. When I call a field of Texas blue bonnets cheerful, I am not claiming that plants have feelings. I am describing how they make me feel. When I look at the self-portrait of Marie-Louise-Elisabeth Vigée-Lebrun and describe it as elegant, I am referring only indirectly to her dress and manner. I also expect the term 'elegant' to capture the classical beauty of her style as a portrait painter. All of these descriptive words are what we call aesthetic predicates. They have the grammatical form "X is A" where X is some object that can be referred to and A is an adjective adapted to describe the aesthetic look or feel of X.

X need not be a work of art. Natural objects take aesthetic predicates. And A need not be an explicitly aesthetic term. Many ordinary emotional terms such as 'cheerful,' 'happy,' 'sad,' and 'frightening' can be used as aesthetic predicates. The first problem in dealing with aesthetic predicates is how to tell that the predicate is being used in an aesthetic way. If I say "David is cheerful," I am describing David's emotional state, but there is nothing aesthetic about the description. If, on the other hand, I say of Allan Ramsay's portrait of David Hume that the portrait is cheerful, I am describing not Hume's emotional state but something about the style of the portrait. Nothing in the grammar alone distinguishes aesthetic predicates from ordinary ones.

We might be tempted to say that the predicate is an aesthetic predicate because the subject is a painting – a work of art or an aesthetic object. That strategy introduces more problems than it solves, however. First of all, many counter-examples can be though of quickly. I can say that the same portrait is square, and there is nothing about the word 'square' that makes it aesthetic. Second, I only defer my problem by introducing the concept of a work of art or an aesthetic object. How do we tell aesthetic objects from ordinary objects? It won't do to say that they are the ones that take aesthetic predicates because then we have gone in a tight analytical circle. Instead we must look to how the predicate is used.

To begin with, some aesthetic predicates are clearly metaphors. Metaphors are figures of speech that allow the meaning of a word or phrase to shift from its ordinary, expected meaning to a different usage. "David is cheerful" uses 'cheerful' in the way we expect it to be used. Whatever it describes, it is describing the ordinary kinds of things that can be cheerful. "This painting is cheerful" acts like a metaphor. Paintings are not the kind of things that have mental states, so we are warned that something unusual is going on with the word 'cheerful' now. I would say the fundamental shift is from an application that is controlled by the object referred to (David's mental state) to one that has to involve the speaker (the person who describes the painting as cheerful) and the hearer (the person who is expected to figure out what a cheerful painting is). In metaphors, the speaker can no longer dictate the meaning of this particular utterance by expecting the hearer to know in advance the kinds of things that are being described. (We all know in advance what cheerful people are. To say that "David is cheerful" only locates David among the cheerful people.) The speaker instead issues a kind of challenge or command – try thinking of this object this way. The result is not likely to be exactly what either the speaker or the hearer began with, but it may well come closer to describing the situation intended than any standard usage that already existed. Clearly, that kind of linguistic cooperation is required if we are to get at some aesthetic perception by means of already existing terms.

Not all metaphors are aesthetic, however. When I describe the atom as a miniature solar system, I use a metaphor, but I do not intend that the atom be taken as an aesthetic object. Moreover, not all aesthetic predicates seem to be metaphors. 'Cheerful' starts out as an ordinary description of a mental state, but the standard use for 'graceful' now is probably aesthetic. (It does not matter that 'graceful' may have acquired its present meaning and use by a long metaphorical process involving the theological and aristocratic senses of 'grace.' We are concerned with the meaning the term has now, not with its history.) That an adjective is used as a metaphor does not mean that it is being used aesthetically, therefore.

It may still be the case that metaphors give us an important clue about aesthetic predicates, however. In order to understand a metaphor, one must refer to the situation being described and relate the speaker and hearer to that situation. Aesthetic predicates have a similar way of involving the speaker and hearer. Consider that we do not really know in anything but a very general way what it would mean to say that a painting is cheerful without having the painting there to look at. If we are told that the painting is square, it is not necessary to look at it to know what is meant. Squareness is well defined independently of looking at a particular square object. Aesthetic cheerfulness is not. We can have a broad idea that cheerful painting belong to a class of things that we think of as cheerful and thus that it is not gloomy, dark, etc. But in the absence of looking for ourselves, we can say nothing that is both positive and specific to this painting. And it is not enough for the speaker who describes the painting to have looked at it and then to tell me that it is cheerful. I really can't know what the speaker meant without looking for myself. So the aesthetic usage of predicates involves the one who understands directly and requires a direct involvement on his or her part. That is typical of what is required to understand metaphors, and it seems essential to aesthetic predicates. In the case of predicates like 'graceful' that have their primary usage in aesthetic contexts, we need only recognize that the same process of understanding that metaphors involve is being repeated with a term that lacks a standard non-metaphorical usage.

The uses of aesthetic language

This would help more if we had a clearer understanding of how metaphors work. It may be that we can only understand metaphors by means of understanding aesthetic predicates, however. In that case, we need a more direct approach to aesthetic predicates. We can observe several things about the way we typically use aesthetic predicates. First, we do not expect them to allow us to draw inferences based on the fact that the predicate applies. Inference drawing is a normal process that we often unconsciously use to extend the application of our language. Assume someone says that Fran is cheerful. We naturally infer that Fran is in a good mood, that nothing really bad has happened to Fran recently, that Fran will not answer harshly if spoken to, and a whole host of other behavioral and emotional conclusions that we can draw. Moreover, cheerfulness implies (informally) that the cheerful person has the same mood that other cheerful people have. I can understand Fran's emotional state by consulting my own memories of cheerfulness. In general, Fran's cheerfulness is going to be similar to mine and to that of others. Just as I do not have to examine a painting to know what its shape will look like when I have been told that it is two feet square, so I do not have to examine Fran's mood to know what it is like when I am told that Fran is cheerful. My own experience of cheerfulness is sufficient.

Contrast that kind of implication-laden use of 'cheerful' with any aesthetic usage. When I am told that a painting by Edward Hopper is gloomy, I know that it is not happy, etc., but I have no idea what it means for the painting to be gloomy until I look at the painting. Then, if the description is a good one, I should be able to recognize what is meant. On the whole, we can draw few inferences from aesthetic language. Some negative inferences apply. A painting that is delicate (aesthetically) is presumably not constructed of thick lines. But negative inferences do not take us very far. From the fact that something is square, I can infer that it is not round, not hexagonal, etc., without any particular knowledge either of what it is to be square or what it is to be hexagonal. Knowing that something is described by some aesthetic predicate does not tell me what the object is like independently of examining the object.

Inferences in the other direction also don't work. Assume that I know that a painting is of two smiling clowns. Can I infer that it is cheerful? Probably not. It all depends on how the smiling clowns are treated. Is a painting all in shades of black and gray not cheerful? Not necessarily. It all depends on what it is of and how it is presented. "Cheerful" can apply to paintings that are totally non-representational. Of course a cheerful painting cannot be gloomy. One aesthetic predicate cannot contradict another. But no set of non-aesthetic properties is sufficient to make a painting cheerful or gloomy. It all depends on how the painting is presented. This leads us to conclude that in general there is no guaranteed relation between a set of non-aesthetic properties and the correct application of aesthetic predicates. No set of non-aesthetic properties guarantees that an aesthetic predicate will apply; and conversely, knowing that an aesthetic predicate does apply (i.e. having understood its application), we cannot be sure that any particular non-aesthetic property is in the thing being described.

This has led some philosophers to conclude that aesthetic predicates are just those that operate independently of any rules of application. We say that they are not rule-governed. Rules govern the application of language in two ways. One is by having a definite set of rules that tell exactly what things are and are not P. Geometrical figures are like that. 'Square' describes something bounded by four straight lines of equal length meeting at four right angles. Such precise rule-governed language is relatively rare because it imposes a precision on our speech that limits its use. A more common form of rule-governed language allows for fuzzy boundaries between obvious central uses. The standard examples are things like calling something a game or saying that someone is bald. We are willing to call all sorts of things games even if there is no one feature that they all share. We say someone is bald if they have no hair, or if they have only one or two strands, or three, etc.; but at some imprecisely defined point we cease to apply the term. We might note that the same thing applies more loosely to all sorts of adjectives. "The sky is blue" applies to many shades of blue but excludes red skies. The central or paradigm case provides an example, and then each of the cluster of cases around that central case shares enough with it that we feel comfortable applying the term to those cases as well. In such cases there are rules in a loose sense of examples that can be extended but no definitions.

Unfortunately, aesthetic predicates do not seem to obey even those looser kind of rules. We might say that a central cases of cheerfulness in poetry is Milton's *L'Allegro*, which begins "Hence, loathed Melancholy." But then a comic poem by Ogden Nash is also cheerful, yet the two poems share only the most general features. Neither is more centrally comic than the other. (Milton's poem is more important poetically, but that is another matter.) On the other hand, we do not want to slip into the error of just saying anything at all. Aesthetic descriptions can be wrong. And we do offer evidence for our descriptions. If someone disagrees with my description of Wyatt's sonnet, "Who So List to Hunt," I can point out exactly what evidence leads me to say that the poem is moving. I just can't generalize from that evidence to any other poem. The answer about aesthetic predicates, then, seems to be that we must look and see in every case for ourselves. Some applications will withstand examination in that way. Others will not. So 'correct' and 'incorrect' apply. But the test is unique to every case. Such terms lead us back in the direction of taste. Those who have aesthetic ability apply aesthetic terms, and others say: "Oh, I see." Those who lack that aesthetic ability not only do not obtain agreement from others; they are themselves inconsistent in their applications of aesthetic terms.

We still do not know what aesthetic predicates really are. We are dependent on a kind of trial and error in which disputes are settled by time and application rather than rules. If enough people agree, an application will withstand further challenges. *Hamlet* is psychologically penetrating. Who can disagree with that truism today? But for a time *Hamlet* was a matter of more critical disagreement. Aesthetic predicates are clearly intended as more than mere appeals to a timeless majority, however. They are very individual judgments that are to be verified by a kind of critical exercise of presentation and insight. The only test, ultimately, is "Oh, I see."

We are left with two problems. First, if aesthetic predicates require some kind of persuasive rhetoric, then there will always be the possibility of changes. We began by looking for some linguistic uses or conventions that would help us to understand what makes something aesthetic. We seem to have discovered only that usage requires persuasion. But there is nothing uniquely aesthetic about persuasion. So aesthetic predicates will still be indistinguishable from others. Second, our test has turned out to be "look and see." But that is just the claim that was made for taste in another guise. We must have a sense that sees. All of the problems of sense theories of taste reappear.

The only improvement comes if an analysis of aesthetic predicates is joined with a theory of critical arguments so that we are not left looking but not seeing. Then a paradox looms. Aesthetic predicates resist all attempts to reduce them to rules or ordered usage. But aesthetic predicates can be used meaningfully only if they are the subject of critical presentations. The complete subjectivity of aesthetic judgment meets the absolute need for critical persuasion. Critics are people who express their own opinions and invite others, on the basis of some kind of evidence, to share those opinions. Just expressing opinions is not enough. A critic must be able to supply reasons. But aesthetic opinions, we have reason to believe, are radically our own. We feel no need to adopt someone else's opinion. Reasons and evidence do not apply to aesthetic predicates in the same way that they apply to measuring or arguing. So critics are usually not considered necessary to having aesthetic opinions. Yet now it seems that we could not even tell that an opinion is aesthetic without some critical involvement. We shall have to see how we can extricate ourselves from this apparent paradox.

Conclusions

To summarize: Aesthetic predicates are specific descriptive terms. They are most commonly adjectives and appear in the form "X is A," where X is the object being described and A is an adjective applied to X. When A is used aesthetically, it operates like a metaphor, though it may not be formally metaphorical. A does not allow us to draw inferences independently of looking at X, nor does A conform to definitions or obey rules for its use. We can only understand A by looking at X for ourselves. We have no sure way to tell that A is aesthetic, however. We depend on critics to make "look and see" more than an empty command. But criticism implies the ability to give reasons, so we are back to the need to give reasons for a kind of linguistic usage that does not seem to be open to reason-giving.

Criticism and Value Terms

One reason why criticism is resisted in aesthetics is that it seems to impose someone else's judgments and values on us. In aesthetics, more than anywhere else, Descartes' observation seems justified: "Good sense is of all things in the world the most equally distributed, for everybody thinks himself so abundantly provided with it, that even those most difficult to please in all other matters do not commonly desire more of it than they already possess." Each individual is satisfied with his or her own judgment. I believe that I have a right to my own opinion about art and what I like to experience in nature. The irony of these observations, of course, is that while I am satisfied with my own judgment, I have strong doubts about everyone else's when they do not agree with me. As the old saying goes, "Everyone is crazy except me and thee, and sometimes I have doubts about thee."

The self-satisfaction and self-referentiality of aesthetic language creates a special problem for criticism. Since I am satisfied with my own judgment and believe it is beyond correction, I don't need some critic telling me what to like or what to look at or how I should think about something. Artists, in particular, usually don't like critics (even though some of the best critics are also artists). What the artist does is personal and productive. The critic is analytical and judgmental. Aesthetics mirrors this split and divides into two camps. The artistic camp views aesthetics as a secondary form of art. Everyone is invited to try their hand. The fewer critical principles there are, the less there is to get in the way. The critical camp views aesthetics as a kind of analysis. It is sometimes called metacriticism. Aesthetics analyzes the language of the analyzer who analyzes art. If we are to talk about art and the aesthetic, we must be prepared to understand both camps. We must be able to look and see for ourselves and express in language what we have seen. And we must be able to understand and defend our own aesthetic language and the aesthetic language of others.

Judgments and aesthetic value

A significant role for critical language is making judgments based on aesthetic values. Aesthetic values are not limited to explicit judgments of goodness and badness. Many forms of criticism try to be "objective." They offer analysis without saying that the work in question is great or not so great. But even the most objective forms of criticism tend to conceal choices based on values. Whenever we make comparisons or select something for analysis, we are involved in judgments that depend in some way on our ability to use 'good' and 'bad,' 'better' and 'worse,' about the objects of our aesthetic judgments.

To begin with, we should distinguish two kinds of aesthetic judgments that arise from criticism. The first is comparative. Its form might be represented as "A is better [worse] than B." For example, we might say that "*Hamlet* is better than *Othello*" or that "Shakespeare is better than Christopher Marlowe." Note that comparative judgments like this establish some frame of reference. In the first example, we compare two plays by the same author. In the second, we compare two Elizabethan authors of tragedies. No frame of reference is absolute. Anything can be compared to anything else. Nothing prevents me from saying "*Hamlet* is better than the color red," for example. However, when nothing obvious is shared, a comparative judgment depends on finding some basis for comparison if it is not to be considered simply absurd. The basis for comparison usually dictates a range of values that should determine the judgment.

Assume, for example, that we are comparing two authors of tragedies. Then there will be a number of things that count as specific values; they are the "good-making" features of tragic authorship. Such features usually include things like unity of plot, moral complexity, verisimilitude of character, appropriateness of language, stagecraft, etc. No list is complete or exhaustive. Every list implies something about the set of values that is being used. Comparison must be based on some agreed set of features that are to be compared. I cannot say that Shakespeare's language is more subtle than Marlowe's without indicating that I think that language is an important good-making feature of tragedies and that subtlety is a good-making feature of language. Then I am at the level of what constitutes subtlety and whether it is more or less present in Shakespeare's or Marlowe's work.[4] What looks to be a straightforward claim about something in the language also implies values. A claim that a phrase is subtle has two parts: (1) the part that refers to some features of the language; and (2) the claim that subtlety is what we should pay attention to in comparing the two writers.

We need to distinguish carefully between factual claims and the value-claims that are attached to facts by the way that they are presented and advanced as reasons for other claims. For example, it is a fact that a line of poetry is iambic pentameter. We can verify that by counting the number of short/long stress repetitions in the line. The line either does or does not have that pattern. The fact in itself implies no value-judgment. But in English poetry, an iambic pentameter line is usually held to be a good thing. It captures the rhythm of our ordinary speech while providing order and linking lines rhythmically. Other meters sound more artificial, choppier, etc. The simple assertion that a line is in iambic pentameter may, in context, indicate that this is taken to be a positive feature of that line. Facts are confirmed by evidence. Values are assigned to facts by some additional theory or choice. A fact just is; a value implies that we ought to do or believe something.

Comparative judgments have the advantage that they indicate some-

4 See the appendix at the end of the book for two passages that might be compared.

thing of their value structure by the things that are singled out for comparison. It is often possible to figure out from comparisons what values are being attached to facts by the mere fact that something has been singled out for comparison. Also, often we can follow comparative judgments even if we do not share the values involved because the factual basis is accessible. For example, I might think that tragedy is a bore and that neither Shakespeare nor Marlowe is of any concern to me. They are merely dead white males best consigned to the cultural archives. That in no way prevents me from determining that Shakespeare used an iambic pentameter line, or that Marlowe had a fondness for exaggerated comparisons. Then I can infer that in the comparison of Shakespeare and Marlowe, the former is considered a good feature and the latter a bad feature. The judgment that Shakespeare is better than Marlowe is a sensible judgment as a result. At that point, I have two alternatives. I can agree or disagree with the specific judgment. If I do, I am willing to enter into the debate about the facts and values that are being asserted. Or I may deny that the comparison really involves anything of value. In that case, I only hypothetically entertain the values. If Shakespeare and Marlowe were important and if language were a sound basis for comparison, then Shakespeare would be better than Marlowe.

The second kind of critical judgment is absolute. It takes the form "X is V" where X is some object or experience and V is some value-term applied to X. Rather than comparing two works or two authors, for example, I might say that *Hamlet* is a great play. That commits me to nothing about other specific plays. It does require that I have some scale of value-terms, however. To say that *Hamlet* is a great play is to place it on a value-scale of some sort. I am also committed to some set of values that implies some standards of application. I might not be able to say very exactly what I mean by 'great,' but if I mean anything at all (other than a vague praise for the play), there is some set of features that I believe *Hamlet* has that makes it great. For example, many of the same features that appear in comparative judgments also might appear in an absolute judgment. I can complete the sentence "Hamlet is great because . . ." with more specific judgments like "it is morally complex" or "it is interesting to watch." Then I am saying that a feature like moral complexity is valuable and having it is one of the things that makes *Hamlet* great. Finally, I must get down to the level of specific features of the play that constitute moral complexity if what I say is to be more than an expression of my positive feelings about the play.

We must be careful here. Absolute judgments are not absolute in the sense that they cannot be challenged or in the sense that they are the only things that can be said about something. We sometimes think that there are things called absolute truth and absolute value that are independent of context. But that is not really a very meaningful claim. Truth is the truth of particular sentences. 'The Truth' is meaningless unless one holds a strong form of Platonism. Sentences (or propositions, ideas, beliefs, statements) are true or false; truth is not a thing. 'The Good' is equally meaningless. Goodness and other related value-judgments apply to particular things. Value-words express our positive feelings towards something, but they do it in a way that implies that we have grounds for our feelings. We expect to be able to validate our judgments with some kind of attention to detail.

We can see that values creep into our aesthetic judgments quite easily and that we have a number of options in how to understand such value-claims. Not all of the options involve any real commitment to the values on the part of the person being persuaded. Value-claims in aesthetics permit a hypothetical position much more easily than in moral philosophy, for example. Say that I concluded that Hitler was worse than Stalin. If that were a judgment made in 1943, it might lead me to agree with Churchill that an alliance with the devil was permissible if it would lead to Hitler's defeat, so an alliance with Stalin was certainly permitted. At the time, such a moral judgment called for action. I cannot, without contradiction, simultaneously make a moral judgment that I ought to do X and also conclude that I have no need to act on X. Moral obligations imply a willingness to act appropriately. But aesthetic judgments imply no such actions. Whatever they are about (preferences, beauty, taste, etc.), I am permitted to be indifferent or to respond merely hypothetically. That is one of the fundamental differences between aesthetic and moral values.

We also expect our judgments of moral value to be consistent with some form of behavior. Moral judgments lead to actions. Judgments of aesthetic value indicate a capacity of some aesthetic object to satisfy desires. I might say that *Hamlet* is great and still not want to read or see *Hamlet*. Judgments about plays do not imply that I desire to see or read plays. But I can hardly say that *Hamlet* is great and yet that I would give aesthetic preference to a not-so-great tragedy. (I might like a lesser tragedy better for all kinds of other, non-aesthetic reasons, of course.)

The fact that I place *Hamlet* near the top of my value-scale does not mean that others must agree with me. What it does mean is that we must treat our disagreement as a real disagreement about the value of the play. If I have arrived at my value-judgment by reference to some set of values that are associated with some set of factual properties about the play, then we have two possible areas of disagreement. We can disagree about whether the play has the factual features, or we can disagree about whether those factual features should be valued in the relevant way. I can deny that moral complexity is found in *Hamlet*, or I can deny that moral complexity is a feature with makes tragedies great. Either way, I am committed to more than just a preference for the play.

The primary difference between absolute and comparative value-judgments in aesthetics rests on a difference in perspective. Comparative judgments require less commitment and give greater guidance. They permit "if" kinds of judgments more easily. Given a set of things and some instructions for arranging them, I can follow the instructions. For example, if I am told to arrange the numbers {1, 2, 3, 4} in descending order, I can do so. Similarly, if I am given a set of plays and a set of value-terms, and I am told how to apply the value-terms, I can arrange the plays from greater to lesser value. Nothing in this procedure requires that I accept the values as described or even that I believe that there are any such values. Comparative arrangements in aesthetics make that kind of arrangement possible by stating or implying how the comparisons are made. Absolute values are more difficult to apply. I can still try hypothetically to understand the application that allows someone else to say that *Hamlet* is great. But I can do so only by finding a way to adopt the perspective of someone who does believe that *Hamlet* is great. There is something a bit odd about saying that *Hamlet* is great but I do not believe a word of the judgment. In that case, an absolute judgment tends to become a different but related judgment: Alex believes that *Hamlet* is great. But that is a judgment about Alex, and it does not require that I know anything at all about *Hamlet*.

The value of feeling

A third sort of aesthetic value is directed toward aesthetic feelings themselves. Instead of saying that something has a value or is ranked above something else, we may believe that some experiences are valuable for their own sake. In these cases the judgment applies differently. It is not *Hamlet* but my experience of *Hamlet* that is valuable. This is what many people would mean by aesthetic value. The value comes not just – not even primarily – from art. Its real source is likely to be nature or creativity or expressiveness, and it is valuable because of what it provides me with. There are, we are told, some feelings or experiences that are worthwhile just for the having of them. They give meaning to life, pleasure to the soul, and sense to our confusion about ourselves. In some cases, aesthetic value in this sense approaches religious experience. It is difficult to deny such experiences, but it is equally difficult to verify or describe them. We can argue about whether *Hamlet* is great. It is more difficult to argue about whether there is value in gazing at a sunset. If we experience the sunset as valuable, it is difficult to see how that can be denied when the value itself is limited to the experience. I might think that Alex should not spend her time gazing at sunsets. But that is a judgment about how Alex should spend her time; it does not contradict Alex's belief that she found the sunset valuable. Nor can I get inside Alex's head and experience her experience. If she says that sunset was valuable and means only that that experience had value to her, I cannot disagree with that in itself. I can, at most, suggest that her values are misplaced and that there are other experiences that would be more valuable, and thus try to shift the question back to a comparative judgment.

The most widely acknowledged value that requires no other justification is pleasure. Some have maintained that it is the only value. They argue that even when we seem to act or desire something other than pleasure, it will turn out that we take pleasure in the results of our actions or the satisfaction of our desires, so pleasure is the ultimate end that leads us to value those acts or objects. Others have replied that that confuses pleasure with the acts or desires. We would still act in the same way without the accompanying pleasure. Our desire is for a specific object; pleasure is only a result. Regardless of how this debate is resolved, pleasure is acknowledged as something that does not need further analysis or justification. Aesthetic value can then be regarded as a special kind of pleasure. Either it is thought of as feeling differently, or, if the pleasure is the ordinary kind, it is regarded as free from other entanglements.

It is difficult to explain a different kind of feeling of pleasure, but we may get some idea of what is meant by considering the pleasure that we take in reading a good book or seeing a good movie. Unlike other pleasures, this pleasure can be repeated again and again. We do not use it up the way we use up the pleasure of food when we have eaten it. And we do not have to think of the consequences either. Reading is not fattening. (Some qualifications might be needed on these observations. Obviously, we can get tired of reading, and reading does have consequences. But the pleasure we take is independent of these external considerations. While we are reading, nothing "real" intrudes.) Such pleasure is sometimes described as "disinterested." It does not involve external interests. Disinterestedness was developed in the course of the eighteenth century first as a critical term, so that one of the conditions for a good critic was that he or she should be disinterested, and ultimately by Kant as a description of aesthetic judgments themselves. Later, disinterestedness comes to be treated as a form of attitude that one can voluntarily assume. The history of the term 'disinterestedness' closely parallels the development of modern aesthetics.

Freedom from outside concerns is often regarded as the mark of aesthetic pleasure. This freedom can be taken in two ways. One way emphasizes the independence from reality of aesthetic pleasure. For example, the death of Hamlet is not a real death, so I can take pleasure in the play without having to worry about the fact that someone has really died. My pleasure in the play is protected by the very fact that it is a play. In this sense, aesthetic pleasure depends on illusion, make-believe, and pretense. A real beggar is a social problem; a beggar in a painting is only an aesthetic object and so is not a problem. Thus I am freed to enjoy aspects of a painting that I would abhor if I saw the real thing. This may account for the difference in our responses to fictional violence in a movie and to real violence in a newsreel. Films about the Kennedy assassination such as Oliver Stone's *JFK* are entertainment. The Zapruder film of the assassination is not. I make an aesthetic mistake if I fail to properly distinguish between the make-believe world and the real world.

The other way of distinguishing aesthetic pleasure regards it as closer to some ultimate reality than ordinary pleasure. In that case, its freedom from real concerns is not make-believe or illusion but elevation. The aesthetic is more real than ordinary experience, not less. For example, a movement called surrealism attempted to take dreams and unconscious desires and correlate them with verbal and visual images to create an art that was beyond ordinary reality. The pleasure available from aesthetic experience according to this approach is never merely the ordinary experience we have. It is a greater reality, a surreality. As the British critic and aesthetician Clive Bell put it shortly before World War I, those who have experienced the cold, white peaks of art cannot confuse them with the warm, cozy valleys of ordinary experience. This kind of pleasure comes close to exaltation, ecstasy, and religious or mystical experience. In either case, the aesthetic pleasure is regarded as a unique kind of experience that justifies the ultimate value of aesthetic experience.

Yet there is something more going on in judgments of aesthetic value along these lines than a simple expression of pleasure in some experiences we have. Clive Bell could not stop with an aesthetic hypothesis about aesthetic experience. He had to go on to a metaphysical hypothesis that postulates that aesthetic experience is the real value for which religions had been striving but which they could not supply. Bell's hypothesis is a bit extreme, but pure aesthetic value seldom is regarded as just a form of pleasure. It provides the sense that our system of fine arts is culturally important, for example. Civilization is a product of aesthetic value as much as moral and economic value. The claims begin to get grandiose and extreme. Artists are the unacknowledged legislators of the world, says Shelley. Aesthetic value comes just before absolute spirit in the history of consciousness, says Hegel (1770–1831). What we are to make of such claims depends to a large measure on how we respond to particular kinds of aesthetic situations. It is difficult to separate the value-claims involved from the instances that produce their justification. Hegel without Beethoven, or Keats and Shelley on aesthetic experiences without romantic poetry, make little sense. Even with aesthetic instances to make them concrete, the values also require the system of philosophy or religion that goes with them. By themselves, the claims for an extraordinary aesthetic pleasure amount to little more than enthusiasm.

Two final distinctions can help us understand how value-terms operate in our aesthetic language. First, the various claims for aesthetic pleasure are claims that aesthetic values belong to the experience itself. We need to distinguish them from related value-claims that belong to other areas. It might be, for example, that aesthetic pleasure makes us better people or that TV violence makes us worse people. The aesthetic experience is a means of getting to some end that is either good or bad. The value in those cases is determined by the end, however. In this example, it is a moral end, and the result is a moral value. Now, we may believe that aesthetic experience should always be subordinate to moral values. That is itself a moral judgment, however. When aesthetic values are subordinated to some other value-system – usually religious or political or moral – we leave the realm of aesthetics. At the same time, an aesthetic judgment can separate aesthetic value from other forms of value. Attempts to isolate aesthetic value are themselves part of a value-system.

Second, we distinguish between something that is good of its kind and something that has value in some way of its own. This is another version of a means–end problem. In this case, however, the end is defined by an idea of what a perfect instance of something would be and particular examples are judged on how they match up with a standard. When judges at dog or flower shows select the winners, they are judging against such standards. A good beagle will match the standard at more points than a poor one. In the case of dogs, the standards can be quite arbitrary. In the case of flowers, there may be more attempt at justification in terms of the aesthetic look of the flower. But in either case, the judgment is not really a value-judgment in the same sense as those we have been examining. 'Good' in these contexts means something like conforming to an ideal. If the ideal is arbitrary or determined by some natural means (the perfect instance of chicken pox), then no implication of value need enter at all. If the standard is determined by some ideal value, then the value of the lesser instances will just be a degree of that value-system. If roses are ideally beautiful, then a good rose will be one that approaches that standard, and the standard will be an aesthetic one. But the intermediate judgment is still not a value-judgment. Whether the rose has all of the points necessary for the ideal is a matter of fact. That is why judging in such contests can have at least a degree of objectivity that is lacking in other critical and aesthetic situations.

Conclusions

To summarize, the problems of aesthetic value are complex. Comparative and absolute judgments require that we relate facts about objects to a value-system. Facts and values are different, but in order to make judgments, some way of relating them must be found. Criticism serves both to analyze the object and to relate facts to a system of values. Critics are sometimes at odds with artists, however. A different range of values attaches to aesthetic experience itself. These experiences are often held to be valuable in and for themselves. One important way of explaining that intrinsic value is in terms of pleasure. Aesthetic pleasure, it is maintained, is either distinctive in its kind or distinctive in being separated from ordinary concerns. Sometimes aesthetic experience is given an even higher value, either as a cultural product or as a quasi-religious form of meaningful experience. Finally, we must distinguish between non-aesthetic ends and the aesthetic means to those ends. This leads us beyond aesthetics back to a moral system or to more arbitrary kinds of judgment (good of its kind).

The Problem of Definition

One of the most common forms of critical disagreement arises over whether something should be considered aesthetic at all. Confronted with a room full of contemporary paintings, many people wonder whether everything in the room deserves the title "work of art." Some performances are intended to push the limits of art. Then whole forms of art are questioned. In the eighteenth century, landscape gardening was considered an art form. Many eighteenth-century gardens survive, but they have grown and changed as well. Can works of art grow and change? What of ordinary objects that end up in museums? Greek wine-jugs were decorated, but their primary use was to hold wine. We place them in museums and treat them as works of art. If their makers did not think of them as art (and perhaps even lacked the concept of fine art as we use it), what justifies us in treating them as art? What of sacred objects in churches? Can they also be art? What of buildings? Is architecture an art form? What of movies that have no author in the normal sense? Can there be art without an artist?

The uses and abuses of aesthetic definitions

These kinds of questions raise interesting issues that have occupied many philosophers. Problems about definitions of art and of critical terms became especially important as linguistic analysis came to dominate Anglo-American philosophy in the mid-twentieth century. If understanding language is the key to understanding concepts, clear definitions would be one way to understand language.

The central aesthetic questions seem to involve critical judgments like the value-judgments we have just examined. However, an important distinction needs to be made. Unquestionably, to call something a work of art is usually intended as a form of praise. Loosely used, it may be nothing more than that. We say of a meal we liked that it was a work of art. A perfect game in baseball may be described as a work of art. Those are extensions of the ordinary meaning of 'work of art,' however. More centrally, when we call something a work of art we intend to place it in a category with other things that we value as art. So, except in rare instances, it would be odd to call something a work of art and not intend to value it to some degree as art.

It is possible to distinguish between the value question and the factual question whether something is a work of art, however. Just to say something is a work of art does not place it anywhere on our absolute or comparative scales of values. So something could be a work of art but not be very good. There are bad works of art that we still would be willing to characterize as art. Perhaps some value is always implied. It would be difficult to conceive of something that I would want to call a work of art but that I would think was totally indifferent as art. However, there does seem to be a sense in which 'art' is used as a classificatory term. Classificatory terms merely place an object in a group or exclude objects from the group. They imply nothing about the relative merits or place of the objects within the group. For example, in order to be in a dog show, an animal must be a dog. So 'dog' can be used as a classificatory term. Of the total animals in the world, some are dogs. That says nothing about whether any particular dog has any merit. In fact, of course, it would not be enough for a dog to be a dog to get in most shows. Additional conditions are prescribed. By itself, the operation of classification does not take us very far. It can be quite arbitrary, for example. We can create classes merely by specifying a set of conditions.

"The League of Red-Headed Men" was an arbitrary class in the Sherlock Holmes story. It turned out to be merely a ruse.

Clear classification requires some set of conditions that determines whether an object is or is not within the class. We have such conditions for dogs and for red-headed men. In difficult cases, the conditions may have to be quite precise and carefully applied. In athletes, the test for gender used chromosomes. When a professional tennis player underwent a sex-change operation, this presented a problem and the test had to be modified. From the standpoint of classification, the important thing is to have some criteria that are sufficient to determine membership. Classification in this sense is an all-or-nothing kind of thing. One cannot be a little bit pregnant or almost a dog. The test must be sufficient to provide a yes or a no.

In the case of art, it seems that this is the kind of test we would like to have. We would like to be able to say of some movies that they are works of art and of others that they are not. Then we could go about our critical business with a definite class of things to work on. Unfortunately, the matter proves more difficult than that. The kind of problems that arise have to do with the nature of definitions. Definitions do a number of jobs in language. Some definitions are stipulative, for example. They specify that a word is to be taken in a certain way. As Humpty Dumpty says to Alice, "When I use a word, it means just what I choose it to mean – neither more nor less." Other definitions are theoretical. They give a meaning to a term within the context of a theory. For example, the term 'force' in physics does not mean just any kind of force. It is specifically the product of the mass and acceleration of a body ($F = MA$). Other definitions are persuasive. When I define 'medicare' as "a wasteful government welfare program that benefits primarily the medical establishment," everything in the definition may be true, but it is hardly an impartial way of identifying the program. The definition is designed to make a classification in a way that persuades others against the program. The most formal kind of definition, however, provides a set of criteria that tell us that a term applies to a thing in such a way that we know in an essential way what that thing is. This is the kind of definition that we would like to have for the purposes of distinguishing one thing from another.

A formal definition provides classificatory conditions that are both necessary and sufficient to locate any object that is a member of the class. A necessary condition says that all members of the class will satisfy that condition. A sufficient condition says that anything that satisfies that condition will be a member of the class. Obviously, some conditions could be necessary without being sufficient, and some conditions could be sufficient without being necessary. For example, being a beagle is sufficient for being a dog and thus getting into the dog show. But all dogs in the show need not be beagles. And being a mammal is necessary for being a dog, but since cats are also mammals, being a mammal is not sufficient for getting in the dog show. To provide a definition, we need some set of conditions that will be both necessary and sufficient at the same time. Then all and only those things in the class will satisfy the definition.

Some objects are easily identified as the result of a system of classification. Biology and chemistry historically developed out of classificatory schemes, for example. So in those areas, formal definitions work well. The necessary and sufficient conditions for some element being oxygen or for some plant belonging to a phylum can be given precisely, in part because the concepts of oxygen and plant species were set up to provide classification in the first place. In plane geometry, the existence of a basic set of rules, called axioms, allows us to easily specify the necessary and sufficient conditions for something being a right triangle. All right triangles are three-sided plane figures with one ninety-degree interior angle. The nature of axioms provides us with the kind of rules we need. Outside of these areas, however, providing formal definitions that can withstand close inspection is remarkably difficult. The Greek philosopher Socrates sought definitions for important human concepts such as justice and friendship. His discussions usually failed to provide satisfactory answers. There is an old story that Socrates and his friends were trying to define 'man.' The proposed definition was "a featherless biped." Someone broke up the discussion by tossing a plucked chicken into the midst of the group and saying, "Behold, Socrates' man."

Socrates' failure to discover the definitions he sought should not be taken as a philosophical failure, however. As Socrates argued, the only total failure would be if there were such definitions but we had not even tried to find them. The attempt to formulate definitions, even if it does not succeed, may increase our understanding of the term and object. Trying to discover necessary and sufficient conditions for the application of a word leads us to consider just which things the word should and should not be applied to and why. Even if we cannot fully define a word like 'justice,' it is useful to know that it involves more than obedience to law (because laws can be unjust) and more than obeying the will of God (because God wills what is just, rather than making something just by willing it). 'Obeys the law' is not a sufficient condition because it would include too many acts. 'Obeys God's will' might be sufficient if God never wills anything that is unjust, but it is not necessary since

God's will is not what makes an act just. There is no c
saying God willed something unjust (Zeus did). We use
help us analyze terms even if we fail to formulate a success

The most obvious aesthetic situation in which we woul
a formal definition arises when we want to tell whether son
or not. We implicitly treat art differently in a number of   and
theoretical situations. Practically, for example, we grant art a greater
latitude than non-art. We do not expect art to fulfill an economic or
material need. We preserve some old buildings even though they occupy
prime commercial sites. We install public sculpture, and disputes arise
over whether it should remain. We exempt art from some legal requirements. Pictures of naked women in museums are not subject to obscenity laws; on billboards, they would be. Theoretically, we approach art
differently. If someone wrapping a building in plastic is art, we try to
see what is happening. If it is not art, it is a public nuisance and we arrest
the person responsible. Unless we have some way to tell whether something is art or not, we do not know which public rules apply, and we
do not know what our proper approach should be.

The practical situations are less important (though more sensational)
than the theoretical ones. A few obscenity and libel cases turn on what
is or is not art, but few of us will find ourselves involved in such dilem-
mas. More commonly, we are genuinely puzzled about how we should
approach some of the more esoteric performances in the contemporary
art world. We would really like to know why and how bricks on a
museum floor should be regarded as art rather than leftover building
materials.

We might attempt to resolve our uncertainty quickly by defining 'work
of art' as any specially made aesthetic object, and then defining an aesthetic object as something that produces or tends to produce an aesthetic
experience. This would tie 'work of art' closely to the ideas of aesthetic
experience and aesthetic pleasure that we discussed earlier. Something
like this understanding certainly is implied by many of the modern uses
of the term 'art.' As a definition, this also has the advantage of preserv-
ing a link between art and other kinds of aesthetic experience. However,
while we clearly want to keep a relation between art and whatever idea
we have of aesthetic feeling, as a definition this kind of formulation does
not get us very far.

The problem is that we need the definition to be more independent of
what is being defined than the notions of aesthetic experience or feeling
and art are. We can see this if we reflect on the kinds of things that guide
our thinking about aesthetic experience in the first place. Two areas are
important: works of art and natural perceptions. Our perceptions of

nature that we call aesthetic are, in turn, just those that have most in common with art. It may even be that nature follows art aesthetically. We tend to view nature as aesthetic in just those instances when it reminds us most of a poem or a painting that we know and find aesthetically pleasing. We make our gardens and landscapes look like paintings rather than the other way around, and we seek out those natural views – flowers, landscapes, seascapes, etc. – that we have learned to look for in paintings and written descriptions. So we get our ideas of what is aesthetic from our experiences of art and certain kinds of natural perception that are closely related to art. If we now reverse the process and define art as an aesthetic object, we have a very small circle. We identify aesthetic objects by referring to our experiences of art and those experiences that are like our experiences of art. Then we define art by referring to aesthetic objects. This is what is known as a circular definition. A brother is a male sibling, and a sibling is either a brother or sister. I have not succeeded in defining either term. Circles in definitions are not always bad. If we can bring in enough verbal equations, we can form a picture of how a word is used and that is a good definition. Linguists and textual critics use this method by assembling as many occurrences of a term as possible and looking for what they all have in common and how they vary. However, a very small circle is not informative. It merely substitutes one term for another without adding anything to either.

We must try to find our way out of the circle. Attempts at definitions of 'art' begin with some obvious attempts to locate art works on the basis of their non-aesthetic properties. For example, a work of art might be defined as an imitation in some medium of an object, intended for pleasure and display. That definition would cover realistic paintings and some music. Novels, plays, and poems could be regarded as imitations of actions or forms of utterance. (A lyric poem could be thought of as an imitation of a speaker actually addressing someone, for example.) "In some medium" eliminates imagined works of art that never get produced; unwritten poems are not works of art. The second clause, "intended for pleasure and display" is supposed to eliminate imitations that serve commercial purposes. A magazine picture of a soup can in an advertisement is not art. Andy Warhol's paintings of soup cans may be.

A simple attempt at a definition like this is not very successful. It is easily criticized from two directions. Remember, a formal definition is supposed to supply both necessary and sufficient conditions. To criticize a formal definition, therefore, we can try to show that the conditions are not necessary and/or that they are not sufficient. If a condition is not really necessary, there will be things that we agree are art, but that do not satisfy the condition. ("If this is art, then it [necessarily] is . . ." will be false.) We say that the definition is too narrow; it would rule out things that we do not want to rule out. It does not include everything that it should. Assume that we are agreed that some non-programmatic music is art. It does not imitate anything. Then our trial definition does not apply to that music, so the definition is too narrow. ("If it is not an imitation, then it is not music" is false.)

If a condition is not really sufficient, then it will include things that we do not feel are art. Applying the condition would say that X is art when we do not think that X should be included. The claim that the condition is sufficient includes too much. We say that such definitions are too broad. They include more than they should. Someone who can do bird-calls may be able to imitate birds, get pleasure from it, and be willing to display this talent on any occasion. It seems doubtful that we want to include bird-calls in art. So being an imitation that is intended for pleasure and is displayed is not enough to make something art. As a condition, it is not sufficient, and our definition is too broad. ("If this is a bird-call performance, then it is art" is false.) Obviously, a definition can be both too broad and too narrow at the same time. It can include too much and also leave out things that should be included. We can only conclude that this definition fails to provide either necessary or sufficient conditions.

As an attempt at definition, two additional points emerge from our example, however. First, we can see one way that we might try to fix the definition. We could add more conditions. Additional conditions might eliminate bird-calls, for example. It would only be sufficient for something to be art if it were (1) an imitation, (2) intended for pleasure and display, and (3) some non bird call condition. And we could add conditions that would be alternatives; it is necessary only that it is either an imitation or a formal expression, for example. Such attempts to improve definitions are likely to be fraught with danger. Every new condition added disjunctively (connected by 'or') to take care of something that we have left out is going to include more things and thus may include too much. Every attempt to narrow the conditions is in danger of leaving out other things that we had previously included. The more conditions we add, the more complicated and specialized the definition becomes. It tends to be adjusted to every new example in special ways. We say that such definitions are ad hoc; they apply only to the cases that we already had to account for, so they do no real work and tell us nothing.

Another problem is that theoretical terms tend to creep into our definitions. Here we tried to define art as an imitation. 'Imitation' is a word whose meaning seems simple enough. An imitation is something that is like something else without being that thing. It is a copy. But applied to art, 'imitation' tends to take on special meanings. In what sense is music or a building an imitation? Does a novel copy anything? To make the definition work, we need a theory of imitation that will describe much more than a simple process of drawing a picture that can be recognized as a representation of something else or making a copy of some other object. 'Imitation' becomes a key theoretical term. The more important the term, the more difficulty we will have in getting into our definition all of the appropriate senses and limitations that the theory prescribes. Definitions have a nasty tendency to lead only to more definitions.

Finally, we may begin to suspect that we have begun in the wrong place. We wanted to distinguish works of art from non-art, so we considered a definition of 'art.' Our problems arose because there are so many different kinds of art that as soon as we take account of one, we have created a problem about another. Not all terms need have a single definition, however. One way to regard definitions is as summary lists. A perfect definition would be provided by a complete list of everything that a term designated. We could define 'citizen of England in 1089' by a census like the Domesday Book. All and only those listed in the book are citizens of England in 1089, so the list is a perfect set of necessary and sufficient conditions. We need only look up any individual to see if he/she is on the list. Anyone on the list satisfies the conditions; anyone not on the list does not. In that case, the meaning of our term 'citizen of England in 1089' is just the list of all the citizens connected by a series of 'ors'. This is sometimes called a disjunctive or extensional definition. We might regard any generic term as having a disjunctive definition made up of more specific definitions. We use some terms to group together more precisely defined kinds of things. In this case, we could treat 'art' as a generic term and try instead to define things like 'novel,' 'poem,' 'play,' 'painting,' etc. It need not be the case that there is only one set of conditions that applies to everything that is art.

However, disjunctive definitions only defer the problem. Unless we can get down to specific names of individuals (like the individual citizens in the Domesday Book), we will still have to be able to supply definitions of terms that satisfy our conditions. That seems to be no easier for 'novel' and 'tragedy' than it is for 'work of art.' At some point, we must begin to suspect that the difficulties in providing definitions for key aesthetic terms indicate that these terms are not very much like 'right triangle' and 'oxygen.' If that is the case, we will have learned a great deal about our aesthetic language, but we should not expect to find formal definitions of its terms.

Essentialism, anti-essentialism, and aesthetic definitions

This is not the place to try out all of the definitions or even all of the major types of definitions. The history of aesthetics provides many different attempts at definitions. Most of them are the product of particular aesthetic theories. All have been extensively criticized. They all share one feature. They assume that works of art and aesthetic experiences are the kinds of things that have some essential set of features. They are therefore essentialist theories. At one time, it was more or less assumed that anything that could be treated philosophically had to have some essential qualities. For example, if there is a moral philosophy, then all morally good acts and rightness of action must have something in common. If there is a philosophy of science, then scientific theories must be about some reality in some essential way that can be described. Essentialist theories do not imply that we *know* the essential features of what we are talking about, but an essentialist about art holds that some set of features must be essential to aesthetic experience and that all art has those features in common. Otherwise, it is maintained, we could not use the terms 'art' and 'aesthetic' meaningfully.

The very idea that aesthetics should be approached in essentialist terms eventually is called into question. This reconsideration of various forms of philosophical essentialism is one of the major contributions of Ludwig Wittgenstein (1889–1951) and his followers. Two lines of argument strike at the essentialist assumption. First, no matter how carefully definitions are constructed, they seem to lag behind what is going on in the art world. If the process of definition were really getting us closer to understanding art, then even if we do not have a perfect definition, we should begin to see what art is and where it is going. We should find that our definitions encompass new art forms as they appear. Instead, new art forms are constantly forcing changes in the definitions. Paintings no longer have to represent anything. Music does not have to obey the rules of harmony. Novels and plays do not have to have a beginning, a middle, and an end. Works of art do not have to be permanent. That our definitions do not account for everything might be no more than a weakness in our philosophical technique. The problem is that our definitions do not even approximate what is going on in the art world. We have to wonder if there are any essential features of works of art.

Second, the kinds of things offered as essential features turn out to be problematic themselves. We saw earlier that aesthetic predicates work more like metaphors than like simple property terms. If that is the case, then looking for non-aesthetic features that will be essential to aesthetic responses is based on a misunderstanding of what aesthetic features are.

Classical writers thought that certain proportions appeared as beautiful to a normal observer. These proportions fit the classical ideas of harmony and beauty. For example, in the eighteenth century, the painter and engraver William Hogarth (1697–1764) maintained that a sensuously curved line was a necessary condition for beauty. He illustrated his theory with engravings. However, like the definition of man as a featherless biped, Hogarth's engravings are easily parodied. Harmony and sensuousness are aesthetic properties described by aesthetic predicates. The attempt to link them to a particular shape of line or a particular mathematical ratio involves us in trying to understand aesthetic predicates again in terms of non-aesthetic properties. Essential definitions fail to capture the aesthetic features.

Under pressure from these kinds of criticism, aesthetics has moved away from attempts to provide formal definitions. Not all terms have to have essentialist kinds of definitions in order to be meaningful. We saw that aesthetic predicates require metaphor-like interpretations and do not follow rules. The nouns that those predicates are describing are correspondingly flexible. To say that some book is a novel is still to classify the book; however, what is included in the class need not have any single feature in common with all of the other things in the class of novels. Things can be added to the class on the basis of similarities to what is already in the class. As more things are added, more possibilities for additions are created. We might imagine beginning with a small group of works – the classical novels of the early eighteenth century. Then in the nineteenth century, historical novels increase the scope of the term 'novel.' As more novels are written, novels that lack traditional plots are taken in. By the time we arrive at the contemporary novel, none of the essential features that were present in the novels at the beginning need be included. The term 'novel' has expanded. It is still a useful class term, however. Things that are not sufficiently similar to the books that are already in the class of novels cannot be added. So works like Truman Capote's "non-fiction" novel, *In Cold Blood*, can be included, but this textbook cannot. It is not enough like a novel to make a plausible candidate.

We call terms that classify things but permit expansion open terms. Open terms are still working classifications. They exclude some things and include others. The difference is that no set of necessary and sufficient conditions applies, so no formal definition of the term is possible. In the absence of a formal definition, different means of determining what a term does or does not refer to are required. We still need criteria, but they must be based on what already exists. So, for example, in order to argue that some new work is a novel, we must be prepared to show how it is similar to other things that are already known to be novels. We work from paradigms to extensions on the basis of criteria of similarity. There will always be a few works whose status will be in doubt in this technique. These are "borderline cases." In time, such borderline cases tend to be either promoted into the classification or excluded from it. At the present time, "novelizations" based on films might be borderline cases, for example. Are they merely expanded screenplays, or should they be thought of as independent works? The matter will be settled not by a definition but by the continued practice of reading and writing such works.

The way to apply open terms in aesthetics depends on examining what is sometimes called the "practice" of the artists and critics who are concerned with aesthetic issues. We have developed a vague but workable concept of art. It is open to amateur and professional workers. The idea of a practice is that what is actually being done is more important than some abstract theories about art. Terms are put to use. They do a job for us in communicating and describing what we do. The activities that involve language and the uses of language determine meaning. So to find out what a term means or how we should provide criteria for classification, we should examine the actual practices as they are going on. Again, this does not mean that everything that is being done is uncritically accepted. That is why borderline cases arise. An easy mistake to fall into in this approach is to look only at contemporary practice. In order not to be chaotic, open concepts must be viewed historically as well as in the present. But instead of looking for essential conditions, we take a different direction. We look at the historical and present use of terms as they occur in the actual workings of people who make aesthetic claims and produce purported aesthetic objects. Then we can make a considered decision about whether a new application of an aesthetic noun is justified.

The recognition of open terms has contributed to a suspicion that traditional aesthetic theory with its expectations of essential properties and definable links between aesthetic and non-aesthetic language is itself a mistake. If we get our aesthetic concepts by analyzing the practices of the art world, couldn't we get along without theory altogether? In that case, we would look to our ordinary intuitions for our aesthetic judgments, and we would sharpen those intuitions by immersion in the art world itself. Modern aesthetics and philosophy of art began in the eighteenth century as an attempt to find a place for feeling in the rational and empirical world of philosophy. Perhaps, the argument goes now, we should declare the end of aesthetics with the end of that modern era of philosophizing. Aesthetics would be replaced by a variety of popular and professional circles, each with its own evolving set of criteria. No fixed limits should be set on such aesthetic freedom.

I think that it is premature to abandon the role of theory, however. Even as we recognize the diversity of aesthetic practices, we should also recognize the theoretical implications of the use of language within those practices. When we use or invent a description for some aesthetic object, we do two things: we single out that object and include it in our practice, and we create the possibility for both positive and negative descriptions based on that practice. For example, say that I describe a new book as a postmodern novel. I have first of all indicated that that book should be included in the category of novel that reaches back to all earlier novels and through them to the history of prose fiction. Whether I succeed in having this book accepted as a novel or not, I have hypothetically positioned it as a novel just by the action of speaking of it in this way. Second, I have combined aesthetic language in such a way that I create theoretical possibilities. Something is or is not postmodern, and by extension, some things are not postmodern in ways that include earlier novels. In effect, my use of a term changes the theoretical character of premodern and modern novels. Novels that before were only modern now also have the additional quality of being not-postmodern. As we build categories and advocate inclusion or exclusion in those categories that we build, we continue to do aesthetic theory.

This way of thinking about theory has opened up additional ways of considering definitions. The kind of definitions that required necessary and sufficient conditions based on non-aesthetic terms proved informative but difficult to construct. Once we have recognized the openness of aesthetic terms, we can return to definitions and include our aesthetic practice in our defining process. An activity like talking about some object in aesthetic terms creates a relation between the aesthetic language and that object. We can look for ways to take that relation-creating process into the definition. Then our definitions would be based not on essential non-aesthetic properties but on essential relations between users of the aesthetic language and what they describe.

One interesting proposal along these lines began with the idea that there are users of aesthetic language who comprise a rough, ill-defined but coherent group called the art world. Then a work of art is just whatever members of this art world single out for talking about as art. Their talk need not make an object a good or bad work of art; they may even fail to convince anyone else to take them seriously. But by being a part of the art world and performing this act of calling something art, they make the thing art. This stops short of just reducing a work of art to whatever anyone calls a work of art because it requires a pre-existing practice in the art world to make the calling possible and because anyone who does call something art takes the risk of losing status within the art world. It also requires that the language being used has a performative function. That is, the object is not just being described, but is being changed by the act of uttering the description. Some language does serve this performative function. Ceremonies, rituals, and some kinds of author- itative declarations depend on it. Typical examples are priests pronounc- ing marriage vows, umpires making calls, and officials awarding status like citizenship. Still, it is a very open, non-restrictive definition based on a relation between language users and objects to which they refer.

In its simple forms, such a definition still seems too broad. It allows in all kinds of things that lack any obvious aesthetic value, and it is not clear that the performative function can be extended so far without some more rigorous criteria for membership in the art world. After all, one does not get to be an umpire by just signing up. One has to be appointed. So the definition probably needs revision. It is not clear that that can be done without losing its advantages.

One suggestion would distinguish between making something an aes- thetic object and making it a work of art. To be a work of art, some- thing must succeed within some complex set of conditions. But to be an aesthetic object, it might be enough to be pointed out in a certain way by a member of the art world. Then the linguistic model required is not performative but imperative. It is a way of extending the linguistic extension of the term by creating a new criterion for its application and inclusion in a class. It would be left to other considerations whether the imperative would be obeyed and the object become included in the practice of the art world. On this view, the operation would go like this. Someone would single out something – say a new book – as an aesthetic object by implicitly or explicitly treating it as a novel. That could be done by an act of calling it a novel, by merely describing it in ways in which novels are described, or by treating it as a novel, perhaps by writing a review of it for the fiction section of a publication. That action includes two parts. First, it classifies the new book. This part is accom- plished as soon as anyone agrees to play by the linguistic rules proposed by the speaker. In effect, the speaker has issued a command, and the hearer has agreed, however temporarily, to play by those rules. At that point, we are operating in the art world and playing by its rules. For better or worse, the book has become an aesthetic object. Then it be- comes a matter of comparison with other things in the classification and the persuasiveness and success of the new book itself. If all (or enough) of the conditions are met, the book succeeds in becoming a novel and, at the same time, changes the scope of what we call novels. The aesthetic object has become a work of art. We are off into the realms of art theory and art history again.[5] All of this seems inescapably bound up with theory, so the announcement of the death of aesthetic theory is premature.

Conclusions

We began by examining different kinds of definitions: formal definitions that require necessary and sufficient conditions, persuasive and theoretical definitions that establish a usage for a term, and open definitions that allow borderline cases and changes in meaning. Definitions are important because we want to distinguish art from non-art. In aesthetics, the search for definitions begins with essentialist assumptions – i.e. that the use of 'work of art' requires some essential characteristic or property. Essentialist assumptions are challenged in contemporary aesthetics, and it is questioned whether aesthetic theory is possible at all. Perhaps we have only a range of practices.

Practices in the art world and relations between members of the art world and possible works of art open up new possibilities, however. A definition of art can be considered not on the basis of essential properties but on the basis of performative language and actions by members of the art world. If that kind of definition proves too simple, it still suggests new possibilities for aesthetic theory. We have worked our way around to having to consider the history and comparative relations of a multitude of aesthetic performances if we are to succeed in maintaining the reality of a distinction between art and non-art. Yet it seems worth doing. We do not want to close ourselves off to any new possibilities. We also do not want to be so open that we lose all standards and distinctions. Some things are art. They succeed in ways that matter to us. Other things are not art. They appear and fade without loss, or they actually corrupt the art world with inferior kinds of things. Telling the difference is a matter of clear distinctions, historical perspective, comparative classification, and finally of judgment and definitions. That is the point of our aesthetic language.

References and Suggestions for Further Reading

Getting started

Beauty

Plato's treatment of beauty and art varies. The description of beauty given here draws on discussions in the dialogues "Hippias Major," "The Symposium," and "Phaedrus," which are available in many different translations. The metaphysical theory of beauty can be found most clearly in Plotinus, *Ennead I.6*. For a modern theory of beauty, see George Santayana, *The Sense of Beauty* (first publ. 1896; New York: Dover, 1955). Two influential treatments of beauty in recent aesthetics are Mary Mothersill, *Beauty Restored* (Oxford: Oxford University Press, 1984) and Guy Sircello, *A New Theory of Beauty* (Princeton: Princeton University Press, 1975).

Taste

Theories of taste were widespread in the eighteenth century. One of the most influential treatments of taste as a sense is Francis Hutcheson, *An Inquiry into the Original of Our Ideas of Beauty and Virtue* (London: J. Darby, 1725); selections appear in several of the anthologies mentioned in the "Suggestions for Further Reading" at the end of the Introduction. The problems of judgment and taste are discussed in David Hume's "Of the Standard of Taste" (1757), which is also frequently anthologized. The identification of aesthetic feeling begins with Alexander Baumgarten, but the most influential separation of aesthetic intuition from conceptual and practical ideas is found in Immanuel Kant, *Critique of Judgment* (first publ. 1790; Indianapolis: Hackett, 1987), particularly §§10–17. 'Taste' in the sense of good taste is interestingly advocated by George Santayana in *Reason in Art* (New York: Charles Scribner's Sons, 1905). Recent treatments of taste include Frank N. Sibley, "Aesthetic Concepts," *Philosophical Review* 68 (1959): 351–73 and Ted Cohen, "Aesthetic/Non-Aesthetic and the Concept of Taste: A Critique of Sibley's Position," *Theoria* 39 (1973): 113–52.

Aesthetic feeling

A psychological approach to aesthetic feeling is central to Edward Bullough's classic Essay, "'Psychical Distance' as a Factor in Art and an Aesthetic Principle," *British Journal of Psychology* 5 (1912): 87–118, which is frequently anthologized. Clive Bell combines aesthetic emotion with a formalist critical approach in *Art* (New York: Capricorn Books, 1958).

Aesthetic predicates

Aesthetic description and metaphors

The range of work on metaphor is extremely wide. A useful anthology is Mark Johnson, ed., *Philosophical Perspectives on Metaphor* (Minneapolis: University of Minnesota Press, 1981). See also Paul Ricoeur, *The Rule of Metaphor* (Toronto: University of Toronto Press, 1977); Philip Wheelwright, *Metaphor and Reality* (Bloomington: Indiana University Press, 1962); and Colin Turbayne, *The Myth of Metaphor* (Columbia, SC: University of South Carolina Press, 1971).

The uses of aesthetic predicates

Among the most influential treatment of aesthetic predicates is Sibley's essay, noted above, "Aesthetic Concepts." See also Isabel C. Hungerland, "The Logic of Aesthetic Concepts," *Proceedings and Addresses of the American Philosophical*

Association 36 (1963): 43–66; and J.O. Urmson, "What Makes a Situation Aesthetic?," *Proceedings of the Aristotelian Society* Supplementary Volume 31 (1957): 75–92. For critical language see Paul Ziff, "Reasons in Art Criticism," in Israel Scheffler, ed., *Philosophy and Education* (Boston: Allyn and Bacon, 1958) as a starting-point. The problems of definition have been discussed very extensively. A good beginning is Paul Ziff, "The Task of Defining a Work of Art," *Philosophical Review* 63 (1953): 68–78; Joseph Margolis, "Mr. Weitz and the Definition of Art," *Philosophical Studies* 9 (1958): 88–94; and Monroe Beardsley, "The Definition of the Arts," *Journal of Aesthetics and Art Criticism* 20 (1961): 175–87. Among the recent works is Stephen Davies, *Definitions of Art* (Ithaca: Cornell University Press, 1991).

Criticism and value terms

The quotation from René Descartes is the first sentence of Part I of his *Discourse on the Method of Rightly Conducting the Reason and Seeking for Truth in the Sciences*; see e.g. René Descartes, *Discourse on Method and Meditations* (Indianapolis: Bobbs-Merrill, 1980). The term 'metacriticism' was introduced by Monroe Beardsley in his seminal text on aesthetics, *Aesthetics: Problems in the Philosophy of Criticism* (New York: Harcourt, Brace & World, 1958; repr. Indianapolis: Hackett, 1981).

Judgments and aesthetic value

Two recent treatments of aesthetic value are George Dickie, *Evaluating Art* (Philadelphia: Temple University Press, 1988) and Alan H. Goldman, *Aesthetic Value* (Boulder, CO: Westview Press, 1995).

The value of feeling

Immanuel Kant distinguishes two kinds of pleasure in the *Critique of Judgment*, §§3–5; "disinterestedness" is Kant's term for distinguishing the aesthetic from everything that has an end. Clive Bell's aesthetic and metaphysical hypotheses are found in *Art*; the analogy to mountain peaks and valleys is on p. 31. Shelley's claim that poets are the unacknowledged legislators of the world is in Percy Bysshe Shelley, "Defence of Poetry," *Criticism: The Major Texts*, ed. Walter Jackson Bate (New York: Harcourt, Brace & World, 1952): 429–35. For Hegel, see G.W.F. Hegel, *Philosophy of Mind* (Oxford: Oxford University Press, 1971).

The problem of definition

The uses and abuses of aesthetic definitions

For help on working with definitions, students should consult one of the multitude of introductory-level logic or critical thinking texts, e.g. Francis Dauer, *Critical Thinking* (Oxford: Oxford University Press, 1989).

Essentialism, anti-essentialism, and aesthetic definitions

The problems of essentialism in aesthetics are discussed by Morris Weitz, "The Role of Theory in Aesthetics," *Journal of Aesthetics and Art Criticism* 15 (1956): 27–35, and Maurice Mandelbaum, "Family Resemblances and Generalization Concerning the Arts," *American Philosophical Quarterly* 2 (1965): 219–28, both of which are frequently anthologized. Hogarth's definition of a beautiful line is found in William Hogarth, *The Analysis of Beauty* (first publ. 1753; Oxford: Clarendon Press, 1955). A "practice" is traceable back to Ludwig Wittgenstein; see his *Lectures and Conversations on Aesthetics, Psychology, and Religious Belief* (Berkeley: University of California Press, 1972). It has been influentially developed by Richard Wollheim, *Art and its Objects* (Cambridge: Cambridge University Press, 1980); and by Arthur Danto, *The Transfiguration of the Commonplace* (Cambridge, MA: Harvard University Press, 1981) and *The Philosophical Disenfranchisement of Art* (New York: Columbia University Press, 1986). The way that language creates theoretical possibilities by its use is discussed by Danto in "The Artworld," *Journal of Philosophy* 61 (1964): 571–84. George Dickie developed the possibilities of relational definitions in *Art and the Aesthetic: An Institutional Analysis* (Ithaca: Cornell University Press, 1974). I have discussed the possibilities of an imperative analysis of institutional conferral and of distinguishing aesthetic objects and works of art in Dabney Townsend, *Aesthetic Objects and Works of Art* (Wolfesboro, NH: Longwood Academic Press, 1989).

2

Aesthetic Analysis and its Objects

Formal Analysis

We must be able to formulate our aesthetic language and theories in the context of the history of art and the current practices of the art world. Aesthetics is not limited to art. As we have seen, some theories start with a concept of beauty instead of art. Even if 'art' is the central term, it can still be extended to cover natural objects. Irrespective of what our theories are, if they are to be persuasive they must be shown to apply to all of those things that the art world needs to take account of. The theoretical judgment might be negative. If we do not think that some contemporary claims for art are justified, the theory can try to show that. For example, we might want to reject such contemporary "art" as pop art and performance art. But that still takes account of the claims. If we think that art extends beyond what the art world currently considers aesthetic, that too can be argued. For example, many popular forms only slowly come to be accepted as art. Shakespeare's drama was a popular form of his day. Now it is regarded as art. Perhaps movies and rock and roll are destined to join the canon. That is something that can be argued for or against by a theory. In every case, such arguments presuppose an ability to perceive and describe what we take to be the aesthetic objects of our theoretical language.

Form and content

One of the most important approaches to describing what we perceive aesthetically distinguishes form and content. At its simplest level, this distinction seems obvious. It is not limited to aesthetic objects. Anything that has been produced by human beings so that it has a meaning implies some distinction between form and content. The sentences of this paragraph have a form, and (one hopes) they also convey something to the reader. The form of a sentence includes its grammar and the system of meanings that are attached to each word and to combinations of words in a language. Sentences that describe or assert something begin with a noun-phrase/verb-phrase form. That form is common to a great many sentences with very different meanings. It is elaborated into many variations that also share formal features with other sentences. For example, the noun phrase may be a simple noun, or it may be a noun plus an adjective, or a pronoun, or more complicated noun phrases. What distinguishes form in this sense is that it can be described in a way that does not require us to say what the sentence means.

What the sentence is about is its content. Content is much harder to describe than form because any description of the content will have to have a content in order to convey what is meant. But then that content will have to be conveyed by some form with some content, and we seem to be off on an endless chain that will never get us to the description we desire. That is why one of the most difficult problems in the philosophy of language is giving a theory of the meaning of sentences. It is also why most critics and philosophers emphasize that any distinction between form and content is artificial and analytical. In practice, form and content not only occur together, they also cannot exist alone. "Pure form" has to be the form of something or it will not be form.[1] Content must be given form or there is no content. Yet the distinction between form and content is intuitively obvious. "That book is blue" does not mean the same thing as "That painting is white," yet the two statements share an obvious structural similarity. If we could not recognize the similarities and differences between sentences, we would have to learn every sentence separately in order to learn a language. So we commonly do distinguish form from content, and we use the distinction to help us describe and understand what we perceive.

The distinction between form and content in language implies some system of conventions created by human beings. 'Created' here should be taken rather loosely. We need not assume that at some time some group of people thought up a language in the way that we might think up a code. But differences in languages and families of languages show us that much of the form of our language could be different. The same content can appear in many different forms, and the form is, to some

---

1 In formal logic, the distinction between form or syntax and content or semantics can be maintained rigorously, and there is no requirement that a syntactic form have any semantic interpretation attached to it.

extent, a matter of conventions that have evolved in the course of our history. Whatever one thinks about the ability of animals to communicate by means of signs only marginally extends language.

While we may be impressed with the order that exists in nature and want to extend our distinction between form and content to it, there are significant differences. Consider the atomic structure of an element such as gold. Certainly, we can say that atomic structure is something that is common to all elements, and the particular order and make-up of this atomic structure is what makes gold gold and not lead. But gold is not the content of this atomic structure. Gold is just gold; it is a kind of thing that has an atomic structure. The atomic structure is a part of the thing. Gold can be gold in no other way. Atomic structure shows no conventional differences or history in the same way that language has a history. Of course, the conventions we have for describing atomic structure have a history; our descriptions depend on the history of our science and our representational models. But then, those are clearly forms that we use to describe some content that we call, in our forms, 'atomic structure.' Our science may be conventional. Nature itself is not. Form thus may be something that is simply perceived, but it may also depend heavily on conventions and a system of representation that has a history. In order to distinguish form from content and to describe the form, therefore, we must pay attention both to what we perceive and to the system of representation we have developed to present what we have perceived. Then we can try to identify the content by describing what this form presents in this case.

Form and content in art

We have been talking about form and content in language because the distinction is often one between how something is presented and the meaning that is presented. However, the distinction between form and content, particularly as it applies in aesthetics, is not exactly the same as that between structure and meaning in language. We can see this if we begin with an example of visual form. Consider Gustave Caillebotte's painting, *On the Europe Bridge* (1876–7), reproduced on the cover of this book. Some formal elements strike the eye very clearly in this painting. It is divided horizontally by the bridge railing that divides the picture-plane and vertically by the central bridge girder. The left side is then occupied by two heavy vertical lines – the black-clad figures of the men. The five segments in the lower right quadrant repeat the vertical lines. Two heavy diagonals cross from upper right to lower left, and one moves from center left to lower right. The space is thus divided rigidly into horizontal and vertical sections that are broken by equally emphatic diagonals. These rectilinear forms are countered by the gentle curve of the bridge arcs that are repeated in the bridge railing. Once one becomes aware of these formal elements, they also emerge as minor motifs in the curves of the hats and the faintly visible repeated forms in the background.

These geometrical forms work to present a mechanical, industrial image. The color is similarly subdued and dehumanized. The painting is in tones of gray and black with only a small patch of blue in the coat partially visible on the left. All three human figures are shown with their faces turned away or obscured. Form in this painting is strikingly geometrical, restrained in color, and simplified in presentation.

When we ask about the content of Caillebotte's painting, it has already begun to emerge from our attempts to describe the form. In this case, the objects are easily recognizable. There is a bridge (a real bridge provides the model, as a matter of fact), and there are the figures of three men. But the content is obviously much more than a picture of three men on a bridge. The geometrical form and the gray and black tones of the painting create a dehumanized industrial image that shows a relation between the formally dressed gentlemen in the foreground and the industrial world that produced this iron bridge. The third figure, perhaps in a worker's blue smock, introduces a slightly discordant element. The way that the left-hand figure is only partially included in the picture frame suggests an incompleteness and a disregard for the viewer who is ignored by the scene. Caillebotte has created a scene that shows both the beauty and the lack of humanity in a monument of the industrial age. The content is an expression of complex admiration and distance that cannot be completely captured by anything but the unique presentation of these forms. This is the kind of ordinary scene that would not have been considered suitable for a painting in an earlier age, but that is transformed by Caillebotte into a work of art by his use of visual forms and his ability to see an aesthetic composition in a social and industrial artifact of our age.

Perhaps others do not see exactly what I have described. Perhaps they see less or more. For our purposes, that does not matter. The process of constructing formal descriptions of one medium (painting) in another (critical language) is obviously difficult and subject to considerable variation. The important point is that one can see the form without knowing much about Caillebotte and without having to describe what the painting is about. The description of the form leads directly to a description of the content. A formal description concentrates on the division of the picture-space, the deployment of the lines and shapes, and the use of color. As that formal description progresses, more and more of the elements of the picture appear in relation to the overall form, and from the formal description a more complex content than simply "three figures on a bridge" emerges. What seemed a quite simple painting using simple geometrical forms and little color becomes fascinatingly and endlessly complicated. To the critic and viewer, awareness of these elements is a necessary step to seeing the painting. To the aesthetic philosopher and theoretician, awareness of what one does in seeing the painting is also necessary.

Many of the formal elements in this painting are conventional. Why do gray and black suggest a dehumanized, industrial setting? In part, the relation is natural. Factories tend to produce smoke that is gray and that obscures the sunlight. But those colors also become conventional ways of representing a more subdued setting. Or consider the use of perspective in this painting. Caillebotte has used a complex perspective to create planes with depth but not the kind of depth that draws the eye into the distance. Rather, there are distinct planes: the background, the bridge, the two men on the bridge in the foreground. That kind of layering fits the geometrical structure, but it also utilizes the conventions of perspective and visual depth that Caillebotte inherited. (Compare Caillebotte's way of showing depth with an equally monochrome Chinese scroll painting, for example.) Moreover, Caillebotte did not simply invent this approach to painting. His use of form belongs to a "school" including other painters who are showing the way that iron and steel and sharp angles can be aesthetically involving in contrast to earlier styles that found beauty in natural curves and softer lights. The shock of Caillebotte's subject-matter here is felt more strongly in contrast to other forms of painting.

Comparison of forms

Form is specific to a medium. In painting, form includes line, shape, color, and the arrangement of space. In music, the medium is sound, arranged in patterns through time. A central formal difference between music and painting is that music is not presented all at once but through a sequence of sounds that are heard in time. At one time, such comparisons of different artistic means were a major part of aesthetics. The Roman poet Horace (65–8 BCE) compared poetry and painting, and in the eighteenth century a frequent topic of discussion was the way in which poetry and the literary arts are related to painting and sculpture. Such comparisons can still tell us a great deal about what form is and why it is important. In order to hear the musical form, one must be able to respond to different degrees of tonality, different speeds of distinct sounds, different degrees of loudness, and, in more complex music, different instrumentation. The patterns of a novel develop sequentially in its plot. In contrast, a painting or a piece of sculpture is present to the eye as a whole. Formal differences determine differences in aesthetic possibilities.

A common element in formal analysis is the recognition of patterns. Random sounds are only marginally musical, and random colors are only marginally painting, although in both art forms artists, particularly in recent art, have tested the limits of randomness. Splatter paintings and atonal, unrhythmic music paradoxically highlight form by defying our formal expectations and thus making us aware of the limits of artistic possibility. They also remind us of how much of our formal response is only consciously present as a totality. We do not, except as philosophers or critics, stop to pay attention to the formal elements of a piece of music or a painting individually. Instead, we assimilate them into their patterns and see or hear a whole, though we can identify the parts when we focus on them. (In psychology, the perception of a whole that is not simply the sum of its parts is called gestalt perception.)

Music does not seem to have content in the same way that painting does. Even if music began as a combination of sounds and words – sung poetry – the musical possibilities do not require the assignment of meaning in the way that language has meaning. Individual words retain their meaning in different sentences. Individual notes are sounded the same, but they have no meaning. Nor does music require recognizable objects in the way that painting can use such objects. Some music illustrates a theme or imitates an emotion, but for the most part such "programs" are not necessary for music, and to many they have seemed artificial and intrusive. Abstract music was accepted long before the abstract possibilities of painting were explored. Yet musicians and music critics speak of musical ideas and the emotional meaning of music. Sometimes, such language is clearly metaphorical and evocative. In the absence of the music itself, the musician attempts to describe in words something that will convey a similar emotional content to the music itself. Yet the need for content remains. Music is not empty sounds. The formal patterns serve some more evocative purpose that is, even if imperfectly, captured by our emotional response and the aesthetic predicates that we use to describe our response. Music is sad, stirring, stately; and we know what those descriptions mean even if they do not correspond exactly to psychological systems. The form/content distinction and the unity of form and content are both marks of aesthetic awareness in the first place. We do not seem able to avoid them at either the practical or the theoretical level.

Poetry combines many of the features of music with language. In many ways, therefore, it presents some of the most complex problems for formal analysis. Because the medium is language, one encounters all of the problems of form and content in language. But poetry is not prose. Poetic form and prose form offer different aesthetic possibilities. We should not overlook the aesthetic possibilities of prose. But the story of the person who was shocked to discover that he had been speaking prose all his life has some point. The forms of prose are natural to our speech and writing in ways that poetic form is not. Poetic form imposes an order of sound, rhythm, and interlocked meaning that contributes to the meaning of the poem. Consider the sonnet by Thomas Wyatt (1503–42), "Who So List to Hunt."[2] The very fact that it is a sonnet tells us several things. For one thing, a sonnet has a formal pattern of a specific length (fourteen lines), a regular rhythm (iambic pentameter: a pattern of five unstressed/stressed syllables per line), and a regular rhyme scheme (abba, abba, cddc, ee). Variations are a part of the scheme. For example, the first line begins with a stressed syllable "*Who* so list . . ." before picking up the regular iambic pattern. Other sonnets have different rhyme schemes but are limited to fourteen lines. One is immediately aware of how ordered and artificial the sonnet form is. It exemplifies our idea of poetry, so that some readers have great difficulty adjusting to freer forms.

If we ask how the form presents the content, we are off into the same kind of reflective explication that we encountered in the Caillebotte painting. Wyatt's poem has a subject-matter at several levels. It is about a deer that is royal property, reserved for the king to hunt. But the poem is also about a courtship that is prohibited. The deer is "she," and the lover – the "I" of the poem – is unable to pursue her any longer. He, like everyone else, will fail in this "hunt." The echo in the prohibition is also religious. The words "noli me tangere" are spoken by Christ (John 20: 17) as a prohibition against a touching of the risen Christ that would violate the separation of the sacred and profane worlds. The woman is out of reach in a deeper sense; the lover is like an ordinary person in the presence both of a royal possession and of a religious mystery.

The language reinforces the connections between the layers of images by repeating sounds: "as she *f*leeth a*fore*, / *F*ainting I *f*ollow. I leave *off* there*fore*". The formal devices of alliteration and rhyme connect the words more closely than they would be connected in ordinary speech. We can identify the formal patterns independently of their meaning in this poem, but they are clearly one of the important ways in which the poem

---

2 Wyatt's sonnet may be found in the appendix at the end of the book.

says what it does say. Without them, it would be impossible to hold together in such a compact and effective space all of the levels of meaning – literal, allegorical, and mythic – that Wyatt presents all at once.

A further level of complexity arises from the sonnet form itself and its historical connection to poets such as Sir Thomas Wyatt. Wyatt did not invent the form. In fact, in this case, he is imitating very closely another sonnet by the Italian poet, Petrarch (1304–74). Petrarch's poem "Noli me Tangere" is about his ideal love. The existence of such a love and its expression in sonnet form is a convention of court poetry in renaissance Europe. By imitating Petrarch and writing a sonnet, Wyatt identifies himself with the whole tradition of courtly love and its conventional expression as a polite form of homage. Moreover, Wyatt may well have been commenting on his own actual situation. Wyatt was a courtier to King Henry VIII, and he was reputed to have had an affair with Anne Boleyn before she married Henry. If this sonnet is addressed to Anne, as many think, then Wyatt is not just commenting in an abstract way on the king's prerogatives. In effect, Anne is beyond his reach because she is the king's, though Henry is subtly reminded that he too may not be able to hold her ("And wild for to hold, though I seem tame"). Form ties together conventions that allow expression of ideas developed in an historical context with the specific history and emotions of the poet and his audience.

Conclusions

The analysis of form and content could go on through all of the media of art. It is a crucial skill for both appreciators of art and critics. For philosophical aesthetics, however, the very existence of this complex interplay of form and content is more important than the specific examples. To summarize, we note several important features.

1 Form depends on the medium and its possibilities. These possibilities vary from one medium to another. They are not the same for sculpture as for architecture, though both involve three-dimensional constructions, for example.
2 The possibilities are shaped by conventions and history. Neither form nor content exists in a vacuum or an idealized space. To appreciate form, one needs to see it in a context. Form is not isolated from history, therefore.
3 Even though form is both specific to a medium and historically situated, formal features can be shared by different art forms. Form is an ordering principle, and similar orders are possible in different media.

Temporal order connects poetry and music. Narrative order connects films and novels. Spatial order connects drama and painting.

4   Form is perceived, but it is not itself the object of perception. We need not mechanically identify the rhyme scheme of Wyatt's sonnet in order to hear it.

5   Finally, form and content are two aspects of a single meaning or expression. In effect, our ability to perceive formal elements that are presentations of aesthetic objects is the basis for all of our claims about art and beauty. The evidence for any theory in aesthetics must come from this basic ability to perceive and analyse art and beauty, and that implies that we can perceive and analyse the formal properties of some perceptual objects that we are aware of in some larger aesthetic context. Formal analysis is thus a skill necessary both for full appreciation of the aesthetic and for supplying evidence upon which we can construct well-founded theories.

Aesthetic Objects

The analysis of form and content leads us to a question about just what aesthetics is concerned with. So far, we have been content to examine our experience in two areas: natural beauty (or other natural aesthetic phenomena) and art. We have seen that both beauty and art raise problems for descriptive language and for definitions. When we analyse form, we must ask "The form of what?" and if form implies content, we must also ask "The content of what?" What is it that we are talking about when we describe a range of experiences as aesthetic? The generic answer is that we are talking about aesthetic objects. We must now try to make that answer more precise.

What is an 'object'?

To begin with, we must avoid some possible confusions. 'Object' is most commonly used to identify physical objects – things like rocks and trees and books and even animate objects like dogs and people. But 'object' can also be used more neutrally to designate whatever someone is capable of thinking about. The number one is an object, but it is not a physical object like a stone. Goodness might be considered an object without even the separate identity that individual numbers have. Goodness only exists as a property of some good thing, yet we can refer to it and think of it independently of any particular thing. Physical objects presuppose that we know a great deal about the object – that it exists, that it belongs to some class of things, that it has a certain kind of reality (the kind that we can sense), that it can be singled out and identified separately from other objects, etc. We may not want to presuppose all of those things about aesthetic objects until we have examined them more closely. So to begin with, we will use 'object' in its more neutral sense when applied to aesthetic objects. In that sense, an aesthetic object is just something that can be referred to by the subject of sentences using aesthetic predicates or that can be the reference for our experiences that we describe in aesthetic terms. We need not presuppose any more than that we can give some account of what we refer to.

That may turn out to be no small task, however. We can think up some pretty bizarre combinations: a beautiful round square or a sky blue pink angel. These kinds of combinations led some philosophers to suppose that there were not just imaginary objects but even non-existent and impossible objects. Not only is there no sky blue pink angel, but such a combination of colors is internally contradictory. It does not just not exist; it literally cannot exist. That stretches the use of 'object' intolerably, so we will limit 'object' to at least logically possible combinations – something that could be referred to in some possible world, if not in this one. That still gives 'object' a very wide scope, and it should allow us to consider any theory of aesthetic objects that has an application to our experience.

Another possible confusion arises from the problems we examined about definitions of art and aesthetic experience. 'Object' does not imply that we can define precisely what we are talking about. In perception, for example, I may have sufficient information to identify something that I see or hear without being able to precisely define what I refer to. There is a considerable difference between being able to identify an object sufficiently to refer to it and being able to describe or define that object. A simple form of identification is to look and point; I may not know much about what I am pointing at, but as long as it remains in view, I can identify it, and I may even be able to pick it out again. Definition and theoretical description are much more difficult. So in order to talk about aesthetic objects, we need not solve all of the problems of definition, though a clear view of what we are talking about should go a long way toward advancing our aesthetic theories.

Finally, 'object' does not mean objective in the sense that something objective is independent of an observer. It may turn out that aesthetic objects depend in some special way on the observer – that they are, in common language, purely subjective. In the nineteenth and twentieth centuries, aesthetics has been dominated by theories of an aesthetic attitude or an aesthetic intuition. These theories include the observer as an essential part of perceiving some object as aesthetic. While a physical object only incidentally involves its being perceived, aesthetic objects are determined by the way that they are perceived. Theories of an aesthetic attitude or aesthetic intuition tend to make the aesthetic object subjective, therefore. According to those theories, individual observers have direct access to those aesthetic objects that they perceive because aesthetic objects are created in the act of perceiving in a certain way or are the result of a certain kind of intuition of the external world. We do not want to presuppose that such theories are correct, but we also do not want to exclude them by the way that we understand 'object.'

Positively, objects can generally be regarded in three ways that are of importance to aesthetics. The first is as ideal objects. Ideal objects take the primary sense of 'object' to apply to some non-physical realm. An ideal object is something that must be thought in order for it to exist. Ideal objects can be located in individual minds, in a single encompassing mind, or in some larger organic whole beyond mind. Ideal objects can become quite mysterious and difficult to imagine in some theories, but we all have common experiences in which we think of ideal objects quite easily. We do not expect to find numbers among the physical objects of the world, yet we easily think of numbers. They are just the kind of things that exist only when thought of. Ideal objects can be identified with physical objects, just as numbers are used to count things. So a second sense of 'object' is physical object. These are the objects that have spatial and temporal location independently of our thinking of them. Materialists reduce ideal objects to physical objects; idealists (in the philosophical sense) reduce physical objects to ideal objects. Both understand the basic distinction between senses of 'object,' however.

A third sense of 'object' becomes important to aesthetics. These are perceptual objects. Perceptual objects are whatever one sees, hears, tastes, smells, or touches, just as they appear in the act of perception. A perceptual object is not the cause of the perception but the object that appears in the perception. So if I see something as round, the perceptual object is round even if the object that caused my perception is some other shape. If I press on my eye so that I produce a color impression, the cause is not something colored, but the perceptual object is a colored image. Perceptual objects are distinguished in that way from physical objects. It might seem that perceptual objects are just ideal objects, therefore. They belong to minds and must be thought. However, perceptual objects always refer to something given in perception. They imply a connection to something else in a way that ideal objects do not. Imagining, remembering, thinking, conceiving are not acts of perception, so they do not give us perceptual objects. Idealists may try to show that just as other physical objects are reducible to ideal objects, so perceptual objects are. But one does not have to be an idealist to understand ideal objects, and perceptual objects are a useful intermediate class of objects to begin with. They are closely related to the empiricist claim that all of our thinking and knowing begins at some point with perceptual experiences, so we might think of perceptual objects as the fundamental empiricist sense of 'object.'

Aesthetic objects

Aesthetic objects, then, are whatever we are talking about when we use aesthetic language or whatever we experience when we have experiences that we want to classify as aesthetic. The idea of an aesthetic object is neutral with regard to the nature of the object until we begin to fill in details with some aesthetic theory. That is one reason why, in spite of the difficulties in constructing theories in an area such as aesthetics, we cannot avoid some kind of theory of aesthetic objects. We will now examine three ways of approaching aesthetic subject-matter – in effect, three kinds of theory of aesthetic objects, though each involves much more than just a theory of aesthetic objects. The three are imitation theories, expression theories, and theories of imagination. They correspond roughly to the three basic senses of objects: physical objects, ideal objects, and perceptual objects.

Imitation

Perhaps the most obvious way to approach aesthetic objects is as imitations of something else. Imitation theories developed in classical philosophy as a part of more comprehensive theories of the good and beautiful. Plato, Aristotle, and Plotinus each considered the role of imitation both in relation to art and as part of their exploration of ethical issues and metaphysics. Imitation theories in the later classical period were also part of the rhetorical tradition that investigated the conditions for effective speech and writing. In the middle ages, imitation was part of an allegorical scheme that linked the natural, human, and sacred worlds in a single repeating cosmos. Imitation continued to be the primary form of aesthetic theory through the neo-classical period in the seventeenth and eighteenth centuries, but during this period imitation was increasingly narrowed in its application and supplemented by a new psychology based on the association of ideas and modeled on the successes of the natural sciences.

Imitation theories begin by distinguishing the object as presented from some more basic object to which it is related and from which it gets its form. When we look at a painting, we see two things. We see the painting, and we see what it is a painting of. The painting is one thing; what it is a painting of is prior to it, both in the sense that the painting depends on what it is a painting of causally and in the sense that the painting is formed according to what it is a painting of. Even if the painting is non-representational (and there have been non-representational paintings ever since Roman wall-painting, at least), we think of the painting itself as one thing and of the colors and forms as something that the painting shows. A simple account of the painting as an aesthetic object then is just to say that it is an imitation of something else. Similarly, other representational art such as sculpture is easily conceived of as an imitation. There is David and there is Michelangelo's *David*. The statue is not the person, but it is an imitation of the person. Aristotle defined drama as an imitation of the actions of men. The events on the stage are not the same as the events they depict, but they are like them. In novels and poems, we have to recreate the events in our minds, but a poem can be thought of as an imitation of a form of speech, and a novel is in many ways an imitation of a history. Music might seem an exception, but even music is often thought of as imitating either natural sounds or, more frequently, emotions or motion. A waltz may do both – its sweeping rhythms depict both the motions of the dance and the joy of the dancers. The central cases of aesthetic objects for imitation theories are representational. Representational painting and sculpture and drama are the paradigms. Then the theory can be extended to cover less obviously representational cases. All aesthetic objects are imitations according to these theories; our questions concern what is being imitated.

From classical Greece through the eighteenth century, artists and philosophers alike took for granted that art was essentially imitative. The complexity of their theories came from what was being imitated. For example, theories of allegory suggested that it was possible to imitate more than one thing at the same time because everything had multiple meanings. A birth was a birth of that person, a renewal of humanity, an emblem of innocence entering the world, and a repetition of the act of divine creation. The single event imitated each aspect of its meaning simultaneously. Other imitation theories rejected allegory and substituted different accounts of how and of what imitation took place.

The fact that the practice of imitation includes more than simple pictures and acting warns us that imitation is more than just copying something. A copy can be regarded as a minimal case of imitation. A mirror produces a copy by reflection. The reflection is related to what it is a reflection of by the laws of optics. A video tape stores information electronically and uses that information to produce a new image that corresponds to the original in a systematic way. From one copy to the next, all that matters is the preservation of the information. However, an imitation need not be a copy. Thomas Wyatt's poem is an imitation of a poem by Petrarch, but it is not a copy of Petrarch's poem. And it is not a copy of anything that Wyatt ever said to anyone either. In spite of the fact that a sonnet might be said to imitate speech, it is not a copy of any speech. A camera may be used to produce a copy of a scene, but what the camera produces need not be simply a copy. The photographer controls the light, the focus, and the arrangement of the scene itself to produce effects that cannot be generated by what is being photographed independently of the photograph. One distinction between a copy and an imitation is simply that some imitations are more than their original. The most that a copy may do is everything that the original did. An imitation may do more than the original did. All copies can be thought of as imitations, but thinking of all imitations as copies is a mistake.

This leads to a further distinction between art as an imitation and a copy. Copies may be natural or they may be artificial. A mirror produces a natural copy. A digital camera produces an artificial copy that has to be "interpreted" by a computer chip in order to be recognizable. Both have in common a precise, systematic way of getting from original to copy and then understanding the copy as a version of the original. Even when we are unaware of the moves, we implicitly know how to learn which is original and which is copy. But art as an imitation provides no sure route back to what is being imitated. One has to learn the conventions of imitation before understanding the object of the imitation. "Learning the conventions" may be unconscious and natural. We learn to see according to a binocular system that quickly adjusts to anomalies. If one wears glasses that reverse images, it takes only a little while for the brain to switch the images right side up again. Perspective, harmony, and narrative conventions all are learnable without any self-conscious awareness of what the conventions are. The point is that the conventions are themselves part of an artistic imitation, so that being able to understand the conventions is not necessarily the mechanical, systematic process of more limited copies.

It can be quite difficult to tell what is being imitated, as a result. A copy corresponds to and repeats the information in the original. In principle, then, it is always possible to discover what the original is by examining the copy. But an imitation that aspires to be art has its own ends apart from the original. So the relation between original and imitation may not make it clear what is being imitated. For example, in classical theories of art, the original is a form, and it is a matter of debate how such forms can be known. Some philosophers held that they could best be known by the mind itself that could examine clear and distinct ideas of its own. In that case, imitations are always less than their original in the sense that they cannot be as clear and distinct as the ideas of the original itself. Artists would produce imitations that tried to be more than copies, but the imitations would always also be less than the intelligible form itself. An imitation depends on a confusion or distraction produced by the conditions of imitation. Other philosophers argued instead that forms are known only by the actual instances in which they appear. In that case, imitations in art might have the advantage of purifying and combining elements to show the ideal in a way that non-artistic actual forms cannot. In both cases, what is being imitated remains mysterious – either because it cannot be fully present in the imitation or because it can only be fully present in some confused imitation.

It is also not clear what is being imitated in some other art forms. Even if music can be thought of as imitative, it does not imitate only natural sounds. Instead, music has to be thought of as imitating motion by its rising and falling, or the rhythms of some larger harmony, or even the emotions themselves – happiness and sadness, joy and grief. But the objects imitated remain more general and vague than the specifics of the music. No one can listen to a piece of music and say from the music alone that it is about some specific incident or any particular non-musical content. Similarly, an abstract painting can be said to imitate form and color, but apart from the painting, form and color prove unidentifiable. One cannot identify the object being imitated independently of the imitation in such cases. Trying to bring all art under a theory of imitation turns out to require quite a bit of ingenuity.

According to imitation theories of aesthetic objects, all aesthetic objects are imitations, but not all imitations are aesthetic objects. Some imitations are merely copies made according to more or less mechanical and systematic forms of representation. In order to function as an aesthetic object, an imitation must do something more than just copy an original, and that "something more" is often difficult to identify. Why are some photographs aesthetic objects and others merely snapshots? Why are some films works of art and others merely entertainment? Is every fictional prose work an aesthetic object? Imitation theories must account for the differences in our intuitions of different objects by reference to something in the imitation and to what is imitated, and that pushes the limits of our concept of imitation.

As we have seen, allegorical imitations may have a multiplicity of objects. The tendency of imitation theories is toward such muliplicity. A does not just imitate B. B itself might be an imitation. Wyatt imitates

Petrarch, but Petrarch, according to an imitation theory, must be imitating something else. One way to account for the differences in imitations is to try to imagine levels of reality. Which is more real: the mirror image or what is reflected? The answer seems obvious. If a painting is thought of as a bad mirror image, then the mirror image is "more real" than the painting by the same reasoning. Works of art turn out to be less than other imitations and one gets a negative theory of art. But the order can be easily reversed. Both Egyptian art and cubist art break down an image and show more than one view at once. They look less like what they imitate, but they in fact show more. So instead of being inferior, in reality they are superior. Images that look ideal remove the imperfections and present something that is "more real" than anything that can be found in nature. By a simple reversal of the argument, art has gone from being less real to being more real. Then the "something more" of aesthetic objects comes from the ability of some imitations to supply what is only fragmentarily present in natural occurrences of the object.

This kind of reasoning reveals one common feature of classical imitation theories. They locate aesthetic objects somewhere on a scale of more or less real and use the concept of imitation to explain what and how the scale works. The variations in the theories come from the differences in describing what is real and how the scale is constructed. If one finds it convincing to talk of reality in this way, then imitation theories gain a great deal of plausibility as a result. Aesthetic objects are explained as a part of a metaphysical system – a system of what there is and how it forms a world. When such metaphysical systems become harder to accept, imitation theories begin to seem more and more vague as soon as they get away from simple copies. That is what happened under the pressure of the scientific revolution in the seventeenth and eighteenth centuries. Imitation theories were gradually pushed aside by theories of aesthetic expression.

A second common characteristic of imitation theories is that an aesthetic imitation is something that has to be made. Let us reconsider the case of a reflection in a mirror. If the reflection is a chance occurrence in a pool of water, the reflection may copy what is reflected, but it will not be an aesthetic object. But what if the pool is placed so that it catches the reflection – as the reflecting pool at the Washington monument does? Then, even though the reflection itself is natural, the arrangement has been created by someone for some effect, and the reflection is more than just a copy. The idea is that some things are what they are from causes that occur naturally. Trees grow into their natural shape according to what kind of tree they are and natural forces. Other things have to be arranged according to some pattern. Imitations belong to that latter kind.

Then, if the form and purpose of the imitation are aesthetic, the imitation will be an aesthetic object. On this theory, aesthetic objects are made things that have some aesthetic effect or purpose.

One problem, of course, is how to say what makes some effects or purposes aesthetic. One technique in psychotherapy is role-playing. Most people would not consider such play-acting aesthetic. The theory of tragedy formulated by Aristotle (384–322 BCE) says that pity and fear are transformed into some higher purpose by "catharsis" – which seems to mean a kind of ritual purgation that takes place both in the play and in the audience. This is considered a clear instance of something aesthetic. Yet it is hard to see how it differs from the psychodrama of a therapist. Both involve pretending, and both are intended to have some beneficial effect on the pretenders. The difference must be found in subtle distinctions. The audience is detached from the tragedy in a way that the role-player cannot be. The tragedy itself does not directly involve events in the life of the audience. One of Aristotle's claims about tragedy was that the old, well-known mythological and legendary plots made the best tragedies. If imitation theories are to work, they must be able to distinguish aesthetic effects from other effects, and this can involve quite detailed analysis. We will look further at some of the possibilities for such analysis when we consider the relation of an aesthetic object to the audience in chapter 4. For now, we only note that for an imitation theory to work, it must be able to distinguish imitations from copies and aesthetic imitations from non-aesthetic imitations.

An obvious objection to the claim that aesthetic imitations belong to a class of made things is the pleasure we take in natural objects. Sunsets and landscapes and starry skies seem to be aesthetic objects, but they are not made things. So if natural objects are sometimes aesthetic objects, and aesthetic imitations are made things, then it cannot be the case that all aesthetic objects are imitations. The theory of imitations would be refuted. This objection is so obvious that it can hardly have been ignored by serious philosophers who argued that aesthetic objects were a form of imitation. Imitation theorists have had two ways of escaping this objection. One is simply to deny that natural objects are ever really aesthetic. They may be like aesthetic objects in many ways, but, the argument goes, they differ in two important respects. They are not related to a mind, and their effects are qualitatively different. So, while we may associate natural beauty with aesthetic experience, it is really different. The other is to find a way to show that natural objects are imitations in aesthetic cases. This can be done either by discovering a creative intelligence that makes nature, or by reversing the priority so that nature is understood to be imitating art rather than the other way around. Either the effects that natural objects produce are not really aesthetic, though they may be very similar, or they are aesthetic because we see some natural objects as if they were really either made things or works of art.

Consider the claim that natural objects do not really produce aesthetic effects. This can be either a straightforward claim that if we examine our experience closely enough, we will find differences, or it may be a claim that we are fooled by our language and expectations into thinking that we have had an experience that we really did not have. In the first case, we could clear things up by reflecting more carefully on our experience. In the second case, we would have to be convinced that we did not really feel what we thought we felt in certain situations. Since we cannot deny that we felt what we felt – it makes no sense to tell someone that they don't have a feeling when they can feel that they do – the latter case comes down to stipulating that we will only use aesthetic language about non-natural objects. The first case is a matter of experience; but, as we saw in discussing definitions, it is hard to see how aesthetic experience can be distinguished without confusion. The alternative, however, is to remove the claim from testing by experience, and that makes the resulting imitation theory merely verbal. If every aesthetic experience is unique and no theory is really possible, that might not be a bad thing. Some artists and philosophers have thought that might be the case. However, it is premature to abandon all theory just because there is a problem with one version.

The introduction of a maker to account for natural aesthetic objects is a bit too close to being a *deus ex machina* to be persuasive. (A *deus ex machina* – a god brought in from outside the structure to fix things – is philosophically suspect because it is not part of the theory.) The claim that we see natural objects as if they were works of art when we experience them as aesthetic objects is more interesting. The impulse to make art seems to be older than human history. We find cave-paintings and carvings from times well before we have any historical records to help us interpret them. Even if these works had other uses, perhaps in magic and ritual, they are imitations in the sense of something made. When we see the grace of an animal or experience the wonder of a starry sky, our way of experiencing these things is influenced by the representations artists have made. Would we feel the same way about natural things without the poems and stories, paintings and sculptures, dances and dramas we know? We saw above that imitation involves learning conventions of representation. In viewing natural objects, the argument goes, those same conventions continue to apply to the way we see and experience things. At some point in our psychic evolution, the process of reproducing what we see reverses itself, and we see according to the ways that we have learned to reproduce. Then nature imitates art rather than art imitating nature. We respond to natural things as if they were works of art; our experience of them is aesthetic because we take them as if they were paintings or dramas or stories. Clearly, this is sometimes the case. We make sense of our lives by treating them as stories and thus give our actions an aesthetic significance. In the seventeenth and eighteenth centuries, a taste for certain kinds of wild natural scenery that looked like paintings became popular, and people went so far as to construct their parks and gardens to make them picturesque like the landscape paintings they admired. The claim that natural objects can be treated as imitations in the sense of made things extends these cases to all natural objects that are appreciated aesthetically.

We must be careful still to distinguish aesthetic imitations from other kinds of made things. We began with an obvious distinction between the imitation and what it was an imitation of. A play is not the action depicted. A painting is not the scene depicted. But a more complex distinction is needed to make an imitation theory work. Where is the imitation located? Is it the physical object? Then if that object is destroyed, the aesthetic imitation will be destroyed. What of plays or musical performances? How can there be many different performances of the same play or piece of music? How can there be many copies of the same novel? (The same distinction is needed in other theories as well, but it is crucial to imitation theories.) These are not problems that come up with respect to other kinds of making. If I buy a Ford Mustang, I do not worry about the fact that there are millions of other cars with the same name. What I own is my car. But if I see a performance of *Hamlet*, I do wonder if I have seen the same play referred to in critical essays about *Hamlet*. If we want to say that an imitation is something that has been made, we need to be able to say something about the peculiar kind of making that seems to be involved.

Philosophers use a simple distinction to help sort this problem out. It is called a type/token distinction. The type is a singular thing that has an identity. The token is any instance of the type that can occur. We use this distinction quite commonly without thinking about it. The words on this page are types, but they appear as tokens. The distinction is a relative one. That is, it applies relative to something else (just as a distinction between a large and a small elephant is relative to elephants). The words of this sentence that you read are tokens of the ones that I have written. There are, I hope, lots of copies in circulation. Each word is also a token of *the* word. I could not write my sentence without tokens of the words I need. You could not read my sentence without tokens of the sentence, which depends on tokens of the words. Yet different tokens can be tokens of a single type. The same word may be printed in different typefaces. Then we not only have different tokens of that word, we have different types of fonts, each represented by a token of that font. The same physical squiggle on the page can be a token of more than one thing, as well as being a type of itself. Representing the type/token distinction can be a logical nightmare. Yet we use it every day.

To apply this distinction to our present problem, when we are talking about a work of art, we normally will be talking about some type, but we will also have in mind some token or tokens of that type. Somewhere, sometime, Thomas Wyatt wrote his poem "Who So List to Hunt." At that point, a type was created. Since then, there have been many tokens of that poem. When Wyatt took has pen in hand, he presumably wrote English words, each of which, as he wrote it, was a token of some word in the language at that time. Now we have new tokens for those words which may use different spelling from Wyatt's Elizabethan spelling. (Purists about the poem may decide it is important to preserve the Elizabethan spelling.) We are pretty sure that we have *the* poem, even though it is quite different from what Wyatt wrote. We would not be able to make that claim without the type/token distinction.

A number of complications arise. Not all works of art seem to work the same way. A novel has many tokens, but they refer to no one occurrence. The autograph copy, in the author's hand, even if it exists (and it usually doesn't, not just because it is lost, but because of the actions of copy-editors and printers), is just one more token to be judged alongside others. But a painting has an original. Other tokens are copies as well as imitations. Musical scores are different yet. They allow for interpretation and variation. Musical instruments are now tuned differently. Notations about the length of notes depend on different timing. So the relation of type to token varies for different art forms.

A more serious complication arises from trying to identify the type. If the kind of distinction includes an original, then we can fix the original as the defining instance of the type. (We do not want to say that the original is the type because types are not the sorts of things that physical objects are. We would create logical problems about the type being at two places at once if we say that it is a physical object.) Even then, problems can arise. Most paintings have to be preserved and restored. Is the original lost with every bit of cleaning or repair? The controversy over the cleaning of Michelangelo's Sistine Chapel paintings warns us how serious these problems can be. Some scholars claimed that the cleaning removed elements that Michelangelo intended to be part of the painting – either by including them in the finishing layers or by anticipating the aging of the painting. Others maintained that after centuries, the only way to see what Michelangelo had painted was to remove the older attempts at preservation and the accumulated centuries of grime. The problem is made more acute because it is usually not possible to go back or to stand still. If nothing is done, the work will continue to deteriorate. If something is done, the process is irreversible. But at least in the case of paintings, we know where we are.

For novels and musical scores, different problems arise. Does a single printer's error make one token any less the novel than another token? If it doesn't, why do we worry so about having accurate texts? If it does, how can we ever be sure we have read the same novel? When does a truly bad, amateurish performance of a piece of music cease to be that work? Have I ever heard Beethoven's Fifth Symphony if the only performance I have ever heard was by a junior high school band on a portable tape recorder? In spite of some heroic efforts on the part of some philosophers to choose one definitive answer to these questions, there is probably no such choice. The boundaries are fuzzy. The tokens must be enough like the type to do the job, but we cannot say precisely what "enough" is except on a case-by-case basis. More important, the identity of the type must be clear enough to be sustained, but again, 'enough' cannot be precisely defined. At some point, a painting is just lost, even though we may have descriptions of it and even have bits and pieces of the original. But that point is not reached every time there is a chip in the paint. In these matters, we live in a less than perfect world; the theory itself does not allow the kind of precision that other objects have.

All of this means that an imitation theory that focuses on made things is not just about one physical object located in space and time at a particular point. Making is a complex process that makes both types and tokens at once, and the theory of aesthetic objects has to try to sort out just what is being referred to at any point. The plausibility of a particular theory that aesthetic objects are imitations will depend on how clearly it can make the distinctions and provide the identities for aesthetic objects. One of the basic problems for any imitation theory is that it has difficulty saying what the aesthetic object is in distinction from what is imitated and the tokens that are provided. It looks as though either one should always prefer the thing imitated to the imitation, or it should not matter as long as one had some token that was sufficient to provide the type of the aesthetic object. But neither seems to be the case. We value the painting more highly than what it is a painting of, and we value the original more highly than a perfectly indistinguishable reproduction. Imitation theories have problems explaining why that should be the case because they have problems explaining what the aesthetic object is apart from either the original that is imitated or the token that is produced.

The value assigned to aesthetic objects by imitation theories can arise in two different ways. One is from the underlying metaphysics. We have just seen that art might be better or worse than other things depending on where the imitation is located on a scale of realities. In a metaphysical system, being "more real" is usually desirable, so value is attached to an aesthetic object depending on where the metaphysical system locates that object. Art in general can be compared to other kinds of things. If art is thought of as less real than a useful version, then the useful object is the better one (Platonism). If art is thought of as more real than the useful object – perhaps because it provides the ideal case that the actual thing can never quite live up to – then art is more valuable than "merely" useful objects (neo-Platonism). Similarly, different specific art forms acquire their value from the system. If painting is better at imitating reality than novels, then paintings are more valuable aesthetically than novels. And if one kind of painting is better at imitating reality than another, then that kind is more valuable. At times in art history, for example, mythological paintings and history paintings were considered more valuable than landscape and still life paintings. The problems come in deciding which is the better imitation. On one theory, a glossy bit of photo-realism may be the better imitation. It just looks more like what it imitates. On a different theory, however, that may be merely mechanical copying. The better imitation is the one that shows more and that may require idealization or abstraction. One can find examples of all of these theories in the history of aesthetics and art theory.

If it seems that we are just multiplying possibilities without getting any closer to an adequate theory, remember that we are trying to understand the different ways in which aesthetic objects can be identified. Until we know what the possibilities are, we cannot criticize the theory. We may not be able to reach a final judgment, but we can eventually decide that some theories are themselves better than others.

Imitation theories should not be dismissed lightly. They capture many of our strongest intuitions about art and beauty, and when they have problems, as they do, they are interesting problems that are basic to our desire to know what aesthetics and art are all about. Among the strengths of most imitation theories is their ability to connect up art to other kinds of things. Imitation theories of the aesthetic try to say how art and aesthetic objects, as either ideal objects or made things, fit into our larger scheme of things. That is why imitation theories are most successful when they are related to some metaphysical theory. They tend to succeed or fail depending on our judgment of the metaphysics that supports them. If we find Platonic forms acceptable, then a form of imitation theory of art that says that art is some way of presenting (imitating) Platonic forms – either better than other ways or worse than other ways – makes sense. If we start with a metaphysics that tells us that things can only be made according to some prior understanding, then it makes sense to locate aesthetic objects as a kind of making – either more effective than others or less effective or having its own special ends. But if the ability to supply a metaphysical system itself becomes suspect, as it has in some forms of modern philosophy, then imitation theories of art also tend to be suspect. If they are the only contenders, then the conclusion is that no theory of art is possible.

We have seen that imitation theories have difficulty incorporating some kinds of aesthetic phenomena. Natural beauty does not fit well with imitation as making. We either have to supply a creator (God the artist) or find ways to include nature. Those ways of adjusting the theory stretch the theory, perhaps intolerably. Imitation theories tend to become quite obscure about what aesthetic objects are. They are not the tokens and not the physical objects, but what they are depends on some hierarchy of reality that is very hard to identify and explicate. There are ways to meet all of these problems, but they also stretch the theory and make it more and more obscure. But the most serious problem for imitation theories is simply the history of art. Again and again, it presents us with art that just does not seem to be imitating anything. The explosion of kinds of things that contemporary art wants to treat as art provides many examples. Performance art does something; it does not imitate something else. Political theater seeks to change the world, not imitate it. Painters drip paint and use found objects. Sculptors pile up earth. Writers turn their own lives into works of art. We might try to dismiss some of these instances as avant-garde failures, and certainly some are. But we are also led to suspect that religious art in past ages and music and oral poetry never were very concerned with being imitations.

Imitation theories have tended to fade with the abandonment of the metaphysical systems that supported them. They survive in two forms. One is the popular imagination. It is still hard not to see much art as somehow transparent to either some other object or some transcendent meaning. The other is in theories of symbolism and language. Because language and conventions (including the special languages of art) are so important to our ability to understand anything, we tend to look for an analogy to language in art. We speak of music as a language of emotions and painting as a language of forms, for example. Symbols and symbol systems imply that they are symbols for something, and that easily takes the form of saying that symbols represent or imitate what they are symbols for. If, the claim goes, all art is symbolic and dependent on symbol systems, then a kind of imitation theory survives. However, it is possible to construe these symbol systems differently, and we turn now to an alternative kind of theory – theories of expression.

Expression

Expression theories are the logical competitors of imitation theories. They are always implicit to some extent in even the most metaphysically formed imitation theories because some means must be found to make the theory itself evident. Expression theories start with the mind, and they understand aesthetic objects to be related primarily not to other objects, as in imitation theories, but to some mind. The most important relation is of one mind to another, and the aesthetic object is the means of making that connection. Rhetoric, the art of speaking and writing persuasively, was an important aspect of classical cultures. The rhetorical tradition in classical philosophy relied on imitation to explain the ideal models for speech and writing, but at the same time it focused on effectiveness of communication in a way that called for the effective expression of ideas. Rhetoric taught students by providing models that could be imitated. A complex system of figures of speech grew up, each of which served a specific communicative function to express certain kinds of ideas. For example, metaphors and similes added novelty to ideas and thus made them more expressive.

However, the rise of expression theories in aesthetics only becomes prominent after the renaissance. Two factors contributed to a shift away from imitation to an emphasis on expression. First, the individual thinker became more important. Initially artists and then philosophers and critics shifted from an emphasis on the person as a type repeating a universal social order to the person as an independent individual bound into society by his or her physical, mental, and emotional abilities and a kind of contract. In that situation, the expression of the thoughts and feelings of the individual takes on a new importance. Second, the psychology of the mind changed. Rather than the mind itself being thought of as a reflection of a greater intellect, as it was in classical and medieval philosophy, the mind was thought of as a bundle or collection of ideas provided by experience and held together by natural and acquired associations. Such a mind exhibits its internal associations by finding symbols and forms for its own expression. It knows itself, in part, at least, by means of its external projections of its interior associations. Art becomes a way for the artist and the audience to know their own minds. In the course of the eighteenth and nineteenth centuries, expression gradually displaced imitation as the principal way of accounting for aesthetic objects.

Expression theories begin with minds and ideas that form minds. Ideas, at least in modern thought, are mind-dependent. If we ask where ideas are to be found, the answer is almost certainly going to be that they are in someone's mind. That can be a little misleading. "In the mind" need not mean "in the head." Ideas are not the kind of things that have spatial locations, except in some extended sense. We also think of ideas as belonging to texts and to symbols. A particular symbol like a flag represents or embodies an idea. So it makes sense to say that ideas are not in minds but "in" the symbols. Symbols, in turn, are used in complex ways to make texts – books and essays, poems, and plays – and by extension in non-verbal symbol systems as well. If we could not incorporate ideas into such systems, it would be hard to see how we could share ideas without some form of telepathy. Nevertheless, our fundamental way of approaching ideas is psychological.

When our modern psychology of ideas began to become dominant, it gave new impetus to an alternative way of thinking about aesthetic phenomena. The mind was conceived as whatever ideas it had. We acquired more ideas as we went along. Along with ideas go feelings, regarded either as ideas themselves or as the qualitative accompaniment of ideas. And aesthetics, it was held, was about the feelings that we have. So aesthetics, like ideas, was mind-dependent.

An aesthetics based on feelings and mind-dependent ideas is radically different from one based on imitation. The most important thing is not an object but some psychological state. Such states are difficult to examine and even more difficult to describe. It might seem that one need only reflect carefully and one would have to know what one was feeling. Our minds are seldom so clear and uncluttered, however. Even when they are and we "know what we like," it may not be so clear why we like something, or how it relates to other things that we like or what the significance of our liking it is. All of those elements go into an aesthetic theory. We need to be able to distinguish aesthetic feelings from other feelings. We need to know what the mind itself is and how it can sort its ideas. Above all, if our aesthetics begins with our ideas and feelings, then we need to be able to find something that makes those ideas public and communicable. Otherwise, our feelings will remain nebulous and private. If imitation theories have difficulty explaining natural beauty because nothing seems to be made in the requisite sense by nature, an aesthetics of feeling and ideas has difficulty explaining works of art. They seem, at best, dispensable means to a felt end. If the feelings and ideas could be obtained some other way – by electrodes or drugs, for example – we would not need art at all.

Expression theories of aesthetics arose to meet those challenges and answer those questions. An expression theory usually has two main features. First, the mind is its own end. What is known and what is felt pleasurably make our minds what they are. Second, some feelings and ideas are more important and basic than others. We are aware of qualitative differences in what we feel. Some ideas provide the basic building blocks for our more complex ideas and notions. To say that something is expressed by someone, then, is to say that something is known and felt by someone and what is known and felt can be understood as the way one mind comes into contact with another mind and with the external world. Everything that we know and understand begins with this impulse toward expression. When it is successful, it gives us a way into our common world. When it is not, we slip back into an incoherent private world without communication or understanding of anything except our own raw feelings and instincts – a kind of autism.

Expression is fundamental because it allows us to give form and content to our ideas and feelings. Expression theories imagine two kinds of mental states. The first is confused and incoherent. It is like a baby that can only cry out for satisfaction of its most basic desires for food and comfort. Or it is like an animal that can assimilate data and react but cannot give extensive form to its experiences, so that everything remains at the level of immediate stimulation and learned stimulus and response reactions. The second kind of state is coherent and organized. It is able not only to produce images but also to abstract and recall those images in other forms. It includes everything we call thinking and imagining and remembering that goes beyond mere instinct and automatic behavior. It preserves past experience, projects future experience, and applies those projections to new situations that are only abstractly related to what we have already experienced. Above all, we like that second state. It feels good, and it provides us with confidence and assurance. So our minds desire expression and are satisfied only when they achieve it. And when the mind is successful, it particularly values those ideas that are successfully expressed.

So far, expression seems close to just being able to think. We need to see how a theory of expression forms the basis for an aesthetic theory. The first thing that expression theories insist on is that the pleasure of expression is so basic that it is an end in itself. Our minds want to feel that they understand. In fact, they need the assurance of their own coherence just to be minds. So the pleasure provided by expression is distinctive because it is more basic. I may like ice cream, but if I do not get it, I will not suffer too much. The pleasure that I get from satisfying my desire is limited to the moment and begins to fade as soon as the desire is satisfied. I need food and drink and bodily security, but those needs are common to all animals. They are essentially bodily, and they too cease to be of interest as soon as they are satisfied. But my ability to anticipate and understand is never satisfied in the same way. I constantly need to renew it by continuing to think and anticipate and remember. The pleasure I have in expressive activity is pure pleasure, unchanged by its fulfillment. That, say expression theorists, is what aesthetic pleasure really is. It is the pure pleasure that we have as a result of the mind's own activity.

The object of such pleasure is not what I think or feel, although there will always be something that is the object of my thinking and feeling. The object of aesthetic pleasure is the activity of the mind itself. Satisfaction and fulfillment come with being occupied in a way that is neither too overpowering nor too repetitious and boring. Why this should be called aesthetic pleasure needs some explanation, but the first step is to recognize it as what expression theories mean by expressive pleasure. It is a feeling, produced by ideas and their formation, and it belongs essentially to the mind as such. Without it, we would not be human minds as we know them.[3]

In order to see why these basic feelings of pleasure and ideational coherence are considered aesthetic, we need to understand a bit of the history of philosophy. Beginning in the seventeenth century, one important way that philosophers tried to account for what we know and how we can know it was in terms of clear and distinct ideas provided either by experience alone or by some combination of experience and innate ideas that we began with. Knowledge consists, it was held, of clear and distinct ideas that are themselves perfect and complete. Individual minds play only a secondary role in such knowledge. The clear, distinct, perfectly complete and coherent ideas will be the same for everyone. Once they are discovered, they cannot be doubted, and they have no need for particular instances. They give us a pure philosophical science like mathematics. But such clear and distinct ideas did not

---

3 As a theory of mind, this is very vague. Many different ways of construing what a mind is would be consistent with this kind of expressive theory. For example, a mind might just be a bundle of ideas. Or a mind might be some combination of neural impulses and chemical reactions which is in some way identical with a brain. A mind could even be an immaterial substratum that is beyond our conscious grasp, though it is hard to know what that would mean. We do not need to settle on one theory of mind in order to consider expression theories of aesthetics as long as the theory of mind permits some form of conceptualization in terms of ideas and feelings.

include the feelings of pleasure and the individual senses that each of us has. The term 'aesthetics' was invented to bring those feelings and senses into the pure science of reason, logic, and mathematics. As philosophers became less and less confident that they could supply the philosophical science required by clear and distinct ideas and as more and more philosophers emphasized the dependence of all ideas on experience alone, the aesthetic ideas seemed to be the only ones that remained! So, gradually, aesthetic ideas and aesthetic pleasure assumed the lead role in accounting for knowledge. They formed the experiential starting-point from which science and practical knowledge could be developed. Aesthetics, which began as something that had to be accounted for in addition to clear and distinct ideas, became the prior ground for human knowledge.

The danger for this kind of expression was that it would remain so subjective and private that it could not be considered knowledge at all. Art is assigned a special role in expression theories in making the transition from subjective feeling and experience to other forms. Scientific theories and practical rules and obligations are tied to specific situations. Scientists must account for what actually happens, and in order to do that, they must start with the limited experience available at a given time and place. The most extreme hypotheses in science, such as general relativity, still begin with phenomena that need to be explained, and they only become established theories and a part of science when they are confirmed by being linked to actual phenomena by advances in our powers of observation. Ethical, economic, and political rules are tied to the actual practices that apply to real situations. Art, on the other hand, has two advantages: it continues to provide the same aesthetic pleasure that started the process of knowing, and it is not limited to what actually exists or is known. Art can run ahead of experience and thus anticipate organizations that will become useful. It can use fiction and fantasy. Some mathematics has a similar ability to develop independently of any actual situations and has been felt to be equally beautiful and aesthetically satisfying for that reason. Art, however, has the advantage of using symbols and conventions that can be drawn from our experience and applied to experience again. So art, it is claimed, is a form of public expression.

Expression theories often take a very extensive view of what is art. All language may be treated as art because, it is claimed, all language is expressive of something. When we speak, we use language to give form to our sensory input and our emotional responses to it. So everyone is a little bit of an artist. Such a broad usage is only a way of making a point, however. In practice, art is obviously not just any language or formal presentation of experience and emotion. Only some kinds of presentations are artistic. Those are the ones that are original and expressive.

In order to distinguish them from more ordinary and repetitious presentations, expression theories typically limit expression to a union of form and content that is original and can stand alone.

Every presentation of an idea or emotion cannot be expressive without the term becoming meaningless. For example, consider what happens when someone gets red in the face and splutters angrily. The person is showing emotion, and it is often possible to infer what emotion is being experienced. Yet most expression theories would not consider such exhibitions an expression of the emotion in the sense required by the theory. The person is simply showing symptoms of what is being experienced. It is like a cry of pain or a spontaneous laugh. When the stimulus disappears, the symptoms will disappear as well. When an actor performs in a similar way, however, the same bodily movements become an expression of an emotion. The actor's showing of the emotion is independent of actually having the emotion at that time; it thus qualifies as a way of expressing the emotion. If we could not make some such distinction, then every performance by an artist would imply that the artist was experiencing what the work of art expressed. Musicians do not feel sad when they play sad music. Actors are not angry when they express anger. So expression is possible without having the experience at that time. By itself, that only means that some expression is independent of actually feeling the emotion expressed at that time. But if it is possible to separate the expression in some cases from having the emotion in those cases, then they are two different acts. The expression can stand alone, while having an emotion implies an actual psychological state of someone at that time. We can distinguish the expression from psychological symptoms in that way.

It does not follow that expression is unrelated to having emotions. Actors value experience of emotions and close observation just because that is how they learn to express emotions. Novelists need not have actually experienced what they write about, but many novelists begin with autobiographically based novels. The distinction between actually feeling emotion and expressing emotion is one of form and psychology. Artists learn to express something, especially emotions, by discovering forms. Those forms may be natural or conventional. The connection between smiling and happiness seems to be natural for humans. The connection between a red-check tablecloth in a movie scene and feelings of security and honesty is merely conventional. In that case, a history of associations and other scenes establishes the expressive power of a visual symbol.

Sometimes expression theories go further and argue that it would not even be possible to experience emotions as we understand them without the expressive powers of art that teach us how to separate out what we feel. For example, mating instincts are undoubtedly natural, as are instincts of parents to protect their young. So "love" has a natural sense. But romantic love owes much of its emotional identity to the stories, poems, and songs that grew up in the twelfth and thirteenth centuries. It is at least arguable that expression creates the ability to feel in certain ways as much as having feeling leads to expression.

A key concept in distinguishing aesthetic expression from other emotional manifestations is originality. An aesthetic expression is the creation of a form that either comes from felt experience or allows felt experience to be formed into some coherent, identifiable experience. Once the expression has been discovered or created, it can then be repeated and used over and over. It becomes part of our cultural resources. The repetitions and subsequent uses are only imitations of the original, however. Aesthetic expression itself is never imitation. This is just the opposite from imitation theories. For an imitation theory, it is important to discover how to make a better imitation. For expression theories, it is important to discover something that is not mere imitation. Expression theories make the artist a true creator. Lesser beings depend on artists. Greater artists create whole new forms or ways of seeing. Lesser artists add smaller, but still original, touches and details. Most of us are very limited artists who depend for most of our expressions on others who have supplied us. We are essentially imitators who feel the way we have been taught to feel by the artists in our culture. Originality and creativity are marks of expression, therefore.

A concept closely related to originality is genius. How artists and sensitive aesthetic types are able to express what others can only secondarily experience is a mystery. It cannot be learned or taught. It is different from skill, for example. So genius becomes the mysterious power to produce original forms. When pressed, some psychological conditions for promoting genius may be supplied. Even genius is not untutored. But, it is often claimed, part of genius is just finding a way to learn what is needed. A genius will discover the best master. After having learned what the master has to teach, a genius will go on and surpass the master. The model for this relation is found in renaissance painting. A young painter would be apprenticed to a master and learn his style. The apprentice might even go to several masters in succession. The rapid advances in painting in the renaissance are attributable to a succession of apprentices who surpassed their masters by inventing new styles. Painting changed again and again in the period from Giotto (1266–1337) in the fourteenth century to Raphael (1483–1520) in the sixteenth. Those who succeeded in outgrowing their masters had their own genius. Those who remained at the level of their masters, no matter how good they were,

were mere craftsmen. The model provided by art history is repeated in other art forms in differing ways. Poetry shifts from classical models to freer forms in its search for originality of expression. Genius, it was held, will triumph over adversity and find ever new ways of expressing the felt emotions. Art forms that become imitative and stale will be cast aside by genius. The rest of us will marvel and, in our own way, appreciate the aesthetic possibilities opened to us.

Expression theories need a way to distinguish art from non-art. As long as aesthetic expression is natural and a subjective feeling, it does not require anything more than the best possible conditions for experiencing it. In that respect, expression theories lead ultimately to a kind of idealized approach that is sometimes described as disinterested. Everyone can – indeed must – have their own aesthetic experiences, and the trick is merely to become aware of them and not to lose them in the more complex forms of our lives. However, the kind of expression that produces art has to be distinguished from its imitative repetitions. If art is expression, then anything that does not satisfy the conditions of expression is non-art, no matter how much it may look and sound like art. And similarly, anything that is expressive is art, even if it was not intended as art in the first place. So a beautiful vase is a work of art, even if its maker was a potter who needed the money and made it to carry water. But a poem or play that copies some other poem or play is not art, even if it gives pleasure and can be read or performed in a manner indistinguishable from real art. The ends of expression are self-contained; art gives expression to emotion. The ends of non-art are extrinsic. The work is calculated to produce a known effect by a known means. Such works may be very good at achieving their effects. Contemporary movie-makers rise or fall on their ability to manipulate their medium in ways that will draw large audiences, and directors are rewarded handsomely for their ability to deliver what they promise in advance. But, according to expression theories, such works are not works of art. They are some form of pseudo-art or entertainment. They lack the originality and the intrinsic formal interest that mark true expression.

Expression theories produce two results, therefore. First, they justify a subjective aesthetic experience based on the ideas and emotions which we, as individuals, find pleasurable for themselves. Expression is our innate ability to give form to emotion and sensation and to find pleasure in that form regardless of what we go on to do with our experience subsequently. In this respect, expression theories shift aesthetic experience to the individual, psychological being and make it independent of metaphysical systems and external judgment. But when expression theories come to art, they must account for a projection of form on to some public, stable medium. Then expression theories create a cult of the artist. Originality is a necessary condition for art, and only genius can be original. Our ability to have aesthetic experiences in the first case turns out to depend on artists supplying us with a means to our own expression. We are not as independent as we thought. We learn to be artists in our own conscious life from the artists who supply us with expressions we can use.

There is certainly something attractive about expression theories in aesthetics and art history. They supply an answer to the doubts of imitation theories about the status of art and artists. They make it clear why we do and should value art, because without it, we would be inarticulate in our own felt sensations and slip back into a pre-human instinctive reaction to our experience. Expression theories do not require us to accept grand metaphysical schemes. They begin with our own individual experiences, and their structure comes from our desire to know and understand through our experience rather than from claims about the world and reality as a whole. Expression theories appeal to our sense that whatever else is going on in art, what I actually feel cannot be wholly wrong as long as I feel it. I may be mistaken about how the world is and about what is right and wrong, but my aesthetic feelings are my own and I cannot be wrong about them. And when it comes to art, we all feel that not everything that calls itself art is art, and that some things that do not call themselves art are art. I may not be sure which is which, but I am sure that there is a difference. Expression theories offer a way of explaining that sense that there are distinctions to be made.

Nevertheless, expression theories are subject to at least as many objections as imitation theories. First of all, expression theories have a vagueness about them that seems to be not just accidental but built in. By definition, whatever precedes expression cannot be known because it has not been expressed, and once it is expressed it can only be known in the form of the expression. So no expressive form allows me to describe expression itself. I just have to try to do it, like following a recipe and then judging by the product. That may be fine as long as I know what the ingredients are. However, expression theories are claiming to identify the constituents as well as how they work. So expression theories depend on terms like 'myth,' 'symbol,' and 'metaphor.' What these terms refer to is often quite vague. Genius and originality are described but they cannot be defined. A great deal of philosophical work has gone into making these concepts more precise. It is not to be sneered at. But if a genius is simply someone who can express what others cannot express, then it is always open to a self-proclaimed genius to simply say that she has not been understood because others have not yet learned this new way of expressing. There is just enough truth in that to make us hesitate to reject any such assertion. Yet at bottom, the claim has become irrefutable because no evidence to the contrary is allowed. The sweeping claims that ultimately we are all artists and that all language and presentational forms are expressive become empty because they include too much. Perhaps not all expression theories are subject to this kind of criticism, but they all tend to be vague in just these ways.

As we noted at the beginning of this section, expression theories arose when psychology and philosophy began to center on ideas located in individual minds. 'Expression' as it is used in these kinds of theories is expression of some idea that belongs to some individual. Before the scientific revolution in the seventeenth and eighteenth centuries, philosophy and psychology tended to use 'idea' more extensively and to be less focused on the individual. Art and the kinds of experience that aesthetics deals with were more closely associated with skill and the production of objects. Artists, in particular, were considered skilled craftsmen prior to a shift that began in the renaissance and increased through the seventeenth and eighteenth centuries. They belonged to guilds or craft associations, and they learned their trade first as apprentices. Even the polite arts, such as poetry and music, that were practiced by ladies and gentlemen tended to be formal and provided opportunities to show the skill of the writer. King Henry VIII of England considered himself an accomplished composer of songs, and some of his music is still played. He did not write to express himself but to demonstrate his ability in the arts of the court and to please his audience.

That imitation theories tended to dominate during classical and medieval periods and then to be replaced by expression theories does not limit either kind of theory. Expression theories must claim that earlier artists were in fact expressing themselves, because that is what art does according to an expression theory. Otherwise, the theory would not be a theory of aesthetics but a theory about the history of ideas. Just as earlier sailors may have believed that the world was flat and been able to sail adequately according to their theory as long as they didn't venture too far, so earlier artists may have believed that they were craftsmen making imitations of eternal ideas, and their theory may have worked as long as art was limited to certain kinds of objects. When more is known, a better theory is required. Conversely, an imitation theory must be able to reverse the procedure and explain how expression is just one more complex form of imitation, now able to imitate the interior life of writers and painters as well as external objects and able to respond to new kinds of imitative activity. Theory is not history. Nor should we take the easy way out and think that the choice of theory does not matter

since either will do well enough. Each has consequences that are potentially negative and inconsistent with the other.

Expression theories tend to lose sight of the importance of skill and
craft in the arts, and even to reduce the importance of the arts themselves. Feeling becomes more important than production. Extreme theories have maintained that the actual work of art was merely incidental
to the real expression. The original, creative act was in the mind of the
artist, who might or might not choose to make it public. The myth of
the inarticulate poet and the musical mind that knows no harmony and
plays no instrument arises from expression theories. The danger is that
as the aesthetic experience is pushed further and further back in the
individual psyche, the productive process becomes secondary. Even if a
close connection between the ability to realize an idea in a medium and
expression is acknowledged, the medium may seem merely accidental.
Classical theories had compared poetry and painting, looking for similarities across the arts, but the concept of fine art implies that art is
more basic than the particular form of art. The very idea that one is an
artist rather than simply a painter or poet or musician moves the fundamental concept back a level in a way that reduces the importance of the
final product. Poets should be able to write plays and paint pictures and
compose music because they are all expressions. If they don't, the lack
of particular skills could be remedied with a little time and effort.

The danger in this kind of expressive mythology is that it just does
not correspond to the real activity of the arts or even to the appreciation
of the arts. The ability to produce works of art is the result of arduous
training and hard won skills. Expression theory has tended to promote
"primitive" painting and pop culture, but when these forms are examined carefully, they turn out to be as complex and difficult to achieve
when they are successful as the polished works of high renaissance painting. It is just not the case that the arts arise from some form of interior
expressive force that we all experience. Knowledge of the history of the
forms, mastery of a medium, and the discipline that comes from trial
and error are as important as the talent, genius, and creative originality
stressed by expression theories. If imitation theories tend to be mechanical or metaphysical to the exclusion of the individual artist's personality,
expression theories tend to make that personality the be-all and end-all
of art to the exclusion of history and skill.

The same thing may be said for aesthetic appreciation. The expressive
theorist's ideal audience is described by such terms as 'disinterested,'
'distanced,' and 'unprejudiced.' In fairness, these descriptions are given
special meanings that we will consider in more detail later. Nevertheless,
an expression theory tends to think of the best audience as one that does

not know too much and just lets the work of art or the natural beauty have its effect directly on the individual psyche. A prominent form of expression theory emphasizes communication between the artist or nature and someone. The more direct the communication, the better. Leo Tolstoy (1828–1910) described the process as a kind of infectiousness.

Again, the difficulty with this approach is that it just does not work. Even when we are most open to the effects of new art or to the purity of natural beauty, preparation is necessary. We are enabled to see by what we know. Perception is not a naïve looking; the schemas we have assimilated allow us to process stimuli. To even hear music, one must listen to a great deal of music, and it helps to have acquired the skills of recognizing musical forms. One need only try to read a poem such as Wyatt's sonnet to see how much more is available when one is aware of the sonnet form and the poetic diction that makes the poem different from the prose of an eighteenth-century novelist such as Henry Fielding.[4] The best expression theories find ways to take account of these obvious facts, but they have to depend on special explanations to do so.

A particular problem for expression theories is that they tend to discount critical activity and thus to have a problem with aesthetic judgment. Imitation theories tend to become too rule-bound. When they oversimplify, they judge something good or bad by its regularity and conformity to a set of fixed rules. Then the theory is refuted as soon as artists find ways to break the rules effectively. Expression theories tend to go to the other extreme. Everyone has their own taste and, it is said, there is no disputing about taste. So judgment is individual, subjective, and ultimately without any standards. Anything goes. Of course, it is not the case that anything goes, so expression theories have to find special ways to explain how some things are better than others and why the taste of some people is better than the taste of others. Critics come out rather badly in this process. Their opinions are at best after-the-fact summaries of public reactions or anticipations of how the public will react. One of the best nineteenth-century English critics, John Ruskin (1819–1900), thought that because art was difficult, it would always take a long time for the public to figure out what was good and what was bad. A critic's job was to anticipate that eventual judgment and make it easier. But the critic, according to expression theory, really can never do anything more than any other audience member. In fact, given the preference posited by many such theories for a naïve audience unencumbered by cultural expectations, critics are a negative influence. We should not

4 An extract from Fielding's novel *Tom Jones* (1749) appears in the appendix at the end of this book.

listen to critics too much because they will warp our sensibility. Judgment becomes chaotic and value becomes subjective in such a system.

This may seem like a greater artistic freedom, but it is not. When every subjective reaction is given equal weight, the lowest common denominator will prevail. If everything is as good as everything else, no value can reach beyond its immediate effect. Even if our theory tells us that values are subjective, that does not correspond to the way that aesthetic appreciation has worked. We are drawn to art and beauty just because they seem to provide some extraordinary value and insight; they matter. A theory of aesthetics must explain how and why.

Imagination

Both expression theories and imitation theories cover the same aesthetic phenomena. For example, aesthetic pleasure is accounted for by an expression theory as the pleasure one takes in intuitions that give form to sense and that express the mind's own powers. Moreover, an active mind is neither bored nor overloaded, so it experiences a pleasant balance of its own powers. Imitation theories do not deny aesthetic pleasure, but they account for it differently. They posit a basic pleasure in imitation itself that is related to our desire to know something. Because knowing is essentially grasping a form or idea that is closer to the singular form of the thing itself, imitation is a basic way of knowing. Pleasure in imitation also enjoys the exhibition of skill that imitation as a way of making something employs. It might seem that we could simply combine these two theories. Maybe aesthetic pleasure is all of these things. That will not do, however, because basic inconsistencies between the two approaches make them incompatible. For example, they understand mind differently: the mind cannot be both a creative power and itself a lesser form of some greater power. Expression locates aesthetic experience in the individual. Imitation locates it in the universal.

Frustration with this kind of theoretical indecision leads to a distrust of all theory. One way to avoid too much dependence on theory is itself a theory: a theory of the imagination. 'Imagination' shifts from a negative to a positive term in the course of the history of aesthetics. It had negative connotations as long as it was thought of as essentially fantasy and phantasm. To call something imaginary was a way of saying that it was illusory and thus not real at all. Fantasy was thought of as a kind of mental disease. At best, it was a waste of time and misleading – daydreaming about what was not and never could be. At worst, it was confusion, a turning from real ideas to fantastic combinations such as monsters. This negative sense of imagination is closely related to the positive force assigned to reason and to illumination through union with ideal forms. Imagination seems to be eccentric, irrational, and disordered, and thus entirely at odds with the ordered, rational, and singular realities sought by imitation theory as the object to be imitated.

The negative view of imagination was widely held not only in classical and medieval philosophy but also in early forms of rationalism and empiricism in the seventeenth and eighteenth centuries. As long as some higher standard for knowledge was sought, imagination would be suspect. Plato and Aristotle both understood intellect as essentially unitary and transcendent. Individual knowledge was judged by its conformity to universal forms. Science itself had to conform to the way things must be as reason dictated. That led to some silly scientific mistakes. When Aristotelian philosophy and science were finally supplanted by more direct observation and mathematically controlled predictions in the scientific revolution, imagination still was regarded as eccentric and unreliable because it was not controlled by reason, observation, or mathematically calculable forms. Only gradually did imagination assume the positive connotations that we now take for granted.

It is a short step from the negative to an essentially positive view of the imagination, however. If imagination is thought of not as a kind of mechanical assembling of ideas into fantastic combinations but instead as a power to create new forms, then imagination seems very close to divine power. Imagination can be linked to inspiration, and thus to the creative force that enters poetry and art without being directly controlled by an artist. This power gives imagination its anti-theoretical force. Reason and imitation seek to control the creative process. Imagination breaks through with a kind of divine frenzy or possession that speaks through an artist. There is a fine line between imagination and madness.

Joseph Addison (1672–1719) had already begun to give imagination its more positive sense when he described the pleasures of the imagination in *The Spectator*. Addison associated the pleasure produced by imagination with the activity of the mind. Through much of the eighteenth century, imagination was still regarded as the suspect enemy of reason and neo-classical rules, however. It was not until the end of the century, as expression theories became commonplace, that imagination emerged as an independent force and competitor to imitation. Something like this theory of imagination appears repeatedly in the history of aesthetics whenever rules and academic restrictions threaten to restrict artistic activity. It is prominent in the romantic poets, for example. Samuel Taylor Coleridge (1772–1834) praises the imagination as the divine, creative "I am" that repeats itself in the activity of poets. In contrast, the mechanical assemblage of images is mere fancy. Coleridge's view is typical of much nineteenth- and twentieth-century praise of the imagination as a mystery that casts off the control of too much criticism and theorizing. Yet clearly this is itself a theory of aesthetic activity.

Imagination takes a somewhat more disciplined form in non-romantic expression theories, but there too it is an antidote to too much theory. Imagination can be linked to the free play of the mind and thus to the mind's ability to express itself in new forms that go beyond established categories. Ordinary perception is understood as occurring in expected ways; imagination sees new possibilities because it is not restricted to the rules and categories of what has already been understood. In this sense, imagination is a positive force in science as well as in aesthetics. Old science follows established paths. New science breaks with established paradigms. It is very much like play, except that it is productive of new understandings.

Imagination can also be viewed as a way into the deeper, hidden associations of the mind. Our conscious minds are constrained by our rational control. The unconscious play of the mind breaks out in dreams and in art. Imagination gives that unconscious expression. One way to distinguish between art and non-art, therefore, depends on a theory of imagination. Art is imaginative. Non-art is conscious manipulation. Art is free. Non-art is controlled by other, already established ends. In expression theories, imagination has become not only a positive force but almost the criterion for authenticity of the product.

All positive theories of imagination share a deep ambivalence toward theory that approaches an internal contradiction, however. On the one hand, to be imaginative, something must be beyond the control and explanation that theory offers. On the other hand, imagination is used as a theoretical category that cannot be dispensed with. So 'imagination' becomes a theoretical term like 'force' in physics. Appeals to the power of the imagination want to have it both ways. The result is that imagination seems to explain more than it really does. In many cases, the appeal to imagination amounts to little more than a claim that some experience should be regarded aesthetically because it is different. In early empiricist theories this was simply the "I know not what" of feeling. So imagination often slides back into obscurity. Interesting attempts in psychology to give imagination more behavioral content may still illuminate aesthetics. For the present we have only promises, however.

A restricted positive sense of the imagination combines easily with expression theories. The strongest theories of imagination break with expression theories, however, because they distrust the dependence on symbols and forms that are characteristic of theories of aesthetic expression. Imagination must be a free play in these theories, and they are

anti-theoretical theories as well. It is best to regard appeals to the imagination as a separate attempt to provide aesthetic explanations, therefore.
If 'imagination' becomes the central aesthetic term, one is nearing the
limits of philosophical aesthetics: a psychology of the imagination is
more important than the metaphysics of imitation or the epistemological
theories of expression, and psychology replaces philosophy as the best
way to investigate aesthetic phenomena.

Conclusions

Aesthetics is about both art and natural phenomena that have been characterized as either beautiful or expressive by competing theories. Aesthetic objects are those that provide the points of reference and identity
for theory. 'Object' need not be limited to physical objects. Aesthetics
is concerned with physical objects when it looks at concrete forms, but
it is also concerned with abstract and ideal objects, just as other kinds
of knowledge such as mathematics are, and with perceptual objects that
are independent of their causes and effects. If we take 'object' in the
broadest possible sense, we can understand competing aesthetic theories
as different ways of accounting for what aesthetic objects are and how
we can know them.

Three broadly defined kinds of theories have dominated aesthetics.
Imitation theories begin with metaphysics – what there is – and identify
aesthetic objects as imitations of more basic realities such as forms or
real, useful objects. Imitation is more than copying, therefore. It is a
way of making something so that what is made is related to something
else that is regarded as more real. Thus imitation theories require a
metaphysics that tells us what is real and what is more real than something else. Aesthetic objects can then be located either higher or lower
in relation to other things that are part of the universe of things. Expression theories become prominent when the metaphysics that supports
imitation theories gives way to questions about how we know things
scientifically and directly. Expression theories relate an individual mind
to the world of things, ideas, and experiences. Very powerful expression
theories make aesthetic objects and aesthetic expression virtually coex-
tensive with knowledge itself. More modest versions think of art as an
activity of a mind that takes pleasure in its ability to order and make
public and concrete its own ideas. In their various forms, expression
theories explain aesthetic phenomena – art and beauty – in relation to
ways of giving order to what we know. Finally, one part of expression,
imagination, is sometimes regarded as so important that it should be
considered the basis of a separate kind of theory. Imagination is seen as

the creative ability of the mind to project itself and to form new objects. Imagination is then both creative and playful, actually bringing into being things that did not exist before and could not exist without an artist's activity.

Imitation theories are criticized because they require a metaphysics of forms if imitation is to be a significant form of making. If imitation does not have that significance, it becomes mechanical copying. Imitation theories are strongest in accounting for the role of skill and the presence of art objects. Expression theories are criticized because they tend to place their claims beyond testing and to focus solely on feelings to the exclusion of skill and physical objects. If expression is what produces aesthetic objects, there is a tendency to dismiss actual art works as mere intermediaries, means to the end of occupying the mind and creating aesthetic experience. When imagination becomes a theory in its own right, it appeals to some often mysterious operation or faculty that cannot be otherwise described. Investigations of the imagination then either become mysterious or, if they are carried on empirically, move into the realm of psychology.

In considering all three types of theory, it is important to keep in mind that the sense of 'theory' here is that of competing explanations of aesthetic objects and experiences. Each theory must account for as much of the agreed subject-matter as possible. One cannot simply combine such theories because they are incompatible in the explanations they give of what we have before us – art and natural beauty.

Both formal analysis and the competing theories about aesthetic objects lead us to focus on what aesthetics is about. Form and content allow us to speak analytically about our experience. Imitation and expression theories provide competing accounts of what we experience and how we can experience it. Imagination as a theory cuts across those possibilities to free aesthetics from theory, but it is itself a theory none the less. We must now see how that analysis and those theories apply to the concrete relations that form the art world.

References and Suggestions for Further Reading

Formal analysis

Form and content

A collection that includes work on both scientific and artistic form is Lancelot Law Whyte, ed., *Aspects of Form* (Bloomington: Indiana University Press, 1971).

Form and content in art

The form/content distinction with respect to visual art and the methods of formal analysis used here follow roughly the methods of Clive Bell, *Art* (New York: Capricorn Books, 1958) and Roger Fry, *Vision and Design* (London: Chatto & Windus, 1920) and *Transformations* (London: Chatto & Windus, 1926). The example is my own.

Comparisons of form

Horace's formula is "Ut pictura poesis," a poem is like a painting. It is found in "The Art of Poetry," which is available in many different translations. For the comparison of poetry and painting in the eighteenth century, see particularly G.E. Lessing, *Laokoon* (first publ. 1766; New York: Farrar, Straus & Giroux, 1957). The classic argument for pure music is found in Eduard Hanslick, *The Beautiful in Music* (Indianapolis: Bobbs-Merrill, 1957). For further reading on the aesthetics of music see Stephen Davies, *Musical Meaning and Expression* (Ithaca: Cornell University Press, 1994); Peter Kivy, *Music Alone: Reflections on the Purely Musical Experience* (Ithaca: Cornell University Press, 1990), *The Fine Art of Repetition: Essays in the Philosophy of Music* (New York: Cambridge University Press, 1993), and *Authenticities: Philosophical Reflections on Musical Performance* (Ithaca: Cornell University Press, 1995); Jerrold Levinson, *Music, Art, and Metaphysics* (Ithaca: Cornell University Press, 1990); and Aaron Ridley, *Music, Value and the Passions* (Ithaca: Cornell University Press, 1995).

Aesthetic objects

What is an 'object'?

A useful starting-point for thinking about aesthetic objects is Richard Rudner, "The Ontological Status of the Esthetic Object," *Philosophy and Phenomenological Research* 10 (1949–50): 380–8. Aesthetic ontology is the topic of Nicholas Wolterstorff, *Works and Worlds of Art* (Oxford: Clarendon Press, 1980). For the problems of identifying objects, see P.F. Strawson, *Individuals* (London: Methuen, 1959). For further discussion of aesthetic attitudes, see the section on "Critics and Criticism" in chapter 4 below.

Aesthetic objects

Two basic theories of imitation are that of Plato in *Republic*, book X, where imitation is treated as a hierarchical concept, and that of Aristotle in his *Poetics*, where 'imitation' has the sense of a made thing. Both works are available in many different translations. For a concise statement of the medieval allegorical scheme, see Letter X in Dante Alighieri, *The Letters of Dante* (Oxford: Oxford University Press, 1966). For music as a form of imitation, see e.g. Susanne K. Langer, *Philosophy in a New Key* (New York: Mentor Books, 1942), chapter 8.

The differences in symbolic representation characteristic of different art forms are discussed by Nelson Goodman, *Languages of Art* (Indianapolis: Hackett, 1976), particularly chapter 5. Expression theories emerge by the end of the eighteenth century, but two influential twentieth-century forms are Benedetto Croce, *Aesthetic* (New York: Noonday Press, 1968) and R.G. Collingwood, *The Principles of Art* (New York: Oxford University Press, 1958). A different form of expression theory is found in some successors to Kant, particularly Ernst Cassirer, *The Philosophy of Symbolic Forms* (New Haven: Yale University Press, 1953) and Susanne Langer, *Feeling and Form* (New York: Charles Scribner's Sons, 1953). A contemporary version is found in Alan Tormey, *The Concept of Expression* (Princeton: Princeton University Press, 1971). Many of the elements of expression theory have their origin in Immanuel Kant, *Critique of Judgment* (Indianapolis: Hackett, 1987). For genius, see particularly §§46–50. The fully developed sense of the aesthetic as "disinterested" is found in §§1–4. Collingwood (*Principles of Art*) makes extensive use of the distinction between art and pseudo-art. Tolstoy's theory that art is a form of infectious communication is in Leo N. Tolstoy, *What is Art?* (New York: Liberal Arts Press, 1960). Ruskin's aesthetic theory appears in John Ruskin, *Modern Painters*, vol. 1 (New York: Wiley, 1885). The positive sense of imagination is expressed by Joseph Addison, "The Pleasures of the Imagination," *The Spectator*, nos 409, 411–21 (New York: E.P. Dutton, 1933) and extended by Samuel Taylor Coleridge, *Biographia Literaria* (London: Dent, 1962), chapter 13. See also Kant, *Critique of Judgment*, §35. For useful treatments of the imagination in romantic poetry, see C.M. Bowra, *The Romantic Imagination* (Oxford: Oxford University Press, 1949) and M.H. Abrams, *The Mirror and the Lamp* (New York: Norton, 1958).

3

The Artist and the Work of Art

Works of art appear in many different cultures and in many different contexts, and they have many different uses. Today the art world encompasses everything from pop art to classical music, from native artifacts to environmental sculpture. Art has always been diverse in its forms and its uses. Cave paintings and prehistoric carved figures have been discovered that pre-date any written texts. We can only guess on the basis of later analogies what role these objects played when they were made. Certainly two possibilities appear very early: such works belonged to ritual and religious contexts, and they were objects of play and enjoyment. We know that works of art served serious purposes. They provided objects of worship and made the gods imaginable. They conveyed religious and dynastic messages. They formed symbols without which cultures would not have been able to identify themselves. Works of art even play a central role in philosophy itself – drama, music, dance, sculpture, poetry, and rhetoric all communicate the ideas, images, and thoughts around which philosophy grew up. But works of art also were enjoyed. Decoration was not necessary for utilitarian purposes, and its conferral of status hardly justified the work and love lavished on it. We desire art because it gives us pleasure. We enjoy a beautiful building, an intricate design, a garden, or a dance. We spend time on poetry, drama, and stories because we enjoy them. Nothing else would justify the work that goes into their writing and performance. We have every reason to believe that wherever there has been time and sufficient release from the necessities of survival, works of art have had these uses. Beyond that, however, we should be reluctant to generalize about what kind of uses and enjoyment art produces. One of the striking features of art is that it does not obey rules or expectations.

We can take one feature to be common to all of these instances of art, however. They did not just happen. They were made in some fashion at some time and place. We need assume nothing about artists in noting that works of art are produced. So considering the relation of the producer and what is produced can offer us a basic way into our consideration of aesthetic phenomena. In doing this we do not pre-judge the status of natural beauty. It will have to be accounted for somewhere in our discussion. We can start with the obvious fact of production of works of art, however, without deciding in advance how all of the pieces of our puzzle will fit together.

The Artist's Intentions

Determining intentions

In approaching an aesthetic object that has been produced in some way, it seems natural to begin by asking what the intent of the producer was. This is particularly true of aesthetic objects because they are not defined fully by those intentions that determine their utilitarian purposes. That is not to say that aesthetic objects and works of art do not have uses. A novel might be used to make money for its author, to inspire actions (like *Uncle Tom's Cabin*), or to explore moral and social issues (like Hemingway's *A Farewell to Arms*), and all of these uses might be intended by their authors. But even when the aesthetic object has a use or multiple uses, we do not start with its use in figuring out what to do with it. Its aesthetic character follows from its being a work of art of a certain kind. Works of art are not like utilitarian objects in this respect. My computer, on which I am writing this sentence, works. That is the primary thing that I need to know about it. I want to know how it works and whether it will do the job that it is intended to do. So the utilitarian intention is to do a job, and when I know what the job is and what it requires, I know whether my computer will do it. For aesthetic objects, on the other hand, it seems to matter more what the producer wanted to do. Perhaps the novelist intended to stimulate action or to create situations that show different possible moral complications. Then the use follows. In art, we tend to let the producer decide; in non-aesthetic, utilitarian objects, we tend to let the job and the user decide. If the question is whether the object is good for its job, we ask the user. But if the question is "What is this about?" we tend to ask the producer. Imagine that someone objected to a novel that it did not improve society. The author might reply that that was not its intent. It was intended to entertain, or to prepare the reader for eternity, or to show the limits of novels. All of those answers meet the objection. If someone objects that a computer is too slow to run today's software, it will not be an effective answer for the manufacturers to say that they intended to make a more leisurely computer. Intentions seem to be a natural part of aesthetic objects in a way that does not apply to utilitarian objects.

We have several ways of determining the aesthetic intention of the producer of an aesthetic object. We can, of course, simply ask. This is not a very satisfactory procedure for a number of reasons. The producer may be unknown, dead, or otherwise unavailable. Or there may not be a single producer. Movies and buildings are acts of collaboration. Whom is one to ask? The producer may not be very good at giving an answer. The ability to make something does not always imply the ability to describe what one has made. On the other hand, in some situations artists have provided us with statements of their intentions. Some movements issued manifestos. Renaissance painters wrote detailed treatises on the art of painting, and in the eighteenth century some of the most prominent painters wrote in detail about what painting involved for them. Artists have also commented extensively on their own work. It would be foolish to deny that what the producer says has some relevance to what is produced.

Often, however, the intentions of the producer have to be inferred from the context and the practice at the time. A painter such as Sir Joshua Reynolds (1723–92) tells us a great deal in his *Discourses* about what he took painting to be and how he thought it should be done. But we know even more from the broader picture we get of eighteenth-century portrait painting by examining the practices of artists and how they tried to present their subjects. For example, most successful portrait painters had apprentices and pupils who were learning the art from them. The design of the painting and the work on the main figure was done by the master, but backgrounds might be entrusted to pupils. That tells us something about the intent of the painter, because it tells us what was considered important and what was considered incidental. It is harder to imagine painters who intend their work as expressions of their own personality allowing someone else to work on the painting than it is to imagine painters who intend their work as some form of imitation doing so. The larger context also tells us something about intentions. In their early forms, some novels made use of broad forms of burlesque and bawdiness (e.g. *The Adventures of Peregrine Pickle* by Tobias Smollett, published in 1751). The intent is clearly to appeal to an audience. Later, more serious novels have a different intent. They want to be true to life, so they establish a different set of conventions and no longer make use of the same exaggerated devices.

Communication: knowing what the artist intended

The search for information about intentions involves an appeal to what is communicated. This leads to a theory that the relation between artist and work of art is based on a desire to communicate something. The aesthetic object is regarded as a kind of language. Sometimes, it is literally made up of language, either spoken or written. But even buildings and music can be said to have a language of their own that communicates the intention of the architect or the composer. What is communicated is something that is first understood (perhaps in the language of that art form) by the producer and then expressed in the appropriate language of the aesthetic object. The purpose of the aesthetic object is to express something, and we learn what that is by asking what is communicated or what the artist is trying to communicate.

This theory has several advantages. First, the analogy with language provides a way to approach works of art. If reading and listening are communicative acts, it is argued, then they should also be communicative acts when we read a work of art or hear it – either literally or figuratively. (We will return to this analogy when we consider the relation of the audience to a work of art in chapter 4.) Second, treating the relation between the artist and the work of art as a communicative act allows us to say that the artist was trying to communicate something but failed for one reason or another. We do not always succeed in expressing our intentions correctly. We have all been misunderstood, either through some fault in our expression or through some failure of communication. As the boss of the chain gang tells Paul Newman's character in *Cool Hand Luke*, "What we have here is a failure to communicate." Not only can there be a gap between intention and communication, but we can know that there has been a failure and sometimes we can figure out what was really intended. Art seems to be like that. The failure can be on the side of either the artist or the audience, and focusing on intentions helps us to bridge the gap. Finally, if the relation between the producer and what is produced is essentially a communication of the producer's intentions, that helps to explain why we consider aesthetic objects and art particularly important. Often, we have no other way of getting at those interior feelings. For example, music can provide an intentional expression of feelings, even if they are not actually felt at that moment by anyone. No other means is as effective. The complex feelings embodied in drama or the feelings of religious awe expressed in paintings would remain private if the intentions of the producer were not communicated in the work. All of these considerations point toward the importance of the relation between the producer and the aesthetic object being understood in terms of some relation between interior feelings or intentions and their expression in the aesthetic object.

Nevertheless, there are three strong lines of objection to taking the relation between producer and aesthetic object to be one of intentional communication. First, there are works of art for which we cannot locate a single producer whose intentions are definitive for the work. We might consider two examples. A medieval cathedral might be considered the work of a master builder. However, the design of a cathedral frequently mixed the styles of several periods. It showed the influence of the bishops and canons. The building itself took decades, sometimes even centuries, to complete and often underwent substantial changes of conception in the process. The decoration and the sculpture that are essential parts of any cathedral were in the hands of various artists and artisans. In a real sense a cathedral can be said to have grown rather than to have been built to a single artistic conception. Yet the result is often both monumental and strikingly effective. One might talk of the intentions of the church or the culture, but there is nothing like a single psychological intention to which we can refer in our understanding and appreciation of the final building.

Or consider the making of a successful motion picture. In the early days of film-making, the entire production – from conception to final editing – might indeed be in the hands of a single producer–director. The parallel between narrative film-making and the storytelling of a novel suggested that films should have authors in the same way that novels had authors. The director seemed the obvious candidate. However, even in early film, the director was seldom an independent author in the way a novelist was. For one thing, many early films were improvised. For another, they followed formulas supplied by popular culture. As film-making progressed and became more complex, the idea of the director as an author became more problematic. In recent film theory, the so-called *auteur* theory of directing refers not to the director as the author of a single film, because that description no longer is plausible. Instead, it refers to a total body of work, the director's films over a period of time, as a single work that is taken to have a coherence arising from the director's vision. When John Ford said "I make westerns," it was not a single western but a whole approach to film-making that gave that simple claim substance. A single film probably owes as much to the producer, the cinematographer, the film editor, and even the distribution system as it does to the director. Seeking something that the director intended to communicate in a film would require a single conscious presence that just does not exist.

Even if we considered these examples as special cases, we would have to account for all of the works of art that were produced as a result of craft with no apparent intention to do anything more than produce a successful, satisfying, and saleable commodity. Potters and vase-painters may have taken delight in producing beautiful objects, but it seems a little much to imagine that they were engaged in some kind of intentional activity of communication beyond producing a fine example of an object to satisfy some potential user. In general, then, while it may be a useful strategy to ask of some works what the artist intended to communicate, intentions by themselves cannot account for everything, because there may not be a single artist to whom we can refer; and even if there is, we cannot always ascribe to him or her a conscious intention to produce art.

Even when there is an artist, an attempt to approach the relation of the artist to the work of art in terms of his or her intentions presents problems. We often have no way of knowing what the intentions of the artist were. Consider how we can know the intentions of an artist. We might have direct evidence in the form of statements, manifestos, or commentary. Dante, for example, explains in some detail in a letter to one of his patrons how he intended his *Divine Comedy* to be read. In a complex work that has multiple layers of allegory, a guide to the intentions of the author is very useful. We have a transcript of a hearing before the inquisition at which Paolo Veronese had to defend his conception of a painting of the last supper against charges that it was too secular. It provides a fascinating glimpse of what a sixteenth-century painter intended to accomplish. But such evidence is rare. We are more likely to have contemporary commentary and indirect evidence from autobiography and documents. Such material, even when it exists, provides only very indirect evidence concerning a work of art, however. We must base our inferences on probabilities that are often little more than guesses. If our ability to appreciate aesthetically were dependent on such information, many works would become inaccessible as our knowledge of their producers faded. What would we make of the anonymous works whose artist remains unknown? If we know little more of Shakespeare than his name and will, does that mean that we do not know his work? Once the artist is dead and records are lost, our external access to intentions begins to slip away.

The most frequent answer to this problem is that we still have the work and that we can infer the intentions of the producer from it. When we hear a stirring march, surely we can infer that, even if the composer was not stirred and the musicians are only performing their crafts, no one could have composed such a piece without intending that the audience be stirred. All this is indeed true. Much of our talk about intentions is in fact concealed talk about how we respond. Given two readings of a poem, we might say that one was the intended reading because most readers could be expected to react in that way. The concealed premise is that an artist can be expected to know his or her craft and to take account of responses. So if there is a clear response, and no evidence that it is accidental or unintended, then it can be taken as the intended response. We rely on the work itself and our knowledge of its cultural context to infer the intentions of the artist. At the New York Independents Exhibition in 1917, Marcel Duchamp exhibited a urinal as a work of art, calling it "Fountain" and signing it "R. Mutt." We know that at that time, the expectations of most people were that art was quite different from porcelain fixtures, and we know that Duchamp knew that. We infer that Duchamp intended his work to be an outrageous comment on the art that was being accepted and exhibited. We use our knowledge of the cultural context to infer the intentions of the artist. That we find the work bland today because much more outrageous things have intervened does not change our inference. However, such backwards inference changes what 'intention' means. We are no longer referring to something in Duchamp. We are referring to something in the work and culture. If it turned out that Duchamp were really an android without intentions, nothing in our interpretation of the work would have changed. The language of intentions is a convenient way of sorting out competing evidence and interpretations in such cases, but it does not really refer to specific intentions of the artist.

Intentions and interpretation

This suggests that reference to intentions and to the artist is a way of giving authority to one kind of interpretation over another. In that case, it would be clearer to cite our evidence for our interpretation directly. The inclusion of the artist is a kind of appeal to authority that is often fallacious. This reflection led a number of critics, particularly in literary criticism, to argue that in matters of interpretation the intentions of the artist were irrelevant. It was not denied that there were artistic intentions. But if they were successful, then the work would be what it is and our response to it would be guided by the work. If they were not successful, then we were left with the work and our response was guided by the work. Either way, as long as we had the work, the intentions of the artist were irrelevant from the standpoint of interpreting the work. When the unavailability of intentions directly and the unreliability of authors as interpreters of their own work were added to that argument, it seemed best to dispense with all talk of intentions in interpretation.

Reliance on the artist's intentions as a critical tool was called the intentional fallacy, and its rejection took on the status of a critical dogma for a time.

In fact, no one ever completely dispensed with talk of intentions or denied that there was an intentional relation between the producer and what was produced. Works of art do not happen by accident, and even if the intention is not formed consciously by a concept of art, it is still what guides the production of the work. The point of the intentional fallacy was to redirect attention to the work and its formal relations that could be exhibited critically. As a piece of critical advice, this was obviously sound. As a piece of aesthetic theory, it was easily overstated. It is one thing to critically restrict interpretation to that for which we have evidence. It is quite another to deny the existence of causal relations that produced the evidence. When Robinson Crusoe comes upon a footprint in the sand, he can infer only what the size and shape of the footprint show. Nevertheless, he is able to infer that the cause of the footprint was another human being and that he is not alone on his island. As critics, we can interpret only what the work shows us, but we can infer the existence of a creative mind with intentions that are represented in the work.

Conclusions

Intentions direct our attention to questions of meaning, and we use our knowledge of intentions to help us understand what is communicated by a work of art. The model of communication treats all art on an extended analogy with language. Intentions are communicated by means of some product, and those intentions can be understood both directly as a form of communication and indirectly from evidence such as explanations from the artist and critics. However, knowing the artist's intentions is not the same thing as knowing the work of art, because there may not be a single artist, and even if there is, the artist may do more or less than intended. Further, evidence for intentions may be lacking because it is lost or never existed even though we have the work. We are guided in our interpretation of a work of art by intentions, but it is a fallacy to equate intentions with the meaning we seek to interpret. Interpretation depends on evidence, and evidence comes primarily from the work itself. Our aesthetic theory can still include the artist as an intentional cause even if we look primarily to the work for what we know of it.

We wanted to know how the producer is related to what is produced. A suggested answer comes in terms of intentions and is explicated in terms of something that is communicated. The problem with that as a theory is not that it does not capture some of the relation but that it cannot be the whole story. We probably want to keep intentions and communication in our aesthetic vocabulary, but we do not want to rely on them alone. The relation between producer and work of art is more complex than that.

Inspiration

If we ask what more than intentions is required for art, the obvious answer is some productive skill. Art in our contemporary sense of a special category of objects and producers has evolved from earlier senses that emphasized productive ability. Artisans were a class of people skilled in a craft. In classical and medieval theories, no sharp distinction was drawn between artisans and artists. The close connection between art and craft was also evident in the structure of guilds (basically craft unions) and systems of apprenticeship. Painters were not sharply distinguished from goldsmiths. Poets might have a special status, but musicians were employed to provide the accompaniment for religious services and special occasions.

Gradually, our sense of art as something made for aesthetic ends and attended to in its own right had to emerge from that classical and medieval union. The emergence of art is part of the emergence of a modern world. In the process the assumption that art implied skill had to be rethought. Inspiration was always part of the equation. Classical theories of inspiration were used to account for the fact that artisans, particularly poets and musicians, produced more than they could explain. The shift to a modern sense of art as something special placed much heavier emphasis on the difference between art and craft, however, and thus inspiration became more and more important. This historical shift discloses some important features of the relation of art to craft and productive skill.

Skill

In his "Elegy Written in a Country Churchyard" the poet Thomas Gray (1716–71) surveys the graves of a village cemetery and imagines that "Some mute inglorious Milton here may rest, / Some Cromwell guiltless of his country's blood." We are asked to imagine that the villagers who have never actually performed great deeds or written great poetry might have done so given a different opportunity. What distinguishes a poet from a silent villager? Gray's villagers, lacking learning and leisure, could not even form the intent to write poetry. But even if they did, intent by itself could not be enough. It must issue in some poem. There must be some product, some artifact, some concrete thing that survives the artist. (Like every generalization in philosophy, this one will be challenged later – by performance art, for example.)

In this respect, we need to distinguish two different kinds of intent. I might have the intention to write a novel when I want to write a novel and think that I can do it. I imagine what it would be like to have completed the work, and maybe I even imagine what the plot and characters will be. That intention remains incomplete because the desire to do something does not imply the actual specific intentions required to accomplish my desire. My intention "to write a novel" does not imply that I have any clue about what actually writing a novel involves. The intention is directed at the end product, not the process. A second kind of intention links what is done to what is attempted. I may actually set out to write a novel. I produce a hundred thousand words with dialogue and events. Now my intention is productive. I intended something, and I can point to it and show it to whoever is willing to read it. Nevertheless, my intention may still fail. Perhaps what I wrote turns out to be autobiographical to the extent that it is a memoir rather than a novel. Or perhaps it is just so badly written and formed that it is a miscellany of episodes or even pure gibberish. The first kind of intention is merely an intention *that* I do something. The other is an intent that issues in some action. But neither intention can succeed without skill. Gray's mute, inglorious Milton would never become a poet simply by wanting to be one or intending to be one unless he also acquired the skill with language that poetry requires.

Skill can be either an overlooked or an overrated part of the relation of artist to work of art. Consider first some of the ways in which it is overlooked. Gray implicitly maintains that the real nature of a poet rests in the ability to feel and experience in certain ways. Poetic feeling is something that sensitive folk are capable of; it responds to nature, beauty, and sentiment. So everyone who has the tender or melancholy feelings evoked by a walk in a country churchyard is, essentially, a poet. In that case, the actual skill involved in writing a poem would be secondary. Any number of anecdotes illustrate this view. Leonardo da Vinci is supposed to have rebuked the prior who objected to his standing before the blank wall upon which he would paint his *Last Supper* by saying that the real act of painting lay in imagining the work. Its execution only came later. James McNeill Whistler replied to John Ruskin's objection that Whistler's highly abstract painting was flinging a pot of paint in the face of the public by citing the culmination of years of artistic experience. If the end result seemed to require little of the skill that Ruskin admired, so much the worse for Ruskin and the public. They lacked Whistler's educated sensibility. The aesthetic theories behind these anecdotes vary. What they share is a sense that skill is an added, independent element separate from art. It serves only to make the work of art more public and available.

Such an attitude is clearly at variance with practice, however. Gray, Leonardo, and Whistler all spent years learning their crafts, and they knew that without the product, there is no art. Most practicing artists acknowledge an intimate relation between acquired skill and the ability to imagine and formulate their art in the first place. The intention to produce cannot be completed without the knowledge of the possibilities and the forms that is only acquired through practice and skill. The deceptively simple drawings of a Picasso or the geometric patterns of a Mondrian do not occur without skill with color and shape. "I could do that" may be a common response on viewing some kinds of painting, but the fact remains that it was the artist who did it. Instead of illustrating how little skill is required, such cases actually illustrate how deeply practice must be assimilated before it can be simplified in such striking performances. Most amateur writing, painting, and acting is overly complex. Professionalism is exhibited in restraint, not excess. So, while skill may be overlooked, it is clearly an essential part of the relation of artist and work of art.

Skill can also be overrated as an aesthetic criterion, however. A different kind of anecdote illustrates the problem. Painters are often praised for their ability to produce lifelike reproductions. (These are called *trompe l'oeil* effects because they fool the eye.) The classical Greek painter Zeuxis is said to have painted grapes that looked so real that the birds tried to peck them. Some painted architectural features of the renaissance are so skillfully done that only from certain angles can the eye tell that they are not three-dimensional. We both admire and enjoy such performances. Actually, there are two different ways in which we admire them. The first values the reproduction as a near-instance of what it reproduces. If one cannot have the real thing, then a painted ceiling or a painted landscape is a good substitute. The more the eye is fooled, the better the painting. The best painting would be one that succeeded perfectly in not being recognized as a reproduction. Illusion comes into play in a second way. This requires that one recognize that what is presented is an illusion. What we admire is the closeness of the reproduction and the skill that produced it; and in order to admire them, we must be making a comparison that depends on our recognizing the difference. Photographs tend to replace painting in the first case; they can perform better than any hand alone the process of reproduction. However, there is a recent movement in painting called photo-realism. A painter produces a painting that is so like a photograph that it may be mistaken for one. This illustrates the second fascination. The painter produces not the scene itself but the illusion of being a photograph of a scene.

Photo-realism also illustrates the problem in depending on illusion. The tendency is for attention to shift from what is produced to the skill itself. Apart from the skill involved, nothing has been produced that was not already available. (This is not true of all photo-realism, which is a complex movement in painting and should be understood in the context of its reaction against movements such as abstract expressionism.) The anecdotes about Zeuxis and other illusionistic painters illustrate something about the artists, not something about their art. The intention involved is not to produce something but to display a skill. We tend to lose sight of the relation between artist and work of art in our focus on the skill of the artist.

Illusionistic painting is only one instance of this focus on skill. The same kind of thing may be exhibited in virtuoso musical performances that are intended to display the abilities of the performer. One is less interested in the music than in the amazing ability of the player to perform the difficult exercises demanded by the composer. Opera singers sometimes insert additional high notes because the audience expects them to show their vocal range. All of these displays focus our attention on the performer and the difficulty of the performance rather than on what is performed.

There is a natural alliance between an emphasis on skill and imitation theories of aesthetics. We take pleasure in our ability to imitate; it seems a basic element in our ability to learn. Children are natural mimics and learn in the process. The common perception that art should be lifelike and produce recognizable products – either written, heard, or seen – undoubtedly owes much to a natural tendency toward imitation. However, skill and the intentions that produce its display are not limited to imitation theories. The feeling that artists should give us a "true expression" of their own personalities, for example, fits easily into an expression theory. The point we need to be clear about here is not that one theory or another better fits our fascination with skill but that in focusing on skill we are looking at a different relation from the one we set out to understand. The relation between the producer and what is produced is replaced by a relation between the producer and the ability to produce. Whatever that may be and however important it may be as a part of the process of aesthetic production, it is not the same thing. We expect works of art to be something more than mere displays of skill.

From craft to art

A parallel distinction may help us to understand the difference. As we noted at the beginning of this section, art, in all of its forms, has always been closely related to craft. For a good part of its history, the aesthetic productive process was part of the crafts. Craftsmen made something, and sometimes what they made was also art. Artists were craftsmen; they belonged to guilds and craft unions. (This is still the case for many performing artists.) At the same time, an implicit distinction between the useful arts and those primarily intended for pleasure or enlightenment was available. Painters, musicians, and even poets and dramatists might be thought of as skilled craftsmen, but they were also accorded a special status because of the kinds of things that they produced.

In the early modern period (the seventeenth and eighteenth centuries), that implicit distinction assumed theoretical importance. The fine arts – painting, music, drama, sculpture, dance, etc. – were elevated above the decorative arts – weaving, pottery, gardening, etc. – which were in turn distinct from the merely utilitarian arts such as lens-grinding, harness-making, etc. The reasons for the explicit appearance of 'fine art' at that particular point in history are complex. They have to do with changes in who supported the arts and how arts were produced as well as changes in the dominant art theory. A rising middle class demanded painting, poems, novels, and plays that earlier would have been limited to an aristocratic and ecclesiastical patronage. Mechanical means of production widened the gap between useful objects and those which appealed to aesthetic sensibility.

Theoretically, however, the primary move was to account for differences in pleasure itself. Some pleasures were thought to be higher than others and thus needed no utilitarian justification. The fine arts were valued for their own sake, while the decorative arts appealed to vanity and the utilitarian arts to need. Aesthetic theory was trying to account for a category of aesthetic experience and sensibility that was believed to be different from other forms of experience and senses. The "something more" attributed to art led to a separate category of art – fine art – which thus required its own means of production.

Beginning in the renaissance, artists gradually claimed a dignity and status not previously accorded them, and their works simultaneously came to be valued for their own sake as somehow special and elevated over other productions. Mere skill was craft; fine arts were something more. That respect for the fine arts has become part of our culture and theory (at least until recently) and is embedded in our aesthetic institutions. One need only consider museums, colleges of fine arts, galleries, and symphony and dance societies to see how completely the idea that fine art is somehow different and special has been accepted.

The difficulty, of course, is to say how art is different if it is not simply a matter of skill. The first thing to note is the role played by rules of a certain kind. In order to be able to produce something, a craftsman must be able to follow a plan. An end product is desired, and there is a means to arrive at that end. The means constitutes the craft. It is a combination of an ability acquired through training and an appropriate means incorporated into the way of working. This combination of means and skill can be thought of as the rules of the craft. Do X, the apprentice is told, and you will get Y as a result. The master is the one who knows how to attain a desired end according to prescribed means.

As we have seen, art involves skill, so art needs rules, and the producer of art needs to know the rules and how to apply them. What one notices, however, is that this procedure by itself tends to produce repetitive instances of the same thing. Alone, rules produce not new art but repetitions of what has already been done. For every masterpiece in painting, music, and literature, there are many lesser works that repeat the work of the master according to some learned way of working. One is led to ask what the difference is between the masterpiece and its lesser imitations.

Inspiration provides a means of moving artists out of the realm of craft and into a special category of producers who are inspired in what they do. Inspiration is a very old aesthetic theory. It can take a number of forms. The gods speak through various mouthpieces – priests, oracles, those who are caught in a divine ecstasy. Artists can be added to that list. The skill of an artist is put to the service of a message that the artist need not understand. That does not deny that the artist has skills. They are necessary for public communication, just as the oracle must be interpreted and the priest must learn to perform the rituals correctly. But skill, on a theory of inspiration, is pointless unless something inspired is there to be communicated. So we are led back to a theory that art is communication, but now it is not the intentions of the artist but some greater source speaking through the artist that accounts for what is communicated.

Inspiration need not be understood in terms of gods and oracles, however. The inspiration could come from the process of history itself. Perhaps we are all part of a movement but are only partially aware of it. On that theory, art is the inspired communication of an embodied spirit working itself out through sensitive souls able to communicate what they feel without necessarily understanding it. History, in the sense of a linear, progressive movement, is a peculiarly modern idea. Classical history sought to place events in relation to the origins of a culture. Modern history gives us a narrative of events. By the eighteenth and nineteenth centuries, the meaning of history had to be found within history. Edward Gibbon's *History of the Decline and Fall of the Roman Empire* (1776–88) portrayed a movement of success and decay within history that offered moral lessons. G.W.F. Hegel (1770–1831) went even further, considering history as the embodiment of the spirit of a culture such as that of the German people. If this still seems too supernatural and religious, it can be further "demythologized" into the workings of our individual or collective unconscious. We need refer to no transcendent being or process in order to claim that artists are able to produce works of art because they are inspired to communicate something that they themselves do not understand.

The basic elements of a theory of artistic inspiration place the producer in a mediating position between some otherwise inaccessible idea or feeling and its embodiment in something that is accessible to other people. The artist does not so much produce the work as serve as the means for the work's production. What is produced differs from the products of craft and skill alone by communicating ideas and feelings too deep, different, or important to be limited by rules. Usually, what is communicated takes the form of knowledge about things that are considered important in themselves – things like good and evil, right and wrong, the nature of our selves, our ideals, and our fears. It might be that what is communicated is a form of experience or feeling, however. It need not be the sort of thing that can be easily put into words or propositions. We frequently cannot express our ideas and values independently of art. A theory of inspiration attempts to account for how art supplies what otherwise would be inexpressible. At the same time, inspiration accounts for the value that we place on art above objects of craft or skill.

If something more than rules is required for the production of art, however, the artist is the one who provides that something more. One way to give greater importance to the artist in the process is to say that the rules do not exist until artists produce works of art that can supply them. Craftsmen are rule-followers; artists are rule-givers. They produce the rules, by example, in the process of producing their works. Others can then follow along behind, repeating the process until its possibilities are exhausted. This is one sense in which inspiration can be said to require genius on the part of the artist. An advantage of a theory of genius is that it once again makes the artist an important part of the process and reduces the need for reference to gods or unknown psychological forces.

Genius originally was just the characteristic personality of some person or group. We retain that sense when we say that someone has a genius for speaking out of turn or for turning up late. In the modern aesthetics that emerged from the seventeenth and eighteenth centuries, 'genius' came to be used in aesthetics to describe an ability to produce things that were ordered and effective before any rules for producing those things were available. We know that there are rules because after the fact we can recognize the regularities and similarities in what is produced. But until genius produces the work, we have no clue about the possibilities. Once the rules of harmony have been incorporated into musical works, we can learn the rules. When a new genius comes along and produces twelve-tone music, we learn another set of possible rules. Before Giotto (1266–1337), western painting followed Byzantine rules that produced wonderful colors and spiritual transparency but little visual depth. After Giotto, a series of painters provided new rules of perspective that are now learned by every art student. It took genius to break with the past and leap ahead where no rules existed. The ability to do that is a kind of inspiration, a new vision. The artists who can discover how to communicate their vision are those we call geniuses.[1]

The limits of inspiration

When theory appeals to genius, a problem arises. Artists do not seem to be very good at explaining what they do. They can do it, and they know how to do it in one important sense of knowing, but they do not know in another important sense. The sense in which they do know is closely related to the rules of their craft. They can explain what they do, and even why they do it, in a way that lets others do the same thing. But the other sense of knowing requires not just the ability to produce an effect but also an understanding of the effect produced. The difference is like the difference between being able to add two numbers and understanding what numbers are and how addition works in terms of set theory. Most people who can do arithmetic could not begin to explain the number system. Most artists, as producers, are in a similar position. If what they produce is somehow different and leads to an aesthetic experience that is important in some way, then the rules of production do not get us to that difference. We are led to conclude that, in important ways, both rules and genius are insufficient to explain what artists really do when they produce works of art.

Some forms of inspiration seem to leave little for the artist to do

1 See also the discussion of genius as a part of a theory of expression in chapter 2.

except be a means to an end. As long as artists were thought of as part of a production system built around crafts, that was very nearly the case and it was sufficient. The status of artists was not very important in the overall scheme of things. The exceptions were the poets, dramatists, and builders whose ability to produce in important public ways gave them special status. However, even they were essentially workmen for hire. But when artists are supposed to be geniuses who can provide new rules, it seems odd that they do not know, in a stronger sense of knowledge, what their works provide.

Bringing inspiration into aesthetic theory can have two opposite effects. On the one hand, it reduces the importance of the artist. The artist is merely a means for communication. Moreover, the artist need not, and on some theories of inspiration cannot, know what is being communicated on the more powerful version of knowing. Thus artists themselves are actually somewhat less than craftsmen, who at least have a role in their own right. The poor artists are dependent on inspiration that may or may not come. Plato's account of the performer of epic poetry, Ion, places him in that position. On the other hand, however, inspiration can be used to elevate artists above other craftsmen. Artists are a society's chosen few, the ones who provide special knowledge and value. They deserve special treatment and honor. When Shelley calls poets the unacknowledged legislators of the world, he claims for them a status above mere worldly politics. When the same theory can produce two such diametrically opposed consequences, we may suspect that there is some ambiguity in the theory. In this case, the problem lies in the obscurity of just what is being communicated by art from whom.

Inspiration had its first significant theoretical use in classical Greek and Roman philosophy. It linked religion and civic performance. As such, it was dependent on the religious beliefs that supplied an answer to the questions about who and what. The gods were the who; the what was a mythic vision of the world with its attendant moral and cultural consequences. We would find it hard to believe in inspiration in that way. Inspiration became important a second time when the roles of artists were expanding after the renaissance and art seemed to offer an alternative to older religious beliefs. Inspired artists replaced priests and aesthetic feeling replaced religion. In the first case, art was the servant of religion. In the second, it became the competitor. In both cases, inspiration conceals uncertainty about the sources of aesthetic significance.

An interesting consequence of regarding artists as inspired is that it implicitly requires that art be interpreted. Critics are needed to tell us what the artist was saying, both because what was said (or done) may be difficult and because the artist may be little help. We have moved from divining the artist's intentions to discovering that they do not matter because the artist does not really know anyway. The influence of this approach can be seen in the simultaneous promotion of art and artists to a special place in society and the feeling that art is somehow beyond the reach of the ordinary person without critical aid. T.S. Eliot and James Joyce are admired just because they are difficult and obscure. Each has become the subject of a critical industry, as have numerous other writers. The same thing happens with music and painting. Ordinary viewers are puzzled by the way Picasso's great *Guernica* canvas looks. They are told that it is great art, but they need considerable help in understanding why.

The fundamental criticism of inspiration as an aesthetic theory rests on its concealed uncertainty and need for interpretation. A theory is deficient if it cannot give an account of its principal terms. A theory of combustion that refers to a "combustible substance," phlogiston, has used a name to obscure its lack of insight into what takes place in combustion. To say that artists create art, and not simply artifacts like other skilled craftsmen, because artists are inspired, or that they have a genius, uses 'inspiration' and 'genius' in a similar way. Nothing is gained by naming an unnameable source. In early modern aesthetics, critics frequently referred to a *je ne sais quoi*, an "I don't know what," as the source of the special beauty that some people or works exhibited. Some people and things just have "it." Much of the work of modern aesthetics has been directed toward replacing that "I don't know what" with something more explicit. Inspiration remains obscure.

Conclusions

We began by trying to see how skill is required for there to be works of art. Art cannot be simply unproductive feelings in inarticulate artists. But skill by itself proves insufficient to distinguish art from craft and artists from artisans. Art require rules, but rules are not sufficient for producing art. Thus we turned to inspiration as a distinguishing characteristic of art. Classically, inspiration is the product of a process of communication in which the artist is the means and the work of art is the end product. It does not require that the artist know, in the sense of understanding what is communicated, what is being done. In modern aesthetics, the role of the artist is enhanced by making him or her the rule-producer rather than the rule-follower. That is a primary characteristic of genius. True artists have genius; lesser artists work out the details; and craftsmen produce only copies and utilitarian instances.

Genius and inspiration prove obscure theoretically, however. They only name what we need to understand. We are unlikely to find the metaphysical and religious underpinnings of theories of inspiration convincing today. We are also unlikely to think that artists deserve the exalted status of oracles, and the suspicion is abroad that art need not be difficult to be great. Nevertheless, we should not lose sight of the reasons why inspiration became important in the first place. The intentions of artists are not sufficient by themselves to account for the production of works of art. Nor is art merely a matter of skill. So the introduction of some *je ne sais quoi* (I know not what) seems inevitable. But by itself, that will not do. We cannot simply label what we do not understand and make it a theory. On the other hand, among the aesthetic facts for which any theory must account are the undoubted value and importance that are placed on art and artists. If inspiration proves less than adequate as a final answer, it has recognized a set of problems and suggested a direction for a solution.

Creativity and Originality

We are still concerned with the relation of artist and work, producer and product. An alternative to understanding artists as inspired conduits for communication is to see them as original creators of new objects or ways of seeing. Creativity and originality are very common ideas in thinking about art. We need to remind ourselves that they are part of an aesthetic theory. The producers of art have not always been concerned to produce something original, nor have they always been thought of as creative. Earlier imitation theories stressed the importance of the relation of the work of art to an ideal model. That model was the original, and the work of art was an imitation. The task of the artist was to come as close to the original as possible, not to add anything to it. Creation, if it played any role at all, was the task not of the artist but of the gods or ancestors. Creativity and originality only become important aesthetically when artists begin to think of themselves as part of the work.

Much of philosophical aesthetics took its initial form in the seventeenth and eighteenth centuries, as we have had several occasions to note. Creativity and originality belong more centrally to the romanticism of the early nineteenth century. Romantic poets believed that poetry itself was a way of shaping a world. They took their task to be truly creative, therefore. Philosophy followed the romantic writers. Romantic philosophy in the persons of Arthur Schopenhauer (1788–1860) and Friedrich Nietzsche (1844–1900) described a world being remade by thought. The dominant nineteenth-century philosophical movement is known as philosophical idealism. Idealists gave priority to mental terms (for example, 'mind,' 'idea,' 'consciousness,' 'spirit,' etc.) in explanation and description. Since thought and ideas were understood as the basis for reality, creative thought and original ideas were possible in a way that older forms of philosophy did not allow. We must now see how creativity and originality are incorporated into aesthetics.

Creativity

We might begin by asking what it means to create something. Two aspects of creativity deserve attention. First, creativity implies the appearance of something new. In classical cosmology and mythology, creation is the time of the beginning. The beginning is especially important because it defines the models and forms for everything that follows. In archaic thinking, that beginning point provides all that really exists; subsequent developments are repetitions of the beginning or what was implicit in it. All things were created "in the beginning." There is nothing new under the sun, and thus creation is not only a starting point but a defining point for everything that subsequently is or can be. To this way of thinking, creation is an original event that can be repeated, both by means of rituals and in the cycles of nature. It follows that there can only be one creation, though it is repeated over and over, unless the old creation is utterly destroyed. A new creation would mean starting over altogether, and that is what happens in cataclysmic events (apocalyptic events) that destroy the old world and necessitate a new beginning.

An alternative to archaic thinking makes the beginning equally important, however. If one thinks of the creative process as essentially temporal and mechanical, then whatever happens later is implicit in the initial conditions. Mechanical determinists imagine the possibility that, given sufficient information, the entire course of history could be predicted. This is a vastly different way of thinking from the archaic vision with its repetition and return. Instead, evolution and entropy – the increasing move from order to disorder – control natural processes. Creation is still a matter of the beginning, but nothing remains the same. Every move away from the beginning results in a new state and cannot be reversed. There is no going backwards in time. This view of creativity emphasizes creation as a starting-point, a beginning. Creation sets time in motion.

Another aspect of creation focuses more directly on the productive process. Consider who a creator is. We commonly distinguish between the inventor of something and its subsequent makers or manufacturers. Edison invented the light bulb. Once it was invented, it could be manufactured and improved. But we do not think of the subsequent making and improving as creative. Similarly, new ideas come along. We think of a scientist who discovers a new theory as creative. Einstein is the creator of the general theory of relativity. That does not mean that the theory was not true before Einstein formulated it, but his was the creative act that gave us the theory. This sense of creativity depends on the newness of what is produced or done relative to what was already made or known. It does not ask so much about the origin as about the presence of something. Every new thing belongs to some prior history; light bulbs did not spring fully grown from Edison's head. They are new because they involve a break with an older way that was not anticipated or predicted.

Both aspects of creativity have their aesthetic versions. The sense of creation as a beginning of time – the once-for-all creation – is captured by artists when they are regarded as special kinds of makers. For example, if repetition of the beginning is the truly creative act, then the epic poets who sing of the time of the beginning are the creative poets by virtue of their relation to that time. So epic poetry and mythological drama appear as more creative than decorative arts or lyric poems. Creation as new production accounts for our sense that each new art form involves some break with the past. When perspective was developed in the early renaissance, it broke with older ways of painting. The early painters using perspective, such as Giotto, may not have been nearly as skilled as their successors. But we think of them as more creative because they broke with the preceding style. The later, more polished painters are less creative because they were working out the details of what Giotto had begun. Both of these senses of creation are important to aesthetic theory, therefore, and both have a place in any developed theory.

Having said that, however, it must be admitted that creativity in aesthetics is much more important when the individual artist is thought of as doing something separate and new than when artists are thought of as repeating the initial acts of creation that belong to a time "in the beginning." A fundamental difference in aesthetic theories exists between theories in which the artist is only a secondary creator at best, and more likely a craftsman following the original models, and aesthetic theories that look to artists as the sources of new ideas and new styles. To say that an artist is creative is much more important in post-renaissance aesthetics than it ever could be in classical aesthetics in the west or in traditional aesthetics in the east. Creativity goes along with the idea that individual acts and expression are somehow new and different every time that they occur.

Mechanical determinism may seem to preclude creativity. Aesthetics offers an escape from that determinism, however. All that is determined is the actual world. Artists as creators offer a world of fiction, illusion, and imagined events that need never take place. Art is, in a sense, freed from the constraints of what actually is to explore what might be and even what never can be. This is not just fantasy and science fiction (although those forms should not be derided as insignificant). In classical aesthetics, Aristotle observed that a dramatic incident that seemed probable even though it was impossible was preferable to one that seemed improbable even though it was what actually happened. But classical aesthetics is still constrained by its need to repeat the older stories that tell the "truth" in its mythological forms. History and scientific prediction and projection free art as well as other forms from reliance on the time of the beginning, but they also tie us to the mundane, predictable world. Artistic production as a form of creation frees us from that predictability. The eighteenth-century novelist Henry Fielding openly acknowledged in his authorial persona that he could shape events in any way that he chose. In the actual world, his hero, Tom Jones, would undoubtedly have been hanged as a rogue. But if Fielding chose to save him, he could do so.

What underlies the importance of creativity in modern aesthetics is its ability to shape experience into different forms. Experience belongs to individuals. However experience is understood, and it is understood very differently by different philosophers from Aristotle to today, it belongs to individuals and defines their limits. My experience may be like someone else's, but it can only be like theirs; it cannot be the same, because it is individual to me. Conversely, I may share many qualities with others – genetic, historical, cultural – but I am distinguished by my experience. If experience is taken to be central to who and what I am, then the forms of experience become central as well. Aesthetics is about experience. The productive task of the artist is then to shape experience. That shape can be creative or repetitive. When it is creative, it gives new forms to experience and opens new possibilities for art. Artists are creators, on this theory, because experience must be given some shape, and one of the primary ways that it is shaped is through the free exploration that goes on in art. At various times, art has been regarded with suspicion as a waste of time and effort or a kind of juvenile pastime that is more play than work. A reply to this charge can make use of creativity. Some play is indeed escape from work and responsibility, but some play is creative. It opens possibilities that could only be tried in art. When a new kind of drama is produced, we have more than just a new form of entertainment. We have a new way of thinking about a problem. When a new style of art comes along, we have more than a new form of decoration. We see things differently. If graffiti becomes art, we look again at buildings and words in a new way.

Perception and language

Creativity in this sense is closely related to perception. Perception is a complex operation. It is more than just looking and seeing. What we perceive is affected by what we expect to see, by what we are attuned to, and by the way that we process sensory input. Let us consider each of these factors briefly. In any perceptual situation, we have certain expectations. It may be as simple as what directs our attention. If I want to know where my glasses are, I will pick them out. I may not notice other things in my field of vision at all. Or if I am an actor listening for my cue to enter, I may not even assimilate the other words that are spoken as I listen intently for one phrase. Expectation can be more complex, however. A physicist has the knowledge to notice things that a non-physicist is not even in a position to see. When new discoveries tell us what to look for, we can see what was always there but was invisible because of our lack of conceptual knowledge.

We are also attuned to notice certain things by our biological and acquired capacities. A bird may notice minute changes in the wind but have no way of noticing a pane of glass because glass was not one of the environmental influences that shaped its perceptual capacities. I have a different range of capacities from my dog. Some of these capacities are "hard wired" in, but some can be affected by changes that are acquired. I become sensitized to certain kinds of noise and then can hear the distinctions. Some languages utilize tonal variation as part of their structure, for example. A native speaker hears them; I do not, but I could learn to.

Finally, sensory input is not received neutrally. It is processed according to schemas that are to some extent natural but that are also learned. The ability to perceive threat or hostility or anger is natural, or at least so well assimilated that it seems natural. But the ability to translate two-dimensional images into three-dimensional images is learned. Different cultures will see the same representations differently because they have learned different conventions of representation. Perception is not just sensory input translated into pictures and images. It requires ways of organizing the input. Some organizational principles are so basic that they define the possibilities of human thought – spatial and temporal location, for example. But we have many other internal schemas also that allow us to fit data into already structured patterns. If we did not have that ability, anything but short-term memory would be impossible because we would have to remember every event separately.

Aesthetic creativity plays a major role in influencing how we perceive and think about what we perceive. One way to understand this is to think about how language itself influences perception. If we have words and descriptions for something, we are more likely to notice that thing, and we can use that language to become attuned to that thing's presence. When we learn a new language or create new words and theories, we change the way we perceive as well. Language and related symbol systems can be thought of as influencing perception, therefore.

Now, one important way of thinking formally about art is using the analogy of language. Some art has an explicit language – either as words, or as ordered symbol systems as in music. But even where there is no explicit language, one of the ways we learn to analyze the form and content of art is to look for its symbols and vocabulary. A painting makes use of such symbols, and so do film, dance, and even architecture. So we can usefully think of languages of art. In order to change ways of perceiving and create new ways of thinking, we could begin with language, therefore, and that means that art is especially creative in a linguistic way. Poetry and novels shape language so that we perceive not just new combinations but new perceptions as well. Painting, music, film, drama, and architecture all lead us to think and perceive in new ways.

The analogy with language can be carried too far. Some aesthetic theories go so far as to claim that all thinking is linguistic and language is essentially creative, so art and aesthetic experience underlie all language and thought. Such aesthetic imperialism stretches our credibility. It depends on dubious claims that unless we have words for something, we cannot think of it, and unless we think of it linguistically, we cannot perceive it. Surely such claims overstate the case. In the ordinary way, we often perceive what we do not yet understand. If the more extensive claims are to hold, they have to extend language to areas of our psychological life that are not immediately accessible. Moreover, they make it difficult to explain how we continue to modify and learn new language, and they frequently depend on speculative histories of linguistic development. However, artists are creative and they influence our ability to perceive. That includes shaping the languages of art.

At bottom, creativity in aesthetic theory is about the relation of mind to its expression. As long as aesthetic theory is content to describe production in terms of craft, skill, and imitation, mind does not enter the theory explicitly. But as soon as we begin to think of the productive process as an expression of something that takes place in the mind of the artist, we need to understand what 'mind' means in that context. Theories of mind and mental activity fall outside the scope of this book. We can note, however, that when we talk of a mind, we might be referring to two different things. One would be the psychological and physiological–neural make-up of an individual that allows us to call that person a thinking being. The other would be the properties of thought itself that we distinguish as rational and intelligent. We need not resolve problems in the philosophy of mind to see that how the mind itself is to be perceived is likely to cause difficulty. We are asking for a perception of that which is doing the perceiving. That is a little like trying to look at one's own face. The best that I can do is to look at some reflection or representation. This difficulty has led aesthetics to consider that the expression of mind is a uniquely aesthetic phenomenon. We take pleasure in it because we are expressing and making intelligible our selves.

Creative mind and originality

Creativity enters into aesthetic theory in two ways. First, the mind needs some means to express itself. Even if it uses natural relations, it must put them to expressive uses. For example, the rising and falling rhythms of music are, in themselves, just sequences of sound.[2] By adapting them to spatial forms and by ordering their harmonic relations, music comes to express emotions so that almost everyone can distinguish happy from sad music. Particular sequences of sound are not intrinsically happy or sad. Yet they express those emotions for us in a way that we learn to recognize very easily. The process involves both conventional schemas and natural possibilities. The discovery and utilization of those forms of expression is creative. Without them, we would not have a way to give such emotions form.

Second, in creating expressive forms, it is often claimed that the mind repeats the kind of actions needed to bring it into existence itself. What distinguishes a mind from something that has no mind? It cannot be just the ability to perform tasks. If we say it is the ability to think, that is either ambiguous (do computers think?) or circular (mind = thinking being). So the existence of a mind is just the creation of forms that express its own being. By shaping perception and giving it form in memory and expectation, a mind as a thinking, conscious being is shaping itself. Art is the freest form of mental activity, analogous to play and perception itself. Thus art brings mind into being.

We have entered into rather murky areas with such formulations. What does it mean to say that a mind repeats the infinite creative act? What does it mean to claim that art is the expression of human minds? If we are not careful, our aesthetic theory will lose its ability to relate to

2 See the discussion of music as a form of imitation and expression in chapter 2.

the analysis of the form and content of specific works of art and its ability to clarify critical theory, which are its real purposes. The importance of these views of creativity rests with their ability to answer the question with which we began this chapter: How is an artist related to a work of art? What is the productive relation that causes us to say that some things that are made are more than just useful objects? Creativity understood as an expression of mind reminds us that the productive process need not be understood solely in terms of a physical making. But we should also not lose sight of the materiality of art. Talk of a creative expression of mind is empty if it cannot also account for the physical objects and their histories that make up the art world.

Creativity is closely related to the value that we place on originality, but they are not quite the same thing. Creativity tells us something about what is produced. Originality tells us something about the history of its production. We tend to value originality because it is a sign of creativity. It is common to criticize an artist for lack of originality or to say that an art form has lost its originality and thus its ability to show us new and creative things about the world. In those cases, what is produced is held to be less valuable than what is creative and original.

A positive value-judgment need not follow from claims for originality, however. What is created could be destructive, and there is no guarantee that originality will offer a better way of perceiving than what went before. Too much originality is merely eccentric and destructive. If we could not rely on some parts of our perception being the same over different actual events, then every situation would be original, but we would be unable to organize thought. Classical aesthetic theory did not value originality in art because originality implied difference from the models and paradigms that were acknowledged as the best examples. Creativity might be important because creation itself is important, but originality would just be deviation and difference. When we make originality an aesthetic criterion, therefore, we must be careful to understand it in the context of a theory that gives it positive value. Otherwise, our belief that originality in art is a sign of productive value will mislead us badly in our judgments.

Conclusions

Originality describes what is made. Creativity describes how it is made. We judge originality in relation to the work of art. Today, it is virtually a truism that art must be original. We should remember, however, that the identification of originality and creativity with art is itself part of an aesthetic theory. In classical and medieval thought about art, different theories were common. Creativity becomes central as a result of more satisfactory understandings of the complexity of perception. Once we recognize that perception is not a naïve looking that merely reproduces what is out there, but that it involves mental schemas, conventions, and language, we are led to theories of the relation of the mind to perception. In that context, possibilities for recognizing creativity arise that are not present to earlier ways of understanding the mind. Creativity and originality become aesthetic terms by drawing on the ability of art to express the mind's own abilities and to expand both the content and the powers of the mind. The value that we place on originality and creativity in aesthetics grows out of these new mental powers.

Breaking the Connection between Artist and Art

Thus far, the emphasis in our analysis of the productive relation between artist and art has given the priority to the artist. Whether artists are thought of as the source of a communicative process or as creative makers of original works, the work of art depends on the artist, and the artist controls the process. This seems right in most cases. Even if one holds a theory in which some force is moving through history or some impulse is found within the process, the productive act moves from producer to product. Although some twentieth-century philosophers have spoken as if "being itself" were an active force, the production of individual works of art requires an artist who does the work of forming and shaping some material into a new form. When we describe the mental relation that produces works of art, the experience of art begins with the experience of the artist, even if they are not the same thing.

Fakes and forgeries

The adequacy of this analysis can, however, be challenged in three ways, as we can see from a consideration of the question of faking and forgery. When originality becomes part of the description of aesthetic objects, mistakes about whether something is original become important. One of the more interesting phenomena in the modern art world is that as soon as a new form of art becomes important, false versions of it also appear. Classical art produced excellent copies, but no one regarded them as fakes because originality was not thought of as one of the defining qualities of art. Once originality assumes that role, fakes begin to appear. Michaelangelo was not only a great artist; he was a great forger. What was permissible in art was in flux in the renaissance. That is why we have so many paintings from the fifteenth, sixteenth, and seventeenth centuries whose painters are difficult to identify. Many can only be classified as "from the school of" because they are neither independent works nor outright forgeries. Once originality and creativity are enshrined by romanticism and idealism, the lines are more clearly drawn. Then something either is or is not an original work.

Every major museum has been victimized by forgeries. Even the best technical tests combined with sensitivity and care on the part of curators are not sufficient to guarantee that everyone will not be taken in for a time. Many forgeries have been exposed later as new tests become available or as the perpetrators become known through other means. However, some forgeries almost certainly remain on display, and major controversies continue about the authenticity of paintings. There are practical reasons to care about such questions. An authentic Rembrandt painting is much more valuable than one done by his studio or by an imitator. More important, our knowledge of painters is based to a great extent on the entirety of their work. We learn by comparing subject and technique across a whole body of work. If work that is not by the artist in question is included in the comparison, we will be misled. A famous case of forgery before and during World War II concerned the work of the seventeenth-century Dutch painter Vermeer. A forger, Heinrich van Meegeren, produced a number of "Vermeers" that were widely accepted as authentic. Only when he was charged as a collaborator for having sold national treasures to the Nazis did van Meegeren confess to the lesser charge of having forged paintings. Today, however, one wonders how anyone was ever taken in by the forgeries. They do not look to most viewers very much like Vermeer's genuine work. A crucial point is that there are not that many genuine Vermeers. As long as van Meegeren's work was being accepted as genuine, it influenced what Vermeer was believed to have done and what we expected his work to look like. Subtract those works, and what remains lacks many of the characteristics ascribed to Vermeer on the basis of the forgeries. These practical and art-historical concerns are only a small part of the problem forgeries raise, however.

Much more important theoretically is why we should care aesthetically and what the implications of the possibilities for forgery are for the way we conceive of art. Not everything that is misidentified is second-rate as a result. Assume, for the sake of the argument, that a work taken to be that of a master is particularly beautiful. Many such instances could be found. Does the work look any different when its misidentification is exposed? Does it give any less aesthetic pleasure? The obvious answers are that it does not, or that if it does, then we were not responding to the work but to something extraneous about it. Or consider a very good copy of a work, perhaps so good that side by side with the original they cannot be told apart. Sophisticated tests might reveal the differences, but to the eye, even of an expert, no difference can be detected. In fact, many museums do have copies of classical sculptures in their collections. Why should it matter which piece one viewed? Our intuitions about the connection of artist and work and the value we place on originality suggest that it should matter. It is harder to see why it matters, however.

Why does originality matter?

Considerable ingenuity has been spent justifying our preference for the original. From the standpoint of knowledge about the artist, only a genuine work can be certain not to mislead us. We could never be sure that a copy, no matter how good, might not misrepresent something as we discover more about the artist through the work. Moreover, what we know about perception reminds us that we may not notice some facets of a painting until we have trained our mind's eye by repeated viewing. Then what has guided our learning will matter greatly.

However, knowledge about origins is not about aesthetic experience. If aesthetic experience is a product of a work, then any difference should appear in our experience of the work. Two lines of argument are suggested. One is to acknowledge that we never respond simply to the work, by itself. Our commitment to originality misleads us in this respect. Earlier periods regarded forgery, copying, and imitation as demonstrations of skill. So what we respond to is a combination of the artifact before us and the context of its production. For example, it makes a difference in our response to learn that something was done by hand rather than by mechanical means. In that case, a forgery or a copy is a lesser instance only if it misleads us as to the context. If it does, it affects our response. If it does not, it should be regarded as classical copies were regarded – as a homage to the original and as something that might even surpass its source.

The other solution is to abandon the idea of aesthetic experience altogether. If works of art are not primarily regarded as things to be experienced by an audience in some particular way, then the problem of copies, imitations, and forgeries becomes a matter of evidence. We would have to determine what is being asserted before we could say whether a forgery made any difference. For example, for many statements, a photograph or slide of a painting is sufficient. Obviously, for some it is not. The same principle would extend to a forgery. If the question were about the influence of one painter's style on another, then a forgery would be misleading. If it were about the effect on an audience, it might not be. Art and the art world produce many different experiences.

What these arguments should do is make us much more careful about using originality as our primary aesthetic criterion for value. Originality is related to the priority of the artist. So some works of art need to be accounted for in terms of something other than their producers. This observation reopens many questions that seemed settled by our approach to art in terms of artists who provide aesthetic experience. One consequence is that we may return to earlier art with a wider perspective. Our interest in classical art, for example, might be based on our own appreciation, not the appreciation that was appropriate when the work was made. Classical and medieval sculpture was painted, apparently quite garishly. That was its original state. It does not follow that we should go back and paint marble statues from Greece and Rome.

Another consequence is that art opens into activities that would otherwise be excluded. If we think of art only as a source of a special kind of aesthetic experience, then only those situations that permit that kind of experience can be conducive to art. But if we think of art more broadly than as an aesthetic-experience-machine, we include many objects for which originality is neither here nor there. In particular, interest in folk art, political theater, and experimental forms challenges the exclusivity of aesthetic experience and artistic expression as original productions of a creative mind. Then we are led to consider originality as only one aesthetic possibility among others.

Forgeries and fakes also draw our attention to other characteristics of the productive process. All forgery and fakery is not the same. The classic cases of museum mistakes are all about physical objects. Two different kinds of problems arise, however. One is that something may be misrepresented or misidentified. A painting is either a Rembrandt or it is not, but it is still a painting in either case. A second problem is that there may be two instances of the same thing. Of two versions of the *Mona Lisa*, one may be the original and the other a copy, or they might both be copies. In a sense, only one painting is at issue. Characteristically, paintings, sculpture, and other art forms where there is a single, physical instance can be copied and a problem can arise over which is the original and which the copy. Other art forms cannot be copied in quite the same way. A novel has many physical instances by its very nature. All are equally the novel. In the printing process, variations may be introduced. Successive editions may multiply variations. Yet we would not say that any copy that was not irredeemably corrupt was not the novel in question. One might produce a fake Fielding novel in the way that van Meegeren produced fake Vermeers or in the way that there are more and more Sherlock Holmes stories, but we cannot produce a fake *Tom Jones* except in a way that might concern a rare book dealer who cares about the physical object. The variations in editions matter, but the book is not like the painting because the book is the kind of work that has multiple instances to begin with. Music is different again. Performances inevitably vary; they are supposed to. But they remain performances of a single work. The score is somewhat like a book in that it can be reproduced without loss, but it is also different because the performance takes precedence over the score as the instantiation of the work. So one cannot have a fake Mozart Second Piano Concerto; anything that was sufficiently close to be called that would by the same token be that work. But one could have a fake Van Cliburn performance of it. Elvis imitators sing real Elvis songs, but they produce fake performances.

Modern challenges to originality and creativity as aesthetic criteria

These examples should suggest to us that the intentional object – the object as it is experienced – is not defined simply by the artist. The kind of object sometimes frees the object from its maker or makes the object depend on other factors in addition to the maker. The difference between a painting and a novel depends not just on what an artist intended to make but on the possibilities that language and visual representation afford. Language has a sequential interpretation according to a culturally established code. A painting does not. So if one simply reproduces the language, one has the novel, but if one reproduces the painting, one does not have the painting.

An interesting variation on this has been discussed by Arthur Danto, who, following a story by Jorge Luis Borges, asks us to imagine a complete version of Cervantes' *Don Quixote* rewritten exactly, word for word, by a new novelist, Pierre Menard, who knows nothing of the original. It would not then be the same novel, Danto argues, because even though it matches exactly, it has a different author who has a different experience and presents the work with a different history. Danto is not trying to convince us that the artist defines the work after all but rather that every work of art is defined by its total history, which is changing. If Pierre Menard's novel has nothing to do with the history of Cervantes' novel, then they are two different novels. Identity of appearance or of language is not sufficient unless we presuppose a relation of the productive process as well. What influences our intuition that this case is somehow wrong is our strong inference that if the language is the same, then the two works must be related by some other historical connections as well. The example asks us to rule that out, but it makes our intuition about the situation very uncertain in the process. However, something even more interesting follows. The very existence of the two works, side by side, would be sufficient to change the second into a copy of the first. Then, paradoxically, the intentional object has changed even though nothing has been done to it physically and its past history has not changed. The two authors had no connection at all; yet now they do because they both produced this work. The only solution to this paradox is to acknowledge that neither the intentionality of the artist nor that of the audience is definitive for a work of art. Art works may change in ways that depend on their material and historical possibilities. Instead of thinking of a work of art as a fixed, timeless object produced by an artist at some single point in history, we may have to think of a work of art as an evolving object with its own history. Physical objects change with time, and even works of art such as music change as the instruments and techniques of performance change. Regarded in that way, the problem with fakes and forgeries is not that they produce the wrong experience or that they mislead us about their origins but that they hide their history from us, and in so doing, they hide an important part of their identity.

A second kind of art makes the connection between producer and work of art even more tenuous. Consider some natural object, a rock or piece of wood, that is taken up and put on display. No one made it. The production process was natural. Yet it can be treated as a work of art. Such objects may seem peripheral in our culture. Our expectations of art identify the most important works as masterpieces, which implies that they are the product of some master. It is easy to imagine a different culture with a different conception of art, however. In that culture, found art might be important in ways that it seldom is in our culture. As long as found art is possible at all, its existence challenges our expectations that art must be the product of an artist working creatively.

The counter-argument to found art points out that found art does not just display itself. It must be taken up and displayed by someone. That someone, the argument goes, plays the role of artist. This is certainly the case, and it implies that art always belongs to some wider art world context. However, it does nothing to save notions of creativity and originality as they came into aesthetic theory. Theories of creativity and artistic expression require that the mind of an artist is communicating and shaping something. That process is absent in found art, so the art cannot be the expression of an artist's mind. Originality implies bringing a new form to a material. That cannot be the case if the form is natural to the material. Found art appeals to the experience of the audience, and it may require someone to act as intermediary by pointing to the possibilities of experiencing this thing in this way. That is a long way from saying that the person doing the pointing creates the work of art or is an original producer of new art.

Found art is closely related to some forms of environmental art on the one hand and to utilitarian objects that become art on the other. In some environmental art, a situation is created in which a natural process is set in motion and then the result is presented as the work of art. For example, a site might be allowed to grow in its natural habitat in the midst of human civilization. The natural development of the site is itself the work. In such cases, an artist is at work, but the kind of work done by the artist does not involve expression of the artist's mind but a cooperation of artist and nature. We have a cooperative work, like film or buildings, but now one of the cooperating elements is not a person at all. Important elements in the work are outside the control of the artist who sets things in motion, so they cannot be expressions of a prior vision of the artist.

Such works tend to be avant-garde and marginal. Utilitarian objects that are taken up into the art world are much more common, however. Pots and glass works, photographs and doodles are commonly recognized as art even when their makers had neither a conception of art nor an intent to express anything. Such works are not limited to visual art. Prose intended only to describe or communicate information may rise to the level of art. It is necessary only that such works be able to be put on display in order for their properties to share the same status as intentional art. Yet they lack all artistic intention. The line between artistic intention and its absence is a fine one. We have already seen that skill plays a role in creation, and that being a craftsman does not exclude being an artist. Nevertheless, it must be acknowledged that in many cases where the end product is art no artistic intent – and thus no creativity or originality in the requisite aesthetic sense – is found. Production and intent remain aesthetic factors, but understanding them as communication, creative expression, and originality requires considerable ad hoc adjustment.

Finally, the most serious challenge to theories of creativity and originality comes from the aesthetics of nature itself. Natural beauty requires no artist, and it expresses nothing in the strict sense that a mind is required for expression. This has led some philosophers to divide aesthetics sharply from philosophy of art. Aesthetics, they hold, is about a kind of experience. Its paradigm is natural beauty, and art is aesthetic only to the extent that it produces the same kind of experience. Art, on the other hand, is imaginative, creative, informative, even politically active. Its task is not to please but to engage the audience. Aestheticizing art is seen as a lesser form of art just because it tries, and fails, to duplicate what nature does better while abandoning art's own ends. There is certainly something to this challenge. In order to include nature in the aesthetics of creativity and active producers, a "supreme artist" is often introduced. God, or the spirit of the age, acting through history, is seen as shaping our vision and presenting us with the supreme forms of art. That kind of appeal amounts to little more than postulating what is not in evidence in order to save a theory, however. It would be better to abandon the theory.

It may not be necessary to break the connection between an aesthetics of nature and works of art so radically, however. Art and nature are more closely related than a complete divorce would allow. For one thing, much of the so-called aesthetics of nature follows art. When we look at a scene and describe it as picturesque or beautiful, our perception is guided not just by nature but by the landscape paintings that have taught us how to view nature. The full extent of this interaction of art and nature can be seen clearly in the arts of landscape gardening and in architecture and sculpture that are site-specific. Our aesthetics of nature is seldom, perhaps never, uninfluenced by our art. Japanese and Chinese scrolls and gardens form a single world of art. The same thing could be said for an aesthetics of natural sound. Bird songs and the songs of whales are beautiful. They produce a response that must be taken account of by theory. But our ability to hear them in ways that are aesthetically significant is influenced by our ability to hear music. Literature does not offer similar parallels only because language is never purely natural. Yet the connections between oral tradition and written composition suggest that there is a continuum rather than a disjunction between art and nature. Our perception of nature is shaped to our vision, and our vision is shaped by art. As our theories of perception have abandoned the idea of a purely innocent eye, we have come to recognize that perception itself is culturally influenced. Among the most important influences are works of art.

Conclusions

Fakes and forgeries force us to reconsider the connection between artist and work of art in three ways. First, the existence of the possibility of fakes and forgeries discloses the contingency of originality as a criterion for art. Second, fakes and forgeries tell us something about the possibilities of works of art: some are fakable in different ways from others and some are not fakable at all, though other kinds of mistakes about their origin may arise. Finally, fakes and forgeries raise questions about aesthetic experience – whose experience it is and whether a special kind of aesthetic experience should be the sole basis for aesthetic theory. When we ask why originality matters, we are led not only to consider earlier theories that did not emphasize originality and creativity but also to recognize possibilities for kinds of art that do not have a place for originality at all – found art, utilitarian objects, environmental art, and natural objects. The importance of distinguishing fakes from the real thing may have more to do with our need to incorporate the history of an object in our perception of it than with the way the object appears.

What follows from these considerations is that we must be very careful about taking ideas of creativity and originality as more than a partial aesthetic. The very idea of a productive process connecting artist and work of art is itself only one part of a complex process that includes a dialectic between nature and culture, perception and understanding. Art is central to that process, and artists are central to the production of art. As we look at different examples, however, other parts of the process may take precedence. We must look to the artist's relation to the audience and the relation of the audience to the work of art to complete the picture.

References and Suggestions for Further Reading

The artist's intentions

Determining intentions

For some of the manifestos by artists, see Herschel B. Chipp, ed., *Theories of Modern Art* (Berkeley: University of California Press, 1968). For descriptions by artists and art critics, see Elizabeth Gilmore Holt, ed., *Literary Sources of Art History* (Princeton: Princeton University Press, 1947). Reynolds' *Discourses* are available in several editions including Joshua Reynolds, *Discourses* (London: Penguin, 1992). For additional information on the aesthetics of the portrait, see Edgar Wind, *Hume and the Heroic Portrait* (Oxford: Oxford University Press, 1986). A useful introduction to the context of the eighteenth-century novel is J. Paul Hunter, *Before Novels: The Cultural Contexts of Eighteenth-Century Fiction* (New York: Norton, 1990).

Communication: knowing what the artist intended

Students interested in the development of cathedrals in the middle ages might look at Otto von Simson, *The Gothic Cathedral* (Princeton: Princeton University Press, 1974). For the aesthetic history of film, see Rudolf Arnheim, *Film as Art*

(Berkeley: University of California Press, 1957) and Sergei Eisenstein, *Film Form* (New York: Harcourt Brace Jovanovich, 1977). For the *auteur* theory, see Andre Bazin, *What is Cinema?* (Berkeley: University of California Press, 1967). Selections from all three are included in Gerald Mast, Marshall Cohen, and Leo Braudy, eds, *Film Theory and Criticism* (New York: Oxford University Press, 1992). For the account of the trial of Veronese, see Paolo Veronese, "Trial Before the Holy Tribunal," in Gilmore Holt, ed., *Literary Sources of Art History*. For more on Duchamp, see Pierre Cabanne, *The Documents of Twentieth Century Art: Dialogues with Marcel Duchamp* (New York: Viking, 1958). The classic essay on authorial intent in criticism is Monroe Beardsley and William Wimsatt, "The Intentional Fallacy," in William Wimsatt, ed., *The Verbal Icon* (Lexington: University of Kentucky Press, 1954). The controversy over authorial intention is carried on in Theodore Redpath, "Some Problems of Modern Aesthetics," in C. A. Mace, ed., *British Philosophy in Mid-Century* (London: Allen & Unwin, 1957): 361–75; E. D. Hirsch, *Validity in Interpretation* (New Haven: Yale University Press, 1967); and Monroe Beardsley, *The Possibility of Criticism* (Detroit: Wayne State University Press, 1970).

Inspiration

Plato raises some of the problems for an aesthetics based on inspiration in his dialogue *Ion*, which is available in many different translations. Aristotle's *Poetics* can be regarded as a handbook on how to write tragedy, though it is obviously much more. In the middle ages, St Bonaventure discusses the place of the arts and crafts in "Retracing the Arts to Theology," in Dabney Townsend, ed., *Classic Readings from the Western Tradition* (Boston: Jones & Bartlett, 1996).

Skill

An important recent treatment of the whole question of artifactuality and agency is Randall R. Dipert, *Artifacts, Art Works, and Agency* (Philadelphia: Temple University Press, 1993).

From craft to art

In addition to the classic work of Paul Oskar Kristeller, "The Modern System of the Arts," in Peter Kivy, ed., *Essays on the History of Aesthetics* (Rochester: University of Rochester Press, 1992), many of the issues relating to the rise of the fine arts are considered in Paul Mattick, ed., *Eighteenth-Century Aesthetics and the Reconstruction of Art* (Cambridge: Cambridge University Press, 1993). For the embodiment of spirit in history, see G. W. F. Hegel, *Philosophy of Mind* (Oxford: Oxford University Press, 1971), *The Philosophy of Fine Art* (London: G. Bell & Sons, 1920), and *Hegel's Aesthetics: Lectures on Fine Art* (Oxford: Oxford University Press, 1975).

The limits of inspiration

Shelley's claim for poets as "hierophants of an unapprehended inspiration" is in Percy Bysshe Shelley, "Defence of Poetry," in *Criticism: The Major Texts*, ed. Walter Jackson Bate (New York: Harcourt, Brace & World, 1952): 429–35.

Creativity and originality

For Schopenhauer, see Arthur Schopenhauer, *The World as Will and Idea* (London: Routledge & Kegan Paul, 1883). For Nietzsche, see Friedrich Nietzsche, *The Birth of Tragedy and the Genealogy of Morals* (Garden City, NY: Doubleday, Dell, 1956), and *The Will to Power* (New York: Macmillan, 1914).

Creativity

The description of traditional ontology and cosmology here is based on the work of Mircea Eliade, particularly *The Myth of the Eternal Return* (Princeton: Princeton University Press, 1954). The distrust of poetry as it emerged from the middle ages is the subject of Russell Fraser, *The War against Poetry* (Princeton: Princeton University Press, 1970).

Perception and language

J. J. Gibson links perception to environment in *The Ecological Approach to Visual Perception* (Hillsdale, NJ: Lawrence Erlbaum, 1986). Rudolf Arnheim explores the way perception affects art in *Art and Visual Perception* (Berkeley: University of California Press, 1974). Ernst Cassirer extends the claims for symbols and language in *The Philosophy of Symbolic Forms* (New Haven: Yale University Press, 1953).

Creative mind and originality

The strongest claims for an aesthetic view of the mind itself are in Schopenhauer, *The World as Will and Idea*, and Benedetto Croce, *Aesthetic* (New York: Noonday Press, 1968).

Breaking the connection between artist and art

Fakes and forgeries

A particularly good treatment of a museum's problems with fakes and forgeries is the volume published by the British Museum in connection with its exhibition of fakes and forgeries from its own collection; see Mark Jones, ed., *Fake? The Art of Deception* (London: British Museum Publications, 1990). On forgery, see Denis Dutton, ed., *The Forger's Art* (Berkeley: University of California Press, 1983).

Why does originality matter?

Nelson Goodman discusses the difference between art that can be forged and art that cannot be forged in *Languages of Art* (Indianapolis: Hackett, 1976).

Modern challenges to originality and creativity as aesthetic criteria

Arthur Danto discusses "the Pierre Menard phenomenon" in "Artworks and Real Things," *Theoria* 39 (1973): 1–17, and the example has been picked up and used in numerous papers since then. The instances of environmental art are described in Alan Sonfist, ed., *Art in the Land* (New York: Dutton, 1983). Allen Carlson has written extensively on environmental aesthetics; see, for example, "Appreciation and the Natural Environment," *Journal of Aesthetics and Art Criticism* 37, 3: 267–75. A different approach to environmental art that emphasizes the aesthetic implications of environment is found in Arnold Berleant, *The Aesthetics of Environment* (Philadelphia: Temple University Press, 1992).

4

The Audience and
the Work of Art

Attitudes of the Audience

Assume that, by one means or another, one is confronted with an aesthetic object. If it is a work of art, the artist may or may not be evident. If it is a natural object or one of the forms of art where the idea of an artist becomes problematic, no artist may be implied. There is still an important relation to explore, however. How is the aesthetic object related to the person who confronts it? Obviously, some of the possible relations are not of aesthetic interest. I might desire the object because it will make me rich or famous, or because it is a family heirloom. The possibilities are endless. One of the central questions of modern aesthetics has been whether some special relation, a peculiarly aesthetic relation, can exist between someone who perceives an aesthetic object, particularly a work of art, and the object itself.

Intentionality

An aesthetic object is what is called an intentional object when it is presented to someone who serves as the audience for the object.[1] As we have seen, an object is anything that can be referred to. An object need not be a physical object that can be touched or kicked like a stone. An

1 The term 'intentional object' is only indirectly related to the sense of 'intention' discussed in chapter 3 where we were concerned with the artist's intention and how it related to the production of an aesthetic object. 'Intention' as it is used there is a mental state or the content of a mental state. In this context, however, 'intention' refers to the direction of thought toward some object of thought. Both presuppose a thinker and something that is thought. The sense of 'intentionality' needed here refers to the content of a thought and not the psychological state itself.

intentional object refers to something that is thought or appreciated or that someone is conscious of. We call objects in thought intentional objects because they are the object of some conscious act or intention of a person who perceives them. 'Intention' here refers to the act of perceiving rather than the intention of the maker that we explored earlier. All objects that can be perceived or thought can be intentional objects for someone, but for some objects their intentional status is more important. Natural objects, such as rocks and trees, exist by themselves. Physical objects in general, even if they are made by someone, are like that. They are what they are by virtue of their form and structure. Having someone perceive them does not change them. It makes no difference to our understanding of the object whether someone is aware of it or not. Other objects, such as words and ideas, are incomplete unless they are related to someone who knows the language or thinks the idea. The difference is that between objects that can be described independently of any intentional state of the perceiver and objects whose description includes someone who is conscious of the object. For the latter, being an intentional object is their primary way of existing. Intentionality is part of the essential description of the objects. A language that no one understands any longer, such as Etruscan, is incomplete. (Etruscan was the language of central Italy before Rome and Latin replaced it. We know something of the grammar of Etruscan, but its meaning is now untranslatable.) The words and sentences still exist, but part of what they are – their meaning – has been lost. Aesthetic objects are that kind of intentional object. Objects such as paintings and waterfalls that are concrete and separate only become aesthetic objects when someone is aware of them, and some aesthetic objects such as musical works have only a secondary physical existence as scores or digital code on a magnetic disk; so aesthetic objects are intentional objects in a fundamental way.

The intentional status of aesthetic objects can be seen clearly in works of art, which are the aesthetic objects that concern us most centrally. There must be *some* relation between a work of art and its audience, at least potentially. The point of works of art is that they be presented, in an appropriate fashion, to someone. At one extreme, we know of things like cave-paintings and the interior decoration of tombs that appear to have been done without any intention that they be viewed by anyone after their creation. Even those extreme cases imply some audience, however. Works of art produced for use in magic, superstition, and religion are there to please, invoke, or propitiate some gods, spirits, or forces. So while there may not be a traditional audience, the work is not meant as an isolated object but as one that presents itself for viewing.

That is what it means to say that aesthetic objects are fundamentally intentional objects. They imply that they are objects for someone (including the person who made them, of course) as well as being simple physical objects, like rocks or plants, whose existence does not point beyond itself unless someone chooses independently to take notice of it.

At the other extreme, some works of art are fundamentally performances. The presence of an audience, even if it is only imagined or a reflexive relation to the performer (where the performer is also the only audience), is part of the work. Art forms such as music and dance imply performance. While there may or may not be a written score, only in a performance is the work realized. Usually the performance includes more than the score by itself annotates. A combination of notes and indications of speed (*allegro*, etc.) still have to be interpreted by a player, and the characteristics of the instruments on which the music is played substantially affect the performance. Dance notation is even less restrictive on the actual movement and visual presentation of a dance. Improvisational works and some recent avant-garde performance art even more completely locate the work of art in the performance. The work may occur only once and may or may not be recorded in some way.

When we turn from works of art to natural objects, a similar intentionality is needed for them to become aesthetic objects. A scene that no one sees may have potentially aesthetic qualities, but it only becomes an aesthetic object when someone looks at it. If, as we have considered earlier, natural objects are viewed in ways that we have learned from works of art, the relation of a viewer to the object is even more clearly essential. When someone looks at an arrangement of fruit and responds to it aesthetically because it has the form of a still-life painting, then the observer's presence is needed to bring that perspective to the relation. Aesthetics is about the way people respond to things. So there has to be some response before anything aesthetic occurs. Even the most scientific theories of aesthetics are closer to human sciences than they are to natural sciences that try to bracket out the observer as much as possible.

Participatory aesthetics

In classical aesthetic theories, art was considered important either because it made possible some relation that would not have been there without the work of art or because it helped to cement a relation that needed reinforcement. Art makes possible a relation between gods and people or between individuals and the collective (tribe, people, nation). By participating in art, one is connected to the source of something larger than oneself. Many art forms are communal – dance, drama, oral poetry, even film. They are not forms that, normally, one participates in by oneself. One is part of an audience, and the audience is affected not only by what is performed but by the presence of others at the performance. That is one reason why live music and movie theaters provide a very different experience from CDs and video. In classical aesthetics, this relation was usually taken to be primary. Private enjoyment would be a lesser, secondary form of aesthetic participation. The unity and participation provided by dance, ritual, music, and drama could not be achieved without the communal experience of art. Sometimes this would take religious forms, but it could also be civic unity or a form of group identity that was achieved.

A second form of participation suggests a lesser but still very important kind of relation. When one enters a cathedral, much of the art work is designed to reinforce what is more directly accomplished by the ritual and practice of the religion. Statues, paintings, stained glass and architecture itself support and teach what the primary rituals and practice make possible. In a similar way, monumental art, historical painting, and many of the forms of poetry – elegies, epitaphs, and orations – all serve to remind an audience of what is important and what has been accomplished by the state or the individual honored. Think of a triumphal monument such as the arch of Trajan or the Washington monument. To look at those works is to be reminded of what it is (or was) to be a Roman or an American. Painting could serve the same function not only by depicting a scene of significance but by showing the patron who commissioned the painting as part of the scene. It was common for the patron and his family to appear along with the saints in religious paintings in the middle ages and renaissance.

Participation on the classical model involved a dissolving of the self into the experience of the work. It could also encompass natural beauty that inspired a religious awe and produced a similar sense of belonging to something present in nature. As an aesthetic theory, this approach is also fundamentally didactic. That means that the aesthetic relation is understood to teach something, and the proper way to approach art is as a kind of intimate knowledge. The advantage of such aesthetic teaching is that it is not too intellectual and logical. It can be experienced directly. Thus it makes possible knowledge of things that are too difficult or even impossible to understand by means of logic or an unaided reason. Christian doctrines such as the trinity require that God be both one and three at the same time. The incarnation holds that Christ was both "very God and very man" in the words of the Nicene creed. These doctrines seem to defy logic, but they could be taught by a direct experience or vision, exemplified in the beatific vision of Dante in paradise.

Similar examples could be cited from Buddhism and Hinduism and probably from most other religions. Secular instances included moral principles and concepts such as honor and justice. In neo-classical aesthetics in the eighteenth century, this didactic aesthetic was summed up in the idea that art should instruct through pleasing. The relation of the audience to the work of art was fundamentally a way of participating in something that was important, but it was also pleasant and therefore easier to accomplish. Nature too could be experienced in that way, but this required more imagination.

We might call this a communal or participatory aesthetic of the audience–work relation. From this point of view, purely private viewing or reading was either corrupt or dangerous because it lacked the communal element. Interestingly, private reading, for example, was regarded with suspicion well into the eighteenth century in many circles because it took people away from their work; it denoted a form of idleness, and it lacked the authoritative interpretation that a public presentation gained from the authority of the reader. The patriarch of the family or the parish priest could be counted on to read aloud only those things that would benefit his audience and be within their understanding. A lone reader could easily choose badly or misunderstand what he or she read. That does not mean that books were not read alone or that paintings could not be viewed alone. It means only that when one was related in that private way, the object of the relation was still understood aesthetically to imply a connection with something greater. The goal was not one's individual pleasure but a pleasure produced and shared, even if it manifested itself only in a single individual.

A participatory aesthetic theory captures some important elements of the audience–work relation. We commonly say that we are "lost" or "absorbed" in a work of art. We enter into its world. We also find works of art significant because they have the ability to create relations. The negative reactions to works of art – censorship and attempts to utilize art for propaganda – also indicate how much we think participation in art can accomplish. If art did not have real effects on its audience, there would be no point in forbidding some art. In fact, among the frequently voiced objections to art were that it was uncontrollable by reason and that it competed with religion. Participation in art could be frenzied, emotional, and too powerful. Art was suspect just because it was effective.

As an aesthetic theory, however, a participatory aesthetic asks us to accept metaphysical assumptions as well. It interprets the communal experience and sense as substantive rather than psychological. We participate in something, and that something is only known in a way made possible by our participation. Such an aesthetic theory is caught in a vicious circle. What does our relation to art accomplish? Unity with the gods, the state, the nation, the people, the other. How do we know what that other is? By participating in it through art. To the believer caught in the experience, such an answer may be enough. To a philosopher who seeks to understand the relation, it must seem that the relation is only explained by reference to a mysterious something that cannot be independently known. If the metaphysics of participation is questionable, the aesthetic theory allied to it is also questionable. Modern philosophy takes up that skeptical attitude toward the metaphysical assumptions of the theory.

Aesthetic autonomy

Modern aesthetics breaks with the classical model. Instead of accepting a metaphysics of otherness and the corresponding participatory aesthetics, it asks whether or not the individual shares some special relation that is aesthetic with a work of art. The motivation for this kind of shift is complex, but it certainly involves an increasing reliance on individual experience in science, political and social structures, religion, and philosophy that began in the renaissance and continues to evolve today. Consider. To be scientific, experiments have to be repeatable. The deciding factor is whether any observer can experience and verify what happened independently of any other person. Confirmation comes only because, at least ideally, any individual observer can see for him or herself. No theory that is testable only by believers can be scientific. Political theory speculated that the modern nation was a voluntary association of individuals who joined together for mutual benefit. 'Democracy' came to mean one person, one vote rather than the classical *demos* (people) expressing its collective will. Religion became increasingly a matter of personal piety. And philosophy depended on ideas, which were individual occurrences in individual minds, as the foundation for knowledge. In this environment, aesthetics too looked to individual forms.

What gradually emerged was a theory of an aesthetic attitude. The fundamental idea is that the way that an audience approaches a work of art – or, in some theories, any object at all – is controlled by a kind of perceptual attitude. One sees and feels differently depending on how one approaches something. At the simplest level, this means only that if one is angry or preoccupied, those attitudes will color one's perception. That much seems obvious. However, the influence on perception may go deeper. We see according to certain ways of seeing: categories of space and time and certain expectations that we bring to what we see – causal expectations, for example. When I see an object floating in the air, my spatio-temporal orientation allows me to place it visually, and my causal expectations cause me to see it as a floating object supported in some natural way that I cannot see rather than as a magical or spiritual manifestation. Anything other than an imaginary ghost would violate too many of my perceptual categories for me to even see such a thing. So modern philosophy accepts that perception is not neutral but is controlled by mental attitudes, most of which are themselves acquired through accumulated experience. Perhaps we are born with some perceptual orientations "hard wired" in genetically – the ability to distinguish objects or to respond to positive or hostile expressions, an attraction to food or sex. But a large proportion of our perceptual attitudes have to be learned as we encounter the world. Most of that encounter can be assumed to be similar for all human beings by virtue of the fact that we are one species and are encountering the same world. But some of our perceptual attitudes will be culturally determined as well. The mixture is a matter of considerable debate.

Given that starting-point, it is not hard to postulate a particular way of seeing or set of attitudes that is peculiarly aesthetic. Then the problem becomes how to describe them and, if possible, find ways to either produce or achieve those attitudes at the appropriate time. Many of the central aesthetic terms that we use are basically attempts to describe an aesthetic attitude and/or ways to enter into perception with an aesthetic attitude.

A fundamental premise of modern aesthetics is that the relation of an audience to a work of art must be disinterested. Disinterestedness means a number of things. It does not mean bored or uninvolved. That would obviously not describe our relation to art or aesthetic objects in general. As we have just seen, such objects are particularly absorbing. So disinterestedness as an account of the aesthetic relation must offer an alternative account of that absorption if it is to replace a participatory aesthetic. Initially, then, disinterestedness posits the audience as a kind of ideal audience. A disinterested audience is not overly partial to the work because of special relations. If the work is by a relative, that must be set aside. An ideal audience would have no such special relation. Equally, the audience must be prepared to accept the work on the work's own terms. If an audience demands that every work be a comedy, it will not be able to view tragedy properly. Disinterestedness, in this sense, sets aside most of the personal factors that might interfere with an individual's being able to approach a work while maintaining the importance of individual experience. It is, in effect, a way of making an individual audience member an ideal viewer without the abandonment of self that makes the participatory aesthetic metaphysically suspect. Such an individual is not an interested party but a disinterested spectator. Just as the best juror should not have a personal interest in the case to be tried, the best spectator should not have a personal interest in the work to be appreciated.

A more elaborate and deeper theoretical version of disinterestedness developed out of this early theory. Interest can be analysed into two types. The first is theoretical. When a scientist succeeds in explaining some phenomenon by a theory, a theory serves as the conceptual framework for understanding a particular experience of that type. Galileo observed an object falling. He explained its fall in terms of gravity, distance, and the square of the time it takes to fall. The particular experience has been conceptualized in terms of a more general theory. When that happens, the particular phenomenon observed is understood as a single instance of a more general phenomenon. Its generality, not its individuality, matters. The interest of the particular occurrence – this pebble falling from the tower in Pisa – is as an instance of a falling object. Such an interest reduces the particular to the general, and it can be characterized as a form of theoretical interest. Science does not look at the singularity but at the potential theoretical interest of phenomena.

The second type of interest is practical. I read a book for some reason. I expect to learn from it, to be able to use what I learn, or otherwise to get some benefit from the act of reading. In general, when we do something or observe something, some use is involved. Even the simple act of looking involves looking at something for some reason, and that reason is often practical. I don't want to stumble over whatever is in my path. Whenever use, benefit, or motivation enters into our relations to something, we can say that it is in our interest to have that relation. This type of interest is directed toward achieving some end or goal, and in general, the goal may be known independently of the means.

These kinds of interest can lead to some subtle further distinctions. The existence of the object matters to them. Theoretical interest cannot be based on illusion, imagination, or mistaken identity. Scientists who do not distinguish between real phenomena and what does not occur will fail to conceptualize correctly. Practical interest cannot be based on non-existent objects either. I cannot satisfy my hunger with imaginary bread. Thinking does not make it so in moral terms. One of the most basic practical interests is pleasure. Some ethical theories hold that pleasure is the only intrinsic value. So my practical interest may be simply to enjoy something. But what I enjoy must be there for me to enjoy. This leads to a further distinction. When my pleasure is based on satisfying a desire, only a real object will do. The pleasure comes from the satisfaction of the desire. But a different pleasure comes simply from perceiving or contemplating the object itself. In order to have a verbal distinction, this pleasure is sometimes called delight, and it is said not to depend on the possession or even the existence of its object. It does not matter if I only imagine a painting or the sound of a musical work provided that my imagination is sufficiently vivid. I can still delight in it. When neither the existence nor the fulfillment of some desire beyond the immediate pleasure of the experience itself enters into the experience, it is said to be disinterested in the special sense that evolves in aesthetics.

Disinterestedness is thus phenomenal; it is limited to the immediate phenomenon that occurs. Interested experience includes more than what is presented in the immediate occurrence of the phenomenon. Both theoretical and practical relations of perceiver to object require something more than the immediate experience. They imply a theoretical framework that already existed and desires or goals that need to be fulfilled. In contrast, disinterested experience is limited to its own immediate occurrence. That does not mean that it is not complex. It does not have to be a simple idea of some quality. When I see a painting or hear a piece of music or read a novel, my experience involves a great many complex ideas linked together. To say that they are merely phenomenal means only that I focus on this experience without depending on *concepts* of harmony or narrative voice or perspective. I may see the perspective because I have learned the conventions of painting; but in the moment of seeing, I do not refer to my theoretical knowledge but depend only on what I experience then and there. This is the sense in which I can be said to be disinterested.

Modern aesthetics claims that this disinterested experience is the peculiarly aesthetic experience. It may well be that as a perceptive aesthetic observer, I go on to utilize my experience in theoretical and practical ways that have much to do with my aesthetic experience. However, when I do, I no longer have a pure aesthetic experience. Aesthetic experience is pre-conceptual, and thus has no need for theory or practical considerations. Disinterestedness is sometimes characterized as an experience of something for its own sake, with no other end in view. It does not deny that an end may come into view later. It does make aesthetic experience the purest form of experience available to us, and thus the form of experience that is before all others logically.

Disinterestedness obviously involves us in quite a lot of commitments about perception and how we come to know things and act on what we know. As a part of an aesthetic theory, therefore, it tends to make aesthetics part of what is called epistemology – the theory of knowing. It assumes that we can make distinctions within experience and between kinds of experience, at least analytically. That may not be the case.

Another consequence of disinterestedness leads in a different direction. If the ideal audience is a disinterested audience, and if disinterestedness is that special relation that is at once pre-conceptual and independent of any of the practical and theoretical assumptions that we eventually will make use of, one might ask how it is possible to be that kind of audience. An ideal disinterestedness is all well and good, but none of us is ever in that state. Disinterestedness thus leads naturally to the consideration of the closest attitude that one can achieve in practice. A theoretical disinterestedness finds its natural extension in a theory that describes how one can assume an attitude that approaches disinterestedness in its relation to aesthetic objects, even if it cannot be said to ever be fully disinterested. Conversely, if an aesthetic attitude is possible, the theoretical principles of a disinterested relation to aesthetic objects for their own sake becomes more meaningful.

A number of ways of characterizing an aesthetic attitude have been suggested. The central term, however, was suggested as a result of psychological studies early in the twentieth century by Edward Bullough. Bullough proposed 'psychical distance' as a central metaphor for an attitude or psychological state that approached disinterestedness. It is important to note the shift from epistemology to psychology. Disinterestedness has to do essentially with how we know things through experience. It claims that while most of our experience is formed either by our theoretical concepts or by our practical interests, a foundation of experience logically precedes those interests. When that disinterested experience is treated in its own right, it gives us aesthetic objects and aesthetic experience. Disinterested experience is identified as such only by analysis; normally, disinterested experience will be subsumed in the more complex relations of our lives. We approach disinterested experience *per se* only in the special circumstances of the theater, the museum, or the concert hall.

The kind of aesthetic attitude that comes to be characterized by a metaphor of psychical distance, however, is essentially psychological. It describes a psychological state that we sometimes enter into and that some objects, most notably works of art but also some natural objects, tend to promote in us. As such, this attitude is one that we can voluntarily enter into with proper preparation and training. Its description depends not on our accepting the epistemology of concepts and categories that underlies disinterestedness but only on our observing states that ordinary perceivers can be found to have in the course of their lives. The verification of an aesthetic attitude should come from being able to assume it and match the description of other observers with one's own psychological experience.

A distanced attitude or, more commonly, a distanced experience finds its ideal model in certain natural situations rather than experiences of art. Bullough, in a famous example, compared it to the experience of a fog at sea. The practical, interested attitude toward the fog is aware of its danger to the ship and the discomfort that the damp and lack of visibility brings. The experience can also be pleasant in itself, however. One's senses are heightened, the fog blankets out the normal appearance and gives an eerie, silent world. Bullough says that in that situation one has "put out of gear" one's ordinary reactions and assumed a special relation to the fog and its phenomenal presence, and that the experience is distanced from the ordinary world as a result. Obviously, such a distanced experience is not appropriate for the captain of the ship or a passenger with a bad cold. It is exactly the right approach to both art and nature for producing aesthetic experience, however, according to Bullough's theory.

'Distance,' then, is a metaphor for a kind of experience. It does not refer to physical distance or historical distance. The metaphor is expected to capture several aspects of one kind of experience that is available to us. It fits the requirements of disinterestedness. It is concerned with neither the practical consequences nor the theoretical causes of the fog at sea. It is an attitude that can be voluntarily assumed, at least if other considerations are not too pressing. And it results in a pleasant experience. It maximizes involvement, providing a heightened awareness of self and of the intensity of the experience, at the same time as it maximizes separation from one's ordinary identity, even to the point of a loss of self-awareness. All of these aspects are taken to be characteristic of individual psychological states. Thus, psychical distance is a description of individual experience, and Bullough's theory claims that that kind of experience is aesthetic experience.

In order to apply the idea of psychical distance to the relation between an audience and an aesthetic object, the metaphor has to be extended again. Some kinds of situations, such as the fog at sea, or the eye of a hurricane, or the surf crashing against a cliff, seem naturally to suggest distanced experience. Those kinds of situations can be thought of as making it particularly easy to enter into the fully distanced state required for the experience. Then, if that experience is aesthetic, some works of art and perhaps some other kinds of natural situations might also be particularly conducive to producing the distance required for aesthetic experience. By extension of the metaphor, those objects or situations would be said to be distanced as well. The metaphor is applied not to individual psychological experience but to the objects that produce it. In principle, anything could be distanced, since achieving distance is a matter of assuming a perceptual attitude toward something. In many cases, however, it would be difficult or almost impossible (and not even desirable). When works of art make it difficult to achieve the proper distance, they are said to be over-distanced or under-distanced. If distance is a combination of involvement and disinterestedness, over-distancing is the state that lacks sufficient involvement, and under-distancing is the state where involvement takes over and the detachment necessary for distance is lost.

Both states can be illustrated by a comic episode from the eighteenth-century novelist Henry Fielding's *Tom Jones*.[2] Tom and his companion Partridge attend a performance of *Hamlet* by the most famous actor of the day, David Garrick. When the ghost appears, Partridge is so caught up in the scene that he is frightened and literally takes the ghost as real. He has lost the distance needed to view a play aesthetically. Tom, however, is more amused by Partridge's reactions than by the play. He also does not view the play aesthetically because his attention is focused on what is happening in the audience. He is not sufficiently involved in the play for his experience to be about *Hamlet*.

Hamlet is a great play, and it is relatively easy to experience it "for itself" rather than in the improper ways that Tom Jones and Partridge experience it. Other objects, even other works of art, are harder to experience in the most effective way. Many people find a painting that is all one color uninvolving. Horror films, with lots of gory special effects, are difficult not to find nauseating. The extended distance metaphor can then be applied to those works. The monochromatic painting is said to be over-distanced. The exploitation film is said to be under-distanced. Applied to objects, under-distancing and over-distancing are properties in the objects that either promote or inhibit distance. The extension of the term should not be confused with its direct application to experience, however. Someone with deep sensibilities may experience a color-field painting aesthetically and someone with a strong stomach and an awareness of the subtleties of film may experience *The Texas Chainsaw Massacre* aesthetically. Or so the theory of a distanced attitude holds.

Theories of aesthetic or psychical distance and variations on it try to describe experience more or less directly in terms of its affective states (how it feels) and the kinds of things that produce it. An alternative approach to describing aesthetic experience begins with perception itself. One of the things that we have learned about perception in modern psychology and philosophy is that seeing is governed by aspects. Some figures can be seen in more than one way. One famous example can be viewed as a duck or a rabbit; another can be viewed as two faces in

2 The passage is reproduced in the appendix at the end of the book.

profile or a vase. The shifts in what one sees are more or less voluntary. One of the lessons drawn from such figures is that no unique way of seeing things is determined solely by the shape of the figure. Exactly the same shape appears as more than one object. Perception involves not just seeing but seeing something as something. What is true of simple figures can be extended to more complex visual examples and to other forms of perception. A different way to approach aesthetic experience would be as one possible aspect of our perception of objects. A normal aspect of an object would appear as a useful thing or as an instance of some class of things. Aesthetic seeing would see the object as "itself" – as the object is when only its immediate appearance (or sound, or fictional or imaginative world) is what one sees. Such seeing is sometimes described as impressionistic or imaginative because it focuses only on the immediate impression that the images, words, or sounds produce. It might be associated particularly with certain kinds of painting, poetry, and music that would be considered especially characteristic of the aesthetic aspect of seeing, but in principle any object could be an aesthetic object if it were perceived according to its aesthetic aspect.

A corollary of this perceptual approach depends on the voluntary nature of aspect perception. In most cases, one can choose to see the duck or the rabbit, the faces or the vase. So, it is argued, aesthetic seeing is a way of adopting a particular perceptual stance toward objects. Works of art are objects toward which it is appropriate to adopt that stance. Nature becomes aesthetic when one perceives it aesthetically. Some things, such as car wrecks and murders (real ones, as opposed to the make-believe of film and fiction), may lack any aesthetic aspect to be seen. Other things are primarily aesthetic objects. Some things may exhibit aesthetic aspects in one situation and not in others, just as some figures can be influenced by other figures around them.

Aspect seeing remains a metaphor, however. Ambiguous figures or figure/ground illusions are quite limited. The claim that all seeing is based on perceptual aspects that are influenced by cultural and contextual factors extends a limited description to a much wider range of experience. When those who adopt this theory speak of aesthetic experience as a form of seeing that we voluntarily adopt toward some perceptual objects, they do not mean that we literally have shifting, mutually exclusive perceptual organizations like the duck/rabbit. That would be too limited and too simple. They mean that our perception becomes aesthetic as result of some more complex perceptual shifts that affect our experience. The descriptions offered are quite impressionistic themselves.

A further development of perception as a model for aesthetic experience simply identifies an aesthetic object as the perceptual object itself.

If perception can be singled out so that we can speak of a perceptual object that is neither the physical object that causally produces the perception nor the psychological state in the perceiver that is the physical result, then one might think of the perceptual object as the aesthetic object. Experience that focused directly on the perceptual object would be aesthetic, just as experience that focused on the causes of the perceptual object would be physical experience in one sense, and experience that focused on the effects on the perceiver would be psychological and thus physical in another sense.

That we can make these distinctions seems fairly obvious. Two very different physical objects may look the same; one might be made of wood, the other of metal. The perceptual object is the same in both cases, so we can distinguish the perceptual object from the physical object. Further, I may have very different feelings about the same perceptual object depending on my mood. So my experience of the object at any particular time is not the same as the perceptual object even though the perceptual object belongs to me in a purely psychological sense. Conceivably, there could even be perceptual objects without any physical objects when hallucinations or imagination is involved. There is no perceptual object without a psychological state, however, so perceptual objects satisfy our earlier condition that aesthetic objects are intentional objects.

It is a little harder to see why and how one could ever focus strictly on the perceptual object, and harder still to see why that object should be considered aesthetic. Just picking out the perceptual object in an ordinary experience does not seem to have much to do with art or art-like experiences of nature. When one reads a poem or novel, views a painting, or listens to music, however, only the perceptual object seems to count. So while all perceptual objects do not seem to be aesthetic, aesthetic objects and aesthetic experience might be thought to be uniquely perceptual. The result would then be a limited kind of aesthetic attitude theory. Some additional factors such as artistic intent or the cultural uses of the object would be needed to distinguish aesthetic experience from other purely perceptual experiences that were not aesthetic.

Aesthetic experience

Theories of psychical distance, aspects, and perceptual objects share the assumption that a kind of experience, directly examinable by an individual by means of introspection, is essential to aesthetics. They then go on to characterize that experience in various ways and to give various instructions for how it might be either achieved or enhanced. They find that the experience depends on an attitude that can be voluntarily assumed, cultivated, and learned. They place aesthetic experience within our direct control, assuming only that we have the time, means, and will. The strength of such theories is that they can be tested by everyone for themselves. They conform to our expectations that art is subjectively appropriated. And they do not require us to accept metaphysical assumptions about God, religion, spirit, or some reality other than the one that is ordinarily available to us. They account for both art and nature as aesthetic objects. They take account not only of modern art forms but also of the same phenomena that classical aesthetics accounted for, and they do it in a practical, as opposed to a theoretical, way. That is, they describe and tell us what to do; they do not involve complex assumptions about what must be the case or definitions that every new art form calls into question. Thus they are serious contenders as accounts of how an audience is related to a work of art.

Nevertheless, theories based on a uniquely aesthetic experience and attitude theories in general have come under increasing attack. The problems begin with the difficulty in identifying a kind of experience. We identify objects by what are called identity criteria. To tell one individual from another, we must be able to pick out that individual and know some properties or characteristics that belong to that individual that are sufficient to distinguish it from others with which it shares many characteristics. When one sees twins, they may look the same. By themselves, one cannot tell which is which. They are separate individuals, though, because they are numerically distinct and no matter how much alike they are, each has some characteristics that the other does not have. One may learn those characteristics, so while I may not be able to distinguish them except when they are together, their mother can. The same thing applies to kinds of things. One can tell dogs from cats and beagles from scotties because each species and breed has identity criteria that are sufficient to distinguish them. Such criteria need not be definitions. There may be many different sets of properties that are sufficient. But if one is to speak of dogs, there must be some set.

When we try to supply identity criteria for kinds of experiences, however, problems arise. In normal circumstances, we identify particular experiences by when they occurred, to whom they occurred, and what they were about. Beyond that, every experience is different because it belongs to the person whose experience it is. Talk of kinds of experience, then, makes sense only if the common features that would be the identity criteria for the kind can be found in what the experience is about. So we might talk of various emotions such as love or anger as kinds of experience because they are about situations where one individual is related to another individual in an identifiable way. This is consistent with the earlier identification of aesthetic experience as an emotion that could be called beauty or a kind of pleasure. But if kinds of experience are emotions, and emotions are identified by the kinds of objects and situations that produce them, then we cannot turn around and identify the objects and situations by referring to the kind of experience. We do not do that with love or anger. The person or thing that we love or are angry with or the situation we are angry about has its own identity criteria. Love can then be identified as the kind of experience where we desire a person or object (in various senses of 'desire'), and anger as a kind of experience when we are hostile toward some person. In spite of the things that are specific to every experience, we can group experiences meaningfully on the basis of the kind of relation that they presuppose.

Aesthetic experience does not work that way. Whether it is characterized as disinterested, distanced, or a kind of perceptual choice, aesthetic experience is supposed to be independent of the identity criteria for the object. Anything could be experienced aesthetically, though it might be harder in some cases than in others. An aesthetic object is defined simply as the object of an aesthetic experience. If aesthetic experience were characterized in turn as experience of an aesthetic object, an obvious circularity would result. So all theories of aesthetic experience have to try to describe the experience directly if they are not to rely on independent descriptions of what makes something an aesthetic object. That can certainly be done on an example-by-example basis. One can imagine what the experience of a fog at sea is like in the particular case that Edward Bullough describes. The difficulty comes when one tries to provide identity criteria that belong to experience itself and not to the particular case. The only criteria are introspective – that is, they can be found only by examining the experience when one has it – and the subjectivity and uniqueness of experience make such criteria inaccessible as criteria of identity that must be public. What one gets instead are either analogies – "well, it is like a fog at sea" – or instructions about how to have the experience – put your practical interests "out of gear." Aesthetic experience appears to be something that each individual just has to feel for him- or herself. It is difficult to see how something so individual can function as a *kind* of experience sufficient to explain our relation to art.

If this argument seems rather abstract, it becomes more concrete when we try to imagine how we would use any of the descriptions of aesthetic experience to settle arguments or difficult cases. If I say that something is not distanced or that it is not art, someone else can always say that the problem is just that I have not been able to regard it disinterestedly or with sufficient distance or that I am blind to its aesthetic aspects. Aesthetic claims would be placed beyond dispute. In itself, that would only mean that aesthetic claims are subjective and that, as was widely acknowledged and is still the common feeling, there are no real disputes about taste – only different opinions and feelings. Before we accept that kind of subjectivity, however, we should be aware of its consequences. It means that both our talk and our feelings about art are not about the work of art at all. They are only about our experiences. We set out to explore the relation of the audience to works of art. The one relation that we would take to be most important, the relation to the work *qua* work, turns out to be non-existent on this analysis. We have other relations – to the work as a physical object, as an object of desire, as a means to an end, etc. – but we do not have an aesthetic relation to the object. Our aesthetics feelings are just about themselves.

This argument is just another version of the problem pointed out by David Hume and Immanuel Kant at the beginning of the attempts to identify aesthetic experience in the eighteenth century. Hume cites the argument that "All sentiment is right; because sentiment has a reference to nothing beyond itself." The subjectivity of experience seems to contradict the objectivity of our aesthetic language and the universality of our aesthetic judgments. In spite of attempts to overcome this problem by turning Kant's theory of disinterestedness into a practical theory of aesthetic experience or an aesthetic attitude, we are still left with the same apparent contradiction between the subjectivity of experience and the need to provide useful criteria for identity if we are to talk of a kind of experience meaningfully. Aesthetic experience, understood as a kind of experience, is either paradoxical or a myth.

That does not mean that aesthetics is not experiential. It means only that attempts to find criteria of identity for a special *kind* of experience lead us back to the place where we began historically. Considerations along these lines have led some philosophers to point out that attitude theories, in particular, simply confuse paying attention to a work of art with what the theory calls an aesthetic attitude. When Tom Jones and Partridge both experience *Hamlet* in wrong ways, they did not under-distance or over-distance the work or lack some other aesthetic attitude. They simply failed to pay attention to the play. Partridge is occupied with his own fear of ghosts when he takes the ghost for real. Later, when he thinks the actor who plays the king is a better actor than David Garrick who plays Hamlet (and who was acknowledged as the greatest actor of his day), because the king says his lines louder and is obviously acting (or over-acting), Partridge is paying attention to the actor, not to the character portrayed. Jones, of course, is paying attention to Partridge.

Their problems arise not through lack of an aesthetic attitude but through paying attention to the wrong thing. The only aesthetic attitude required by a work of art is that one pay attention to the work of art. That may produce aesthetic experience, but it identifies the experience – just as any other experience, such as love or anger – by what is experienced and forces us back to the aesthetic object for criteria that distinguish aesthetic experience from ordinary experience. Aesthetic experience is just experience of aesthetic objects, and we still need a way to explain what makes an object aesthetic.

This critique is reinforced by noting how different the experiences appropriate to different works of art can be. Some art should produce moral outrage. If it does not, it has not been effective. Some art is intended to shock. Some art is a commentary on other art. Increasingly, our contemporary awareness of art has been expanded to reach beyond the forms identified as the fine arts. Our art includes public performance and popular culture. It involves gender, race, and economics. The attempts to characterize a particular aesthetic attitude seem more and more to be the product of too narrow a view of what art and the aesthetic can include.

Conclusions

We began with a discussion of objects and distinguished intentional objects from physical objects. Aesthetic objects are all intentional objects, but so are many other things. We then need a way to separate out aesthetic objects from other intentional objects. We cannot use "being made by an artist" as the distinguishing feature because we have examples of aesthetic objects from nature and from art that are not made by artists.

Classical theories of art and the aesthetic have recourse to what we called a participatory theory. Aesthetic objects and aesthetic experience are ways for an audience to participate in something higher or more important or more valuable. This theory has the advantage of accounting for our sense that art is valuable, but it requires that we accept some metaphysical assumptions about an ordered reality and ways that an individual mind can participate in higher levels of reality that our empiricist descriptions of the world make problematic. Aesthetics was thus led to reformulate its theories in terms of individual experience and individual ideas.

In modern aesthetics, aesthetic experience is regarded as an autonomous realm. That means that aesthetic experience is sufficiently different from every other form of experience to have its own criteria of identity. Several ways to explain that autonomy have been put forward. Aesthetic attitudes characterize aesthetic experience in terms of individual abilities to perceive, either naturally or as a result of training, in a specifically aesthetic way. To try to make that more precise, the experience produced is said to be disinterested, in a sense of 'disinterested' that excludes any theoretical or practical interest or even an interest in the existence of its object. Psychical distance is offered as a criterion for the achievement of that disinterested attitude in practice. Psychical distance can be applied either to the experience itself, or by extension to objects that either promote or make more difficult the achievement of psychical distance. An alternative to the psychological theory of psychical distance makes use of perceptual aspects and our ability to distinguish a perceptual object to differentiate aesthetic experience from other forms of experience.

Yet all of these attempts tend to collapse into either circularity, identifying aesthetic experience by referring to aesthetic objects and aesthetic objects by referring to aesthetic experience, or ad hoc treatments of special cases. For all of their value in pointing out attitudes and perceptual conditions that enhance our ability to perceive and appreciate art, aesthetic experience is very questionable if one means by that some kind of experience itself rather than just a common distinction within experience based on what it is an experience of. So we are led back to our starting-point with objects. We need some way of identifying aesthetic objects if we are to make use of the descriptions that distinterested, distanced experience and aspect seeing offer us.

Much of the plausibility of theories of aesthetic experience rests on the metaphors and analogies that they suggest. There is no need to abandon those analogies altogether. Perceptual aspects and perceptual objects suggest a great deal about how we are able to approach art in an appreciative way. If we were not able to adapt our perception of a work of art to a different way of seeing, or to approach a work of art without reducing it to our prior assumptions, we would be very limited in our experience of art. Art teaches us to see it as it demands to be seen. Our experience of art focuses on what is presented, not on the means to produce an illusion or the external ends to which art can be put. The difficulty comes when we take such analogies and perceptual theories as more than metaphors and aids to appreciation. Then we limit our appreciation to those kinds of art that fit the established models that produced the analogies and metaphors. We also open ourselves to a vicious circularity. For example, perceptual objects require aesthetic intent to produce aesthetic experience, but aesthetic intent is understood as a desire for a kind of experience, and we are back where we started. No such circle is produced if we regard attitude theories and perceptual theories as critical aids rather than criteria of identity, however.

Critics and Criticism

Who are critics and what do they do?

Aesthetic attitude theories tend to be ambivalent about the role of one segment of the aesthetic audience: critics. Criticism, especially as practiced by a professional who writes or speaks about some category of art works, has a complex history. Literature, art, and music, especially, were the subject of critical attention in a broad sense in classical Greece and Rome. Essays and commentaries took the arts as their subject-matter and prizes were awarded in artistic competitions. Professional critics who lived by selling their critical writings and acting as arbiters of taste and judges are a relatively modern development, however. They are part of the widening of the audience for art from church, state, and patron to a public that supports art directly by the sale of art products and performances. In that context, critics also were able to make a living by providing presumably informed opinions that would guide and enlighten the public about current and classical art.

Criticism involves more than offering opinions about what is good and bad. An opinion, by itself, is not convincing. So critical opinion has to be supported by reasons. Reasons imply a theory of judgment, so the practice of criticism is one of the contexts in which aesthetic theory is worked out. Criticism also serves an educational function. A critic is not just recommending or disapproving individual works in contemporary art. Critics interpret works. Critical interpretations explain individual works of art and connect works of art to other works. In the process, criticism contributes to the formation of a body of work that is acknowledged as important. The idea of a canon – a body of work that is taken as culturally authoritative – has become controversial in recent cultural debates. Many feel that the acknowledgment of works primarily by "dead white European males" has excluded more than it should and exerts a stifling influence on contemporary art. Be that as it may, the formation of a significant body of work that is widely acknowledged is a natural outgrowth of critical activity. One of the first critical decisions made is the choice of what to talk or write about. As those choices are validated, some works are acknowledged and others are relegated to minor status. Thus criticism plays a central role in the formation of an identifiable culture. "Neo-classical English literature" or "New York art" are categories that designate styles and bodies of work that share features that critics have identified and codified.

Critics are audience members. At one extreme, everyone who reads literature, looks at visual art, or listens to music acts as a critic. Artists themselves act as critics when they revise, promote, or reject their own work. At the other extreme, the idea of criticism implies a special talent for or sensitivity to some kinds of art. Criticism takes one beyond casual involvement with the work of art. A significant body of critical writing is also personal expression, therefore. Even when the writer's opinions are eccentric or wrong-headed, they can be interesting and informative if they are the product of intense involvement with and sensitivity to some works of art. We may feel that some critics are telling us more about themselves than about their subject-matter, but if they are perceptive, their status as audience members makes them interesting.

All of these critical roles are exemplified in the history of the arts and in contemporary practice. The rise of aesthetics in the eighteenth century saw the rise of a theoretical concern about critics as well. When critics began to exert an influence over what was admired and accepted, it became important to think about what a good critic should be. David Hume offered a description of an ideal critic. A critic should have strong sense, delicate sentiment, wide practice, and extensive grounds for comparison, and should be free of prejudice. Strong sense means the ability to reason clearly; delicate sentiment implies sensitivity to the nuances and details of a work. Practice requires frequent reading and writing. Comparison acknowledges that judgment is based on wide knowledge. And freedom from prejudice distinguishes a good critic from those whose special interests color their judgments. Hume's description suggests one view of a critic as an ideal audience member. Most audience response will not come up to Hume's standard. The audience will be too lazy, too ill-informed, too partial in advance to provide the ideal response to any work of art. Over time, those factors fade or cancel out, however, and the responses that approximate those of an ideal critic survive. Good critics, on this view, are ahead of their time, and their views are validated by time.

Two things should be noted about this view of an audience's response and a critic's role in forming it. First, it does not question the essentially experiential nature of the response. Works of art are to be judged by their effects on an audience. But, since any particular audience will be less than ideal, it takes time for the responses of an ideal audience to emerge from the "noise" of immediate response. Critics are part of that sorting process. Second, the role of a critic in the development of the arts is essentially positive. Critics may disagree and be wrong for a time, but one can judge their competence by other standards, and they will lead the way in guiding taste. Gradually, if critics have the characteristics of an ideal audience, their judgments should be recognized. If they are not, we can learn to look for the complicating factors. Perhaps commercial factors are so strong that only movies with lots of car crashes and special effects can be made. Those factors override the judgment of critics for a time. As other means of producing movies are found, however, car crashes and special effects will seem less important (if they are), and better movies will be recognized for what they are.

The deeper problem with this approach to criticism as a kind of ideal audience is that the idealness of the audience will always require further justification. If people like car crashes and continue to like them, who is to say that that is wrong or inferior? Why should the responses of some small body of elitist critics be the ones that will survive over time? Why should the taste of one culture prevail over that of another? The only way to answer such questions is to support critical opinions with some stronger aesthetic theory. Theories of aesthetic experience and aesthetic attitudes tried to supply that additional support. What made some responses better than others was simply that they were qualitatively different. Aesthetic pleasure was not simply pleasure. It was a different kind of pleasure. At least, that was the claim of the kind of attitude theories we have just examined.

One consequence of attitude theories was that an ideal audience was not identified with Hume's kind of sensitive, reasonable, broadly educated and unprejudiced critic. Such critics are too interested in their own judgment for most kinds of attitude theory. They subordinate their responses to reasons and comparisons. They cut themselves off from new experiences. The result was a hostility toward criticism on the part of many attitude theories.

Two strands of argument contribute to this hostility. First, Hume's critic tends to be conservative. His or her taste is formed by extensive practice and comparison. So any new work of art is judged by standards established by older works of art. The process of comparison and judgment is continuous and changing, but it can only change slowly. Critics tend to have a stake in what has been. Attitude theories were developed along with new movements in art, music, and literature, and they tended to promote the avant-garde. Critics were felt to be opposed to the openness required by sympathetic aesthetic response. To attitude theorists, critics appear judgmental, elitist, and authoritarian. Aesthetic response is personal, popular, and anti-authoritarian.

Second, the ideal audience member envisioned by attitude theories is disinterested in a stronger sense than Hume's critic. According to attitude theories, aesthetic response should be immediate, pre-theoretical, and separated from all practical considerations, including a critic's professional standing. On this view, the ideal audience member is often thought of as a kind of aesthetic innocent or primitive whose response will be uncontaminated by cultural expectations or critical judgments. An attitudinal approach to art acknowledges that we all bring to our aesthetic responses who we are and what we desire, but as much as possible we should leave those factors out of account. Our response will be purely aesthetic when we succeed in bracketing our own cultural baggage, according to this theory. Critics only impose their views on others. They are a positive hindrance to aesthetic response. An attitudinal view that devalues criticism also makes art culturally irrelevant because all individuals are reduced to a pre-conceptual state by their aesthetic attitudes.

Not all attitude theories are completely hostile to criticism. In particular, theories that rely on perception and perceptual objects to explain aesthetic experience have an easier time making room for criticism. One's response is to a perceptual aspect or a perceptual object, but the description of how that response is achieved relies on critical aids. Theory itself is sometimes considered "metacriticism" – that is, the account of what an ideal critical activity involves and the nature and status of critical statements. This approach shifts criticism from the productive judgment that produces taste and opinions to a kind of analytic and confusion-removing function. It tends to be allied with critical formalism.

Critical formalism focuses on those aspects of a work of art that appear in its structure. In painting and the visual arts, it would include aspects like shape, color, texture, and the use of space. In literary arts, it includes aspects of the language and structural elements like the construction of plot and character. In music, it denies that music can imitate emotions or ideas to concentrate on aspects such as harmony, rhythm, and tone. Critical formalism is consistent with many kinds of attitude theories because it selects those aspects of a work of art that are independent of its non-aesthetic uses and associations. The formalist argues that in responding aesthetically one is responding to those aspects of a work of art that are most nearly autonomous. Because most people lack formal skills, critics are valuable guides to perceiving formal aspects. Instead of trying to define an ideal audience and then identifying a good critic as approaching that audience, formalist theories define a perceptual object and identify critical skill as the ability to focus on that object. This approach makes a place for some kinds of criticism, but it restricts critical activity to helping others to see the aesthetic aspects of a work of art as the formalist conceives of 'aesthetic.' Many would want a broader view of criticism, and critical activity certainly seems to include more than most formalist criticism allows.

What do critics know?

Criticism includes judgments that claim to be about the work itself or some aspect of it and claim to be true or false by virtue of that aspect.

One of the most important problems raised by the activity of critics is what critics know. There are two sides to this problem. The first focuses on the critic. What and how much does the critic know? The second focuses on critical interpretations. What kind of statements are critical sentences? Are they true or false, and if they are, is there a single true interpretation by which all partial interpretations should be judged? We will consider each of these problems briefly.

The first critics might be considered the performers and interpreters of classical literature and drama. Their function was to present works such as those of Homer to an audience at a time when reading and viewing drama were likely to be public rather than private activities. The question arose whether such interpretive performances required that the performer understand the work that was being performed and whether the ability to interpret a work well implied any knowledge on the part of the performer. Musicians and actors can be considered critics because they must interpret a work in order to perform it and communicate with their audience. It can be argued, however, that they need not understand what they perform to be effective performers. That would seem to imply in a broader sense that critics could point out features of a work and aid readers and viewers without themselves being particularly aware of the significance of what they explicated. It requires linguistic skill to explain a metaphor, but it may not follow that the person who has such skill feels the effect. A critic could give all of the right guidance to the form of a painting without particularly responding to it. If that is the case, criticism might be a learnable skill without requiring knowledge or understanding of the aesthetic aspects of an object on the part of the critic. On the classical model, the interpreter is possessed by the gods or the artist and does not necessarily understand what is communicated through the interpretation.

This argument can be combined with a second argument that seems to limit a critic's knowledge. An academic proverb says that those who can, do; those who can't, teach. (And those who can't teach become deans.) The more intimate and precise knowledge is that of the artist. Critics who are not themselves artists lack the authority of the artist because they do not know, in one sense of 'know,' what the artist does. According to this argument, only a novelist can criticize novels accurately, and only a painter can understand painting. In a novel by Lawrence Durrell, the artist character gets his face slapped when he suggests that he is thinking of writing a book of criticism. (Durrell himself wrote such a book.) The idea is that criticism is always a lesser, secondary activity. Put that bluntly, the argument is not very convincing. Carried to its conclusion, it would seem to imply that no one in the audience except other artists could ever fully understand a work of art. But then there would be little point in producing works of art.

The adversarial relation between critics and artists points to a real division in the way the relation of audience and work of art is thought of, however. If audience members are conceived of as secondary artists who recreate the work in their own imaginations, then critics are not needed. The re-creation is an artistic act, though perhaps a lesser one because the original artist has performed it first. Critical judgment, particularly that the work is good or bad, is external and interfering. If audience members are conceived of as perceiving the work of art directly, however, then their perception of it may be like other forms of perception and knowledge. A critic is a particularly acute member of the audience. The artist may know much less than the work itself has been able to communicate.

This leads us to our second problem. Critical statements are sentences that seem to be either true or false. They may be more complex, however. "The sky in that painting is blue" and "That novel has ten chapters" are factual statements about works of art, but they would not normally be taken as critical statements. Critical statements range from aesthetic judgments to interpretive statements. They include sentences such as "The narrator is unreliable" and "The *Mona Lisa*'s smile is enigmatic" as well as "The *Mona Lisa* is a masterpiece." Their status as statements is complex. We examined some of the questions at issue here in chapter 1, when we considered aesthetic concepts and language. We must ask now whether the typical range of interpretive statements should be regarded as like ordinary judgments or whether some other way of classifying critical sentences is necessary. If they are like ordinary sentences, then whether they are true or false should be settled by the ordinary rules of evidence. Critics would supply evidence; an audience would judge that evidence; and a provisional judgment to accept or reject the interpretation would follow. That procedure makes critical activity a matter of knowledge. It reduces the disagreement between critics and artists to one between competing critics, because as soon as an artist interprets his or her own work, the sentences uttered are just like other critical sentences.

The problems with treating critical interpretations like ordinary sentences and thus applying to them the ordinary rules about how we know things is that works of art involve objects that do not exist (for example, characters and imagined scenes) or no objects other than what is immediately perceived (for example, pure music and non-representational painting). If fictions do not exist, then our responses to them are peculiar to say the least: Why should we care about people who do not exist?

The most that a critic can be telling us is something about his or her own feelings, since non-existent people and things cannot have emotions or psychological properties. If works of art do involve real things, those are not the things that matter most to interpretations. If what is at issue is some aspect that depends on how the work is viewed, or some perceptual object that depends on individual perception, then every interpretation is relative to the perceiver. So critical interpretations might be viewed as recommendations for perceiving a work of art or expressions about the effects of the work. Then it is their usefulness or their appropriateness to the work, not their truth or falsity (even if they are true or false), that matters aesthetically. At an extreme, interpretive statements might be viewed as nothing more than expressions of approval or disapproval – complex ways of saying that someone liked or disliked a work or some aspect of it. Viewed in that way, interpretive sentences are competing ways of approaching a work and an artist might reasonably expect that his or her way would be given priority. Such authorial authority could never be absolute, however, because an audience member could always prefer his or her own view without contradiction or inconsistency.

Sometimes intentionalists – those who defend the importance of artists' intentions in interpreting a work – claim to be doing so in order that there will be an authoritative interpretation. Anti-intentionalists are depicted as opening the way for any critical interpretation. That division is misleading. One could accept artists' intentions as relevant and still deny that interpretive statements are true or false. The relevance of the intentions would just be one more important way of forming one's own reaction. Or one could treat artists' intentions as just one more way of looking at a work and still hold that interpretive statements are true or false depending on other kinds of evidence. The real issue is whether critical interpretations are the kind of sentences that require evidence at all and, if they are, what the evidence should be. That depends on what the relation of an audience member is to a work of art. If audience members are on their own and priority rests with the appropriation of a work of art by an individual audience member, then the issue would be whether there is an ideal audience or not and, if there is, what its characteristics should be. We are led back to Hume's critic. But if priority rests with the work of art and an audience is expected to perceive that work in some special way, then we are led to a different audience relation. An artist is authoritative not as another critic but as the one who makes possible this aesthetic experience. A critic, if needed at all, should be nothing more than one who clears confusion and points out aspects so that the audience can approximate the aesthetic experience appropriate to the work. By extension, nothing prohibits more than one aesthetic experience from arising from the same work, so more than one interpretation can be appropriate. Any experience that conforms to the conditions of aesthetic perception will be equally appropriate.

The two alternatives with regard to interpretive sentences may not be as exclusive as this presentation would make it appear. Interpretation is a complex activity that serves more than one end. Different kinds of interpretation could be appropriate depending on what a critic is trying to do. It certainly seems to be the case that critics think that they have real disagreements among themselves. More than one interpretation can be interesting, informative, and even acceptable even though, regarded sentence by sentence, each is incompatible with other interpretations that are interesting, informative, and acceptable. It would be a mistake to dismiss critical claims as merely subjective when they should be taken seriously; but critics should never be taken too seriously! The way to sort out what is going on in any particular case is to examine what the relation between the audience and the work is at that point.

Hermeneutics

An interesting way of trying to take account of both aspects of interpretation has arisen in contemporary philosophy. It is called hermeneutics and traces its roots to the principles of biblical interpretation as that enterprise began in the eighteenth century. Hermeneutics recognizes that the audience–work of art relation implies an inevitable circle. An audience is responding to something by interpreting it. So the audience relation is formed by the work. But the work is only a work of art in the full sense when it is being interpreted, and that means that the work depends on the audience. A work is only what an audience says it is. The work is defined by the perception of the audience, and the perception of the audience is defined by the work.

Instead of seeing this interdependence as a hopeless circle, however, hermeneutics sees it as the basis for all interpretation. Principles of interpretation have to be formed by an awareness of both the subjectivity of perception and the objectivity of the work of art. Moreover, both audience and work of art are constantly changing because they meet at a particular point in history. Even if one wants to approach a work of art in its own historical setting, the attitudes and perceptions of the audience are formed by a different historical setting. Thus the interpretive circle is also an historical circle. The past is brought into the present and the present must remain in touch with the past. An interpretation that ignores either the historicity of the work or its history of interpretation will fail to keep contact with the work. But an interpretation that does not acknowledge its own historicity is equally fallacious. In biblical studies, this was understood to mean that both an absolute "historical Jesus" just as he appeared to his disciples and a contemporary Jesus in the guise of a modern man were equally impossible. The text presents both and neither.

Extended to aesthetics, hermeneutics argues that interpretation is neither the ahistorical sentences of a timeless logic nor the subjective relativism that ignores the history of production of the work. The question that remains is whether this laudable attempt to retain both history and truth can be made consistent in interpretive practice. It is much more difficult to find ways to apply it than it is to offer it as an ideal. It may turn out to be only an interesting alternative to Hume's ideal critic as a way of establishing some interpretations as the standard.

Conclusions

Critics form one particularly important kind of audience. They provide both interpretive comments and evaluative comments on a work, and they help to situate the work in relation to other works. One way to view critics is as an ideal audience whose characteristics can be explored independently of specific judgments and whose superior opinions will emerge and be established over time. The critic as ideal audience can appear too conservative and restrictive to be able to respond to new work, however.

Attitude theories tend to be hostile toward criticism because it is seen as too self-absorbed, too intellectual, and too distanced for a proper aesthetic response. There is also a long-standing antagonism between artists and critics. Artists become critics when they comment on their own work, and some would limit critical authority to those who are also artists. Theories that depend on aspects and perceptual objects can make a limited role for critics as guides to seeing, but they stop short of granting critics priority in making aesthetic judgments.

Critical interpretations often act like other true or false sentences, but the intentional, subjective nature of aesthetic judgments raises questions about the status of critical interpretations. The fictional nature of much art, particularly in literature, creates special problems for interpretation and the status of interpretive sentences. They are not factual in the way that judgments about physical or ideal objects are factual. In many situations, critical judgments seem better described as adequate or illuminating rather than true or false. Yet critics do act as if they genuinely disagree. Hermeneutics recognizes the complexity of the critic–audience–work of art relation and the importance of the historicity of both audience and work. Hermeneutics tries to expand the critical circle formed when the work has an effect on an audience and the response of the audience in turn shapes the work to its own point of view so that it is an informative rather than a vicious circle.

Critics are both audience members and productive members of the art world. Much of the complexity of criticism in aesthetic theory arises because the critic must both represent the audience as an ideal member and at the same time be productive of some text as well. We have to interpret not only the work of art but also the critic's writing. As audience members, we find ourselves in the complex position of also being critics, in that we interpret and make choices and judgments, at the same time as we are the ultimate audience that both the artist and the critic presuppose in their activities.

Institutions and the Role of the Audience

The art world

We have had frequent occasion to speak of an art world and of the influence of culture on our aesthetic language and the production of aesthetic objects. Modern aesthetic theory was dominated by various forms of aesthetic autonomy, as we saw in the first section of this chapter. A sustained critique of the assumptions of modernist aesthetics has led many to conclude that aesthetic theory itself is questionable. While most of the modernist concepts continue to be in use and to be informative in specific situations, a comprehensive aesthetic theory seems old-fashioned. A new possibility has arisen based on the concept of an art world, however.

Recent aesthetic theory has turned to the concept of an art world to reformulate what aesthetics is all about. The currency of the term comes from two sources. One source is the effect of economics and patronage in the contemporary world. Successful novels and major paintings command high prices. Those who can afford art and also care about promoting it play a significant role in shaping what is available in the way of contemporary aesthetic possibilities. The other source is aesthetic theory. After the attacks on traditional aesthetic theory, a new interest in theory has arisen from those who are prepared to take a broader view of what aesthetics encompasses. Instead of the isolation and autonomy postulated by most modern aesthetic theory, contemporary theory that looks to an art world sees art and aesthetics as the product of broad cultural relations that are historically situated.

It is time now to consider what the art world really is. In a special sense, the art world is the audience for aesthetic objects. No single audience exists, and no single culture defines art. Wherever art is produced, it is linked to an audience, and the combination of art and audience defines an art world and a culture. The culture is broader than the art world, but it depends on it. Culture is as wide as the jokes that make people laugh and the dreams that form their desires. Many of the things we take for granted are actually part of our culture. History and anthropology show us that they could be different. For example, romantic love – the idea that marriage should be between two lovers – appeared only gradually in the western world. In the twelfth century, courtly love presumed just the opposite – that love and marriage were antithetical. Marriage may serve very different functions in different cultures. Literature, music, painting, and other art forms both shape our expectations and are shaped by them. The troubadour who sings of love responds to a new idea and at the same time gives it currency. How are we to understand this interaction between an art world and its objects?

First of all, we must note that many of the assumptions of modern aesthetics have begun to be questioned. Not the least of these assumptions is the one that lies behind the idea of an ideal audience. Even acknowledging the great variety of tastes that audiences exhibit and the differences produced by age and national culture, we have been assuming that a single way of approaching art can and, ideally, should be shared by everyone. The differences in our approaches can be overcome by imagination. A young, optimistic reader may have some difficulty with classical tragedy, but with effort, each person can enter the world of the work and assume the necessary attitudes to appreciate it aesthetically. Or so we would like to believe.

But what if some divisions are so fundamental that they control our approach? Among the candidates for fundamental shifts in relation are gender, race and ethnicity, and religious belief. We must be very careful here. No one wants to maintain that men cannot read women's literature or that African-American painting cannot be aesthetically pleasing to Asian audiences. But the simple assumption of a universality of aesthetic appeal cannot be accepted uncritically. Ideas are formed in a context; no perception is totally objective and uninfluenced by external factors. That does not reduce perception to a chaos of subjective impressions, but it does suggest that our ideas are not just reflections of an external world in a perfect mirror. If our ideas are not isolated and they are not held universally, we must ask what kinds of factors form them. Claims about gender, ethnicity, and culture must be placed in this context.

Another fundamental assumption of modern aesthetics has been that artists are individuals who produce works of art and that audiences are collections of individuals who respond individually to works of art. We begin with individual creation and individual response and look for common features. We have seen in thinking about the relation of an artist to a work of art that this assumption raises difficulties because some art does not have a single artist behind it. The same may be true of the audience. We may need to think of the audience not as a collection of individuals but as an institution that creates both the work and the responder. Aesthetic theory that tries to account for the diversity of factors affecting our responses to art and aesthetic objects makes use of the ideas of institutions and common practices.

Institutional theories of art

The art world is made up of many kinds of institutions. They include museums and art galleries, public spaces and architecture, book stores and universities, symphony halls and associations, movie studios and theaters. Institutions are constantly changing. Now they include CDs and video tapes. How we look and listen is determined, in part, by the institutions. Video tape requires a different way of looking from a movie theater. Think of the difference between sitting with an anonymous crowd in a darkened theater and sitting with people one knows in front of a small screen. Anyone who has watched a movie on a large screen in a theater and on video knows that there are differences. Images must be fitted to a different format (square as opposed to rectangular), and the same images appear differently. Now we are suggesting that those differences are not just differences in appearance. They affect what kind of audience is available. Some differences, such as those between film goer and video watcher, are relatively minor. The differences between male and female or between cultural insider and cultural outsider are much greater. At some point, the differences approach a difference in actual perception. It is not just that we each see different images. We belong to different institutional worlds.

The aesthetically relevant differences are those that either lead to the formation of different works of art or those that dictate the way that someone becomes part of an audience. At bottom, both depend on a special kind of institutional possibility. We know that some kinds of language have the ability to actually do what they say in the act of saying it. If someone yells "Fire!" they do one thing and say something else. They warn, and they say that there is a fire. The standard examples of both doing and saying at the same time include things like umpires shouting "Out!" and priests pronouncing marriage. What is said and what is done are the same. Such language is called performative language. Institutions can play a similar performative role. What allows a priest to pronounce a marriage is that he or she is a priest and that an institution, the church, sanctions the performance. Otherwise, it does not take place. It has been argued that a similar act takes place when someone in the art world pronounces something an aesthetic object and thus makes it a candidate for aesthetic appreciation.

What has not been so widely acknowledged is that the same kind of act applies to the audience. Someone who goes to a movie theater or to a museum is placed in a relation by the institution that created and shows the movie or displays a painting. When I pick up a novel and read it, if I read it in a way that tries to enter into an aesthetic relation with what I am reading, I am made into a particular kind of reader by the work for which I am an audience. It is rather like being made a citizen or a husband. One does not cease to be what one was before, but a new relation has been created. Many artists in many different fields understand and exploit that relation. When Samuel Beckett writes a novel about existential consciousness, he also is playing with the existential consciousness of the reader. When performance art intentionally refers to the audience, the audience is being shaped, even if it resists, into part of the performance. Such extreme examples only indicate what is a possibility for all audience–art relations.

Institutions also draw on another kind of language. Imperatives are not only used to give individual commands. They also lay down rules. The formulation of rules for some practice and their imposition on others requires that someone have authority to issue orders and commands and that others be prepared to listen and obey. A commander who is not obeyed has failed in a linguistic action. We say that the particular linguistic act has failed even though it may have been perfectly clear what was being attempted. Similarly, one cannot play a game consistently without obeying the rules of the game. Otherwise the game degenerates. The rules of the game operate as imperatives imposed on the players who must obey. The same is true of the institutions of the art world. If an audience will not play by the rules laid down by the artist through the work of art, then both work of art and audience degenerate into chaos. The ability to perform those imperative functions is as much a product of institutional power as it is of performative language. The institutions make it possible to establish rules.

A consequence of this power of institutions is that some institutions may only be available to some people. Only males can be husbands (though perhaps not all married couples have to involve both sexes). So some aesthetic relations may also turn out to be conditioned upon the prior sex or culture of the one who is institutionally related. There may be many aesthetic audiences, and they may not all be equally open to everyone at any time. Some other institutions can be entered by voluntary association or by education and initiation. In many archaic and traditional cultures, initiation played a fundamental role in making a boy into a man and a member of the people. Baptism provides a similar example. If the art world is thought of as an institution, it must be thought of as constituting an audience as well as making something an aesthetic object or a work of art.

In order for these kinds of institutional activities to take place, institutional identity must be sufficiently defined to make possible the performative and imperative acts needed. It is difficult to create new institutions. They have to grow up in ways that reflect their success. Something like the chicken and egg problem applies to the kind of institutional activity needed for an art world. Art is the product of an art world that makes possible both an audience and a work of art by its performative activity. But the art world is created by artists and audiences that succeed in what they are trying to do. Which comes first? No answer is possible, because the kind of process is emergent rather than controlled and sequential. The developed institutions of the art world that we know and the clear examples of fine art with which we are familiar both arise from situations that are much less clearly defined. The difference between cult object and art work, for example, blurs the line between art and religion. The medieval church was simultaneously a religious institution that made sacramental activity possible and an institution of an emerging art world that made art possible.

It follows from these considerations that the institutions of the art world are not timeless. They grow up in certain contexts, and they can also lose their ability to function. For one thing, there are risks in performative actions. If an umpire consistently makes bad calls, he or she will lose status, and if the tasks of umpiring prove too difficult, the game itself will lose status. Museum directors and critics take similar risks. Because one function of the art world is to create the status of audience, when the audience will no longer follow a particular segment of the art world that particular institution loses the ability to even function. Its performative powers depend on its being neither too repetitive nor too far ahead of the audience that it creates. Similarly, imperatives depend on a mutual relation that issues and carries out the commands. One quickly learns the risks in issuing imperatives that no one is prepared to obey.

Early versions of institutional theories of art had problems because they made the art world so broad and inclusive that it seemed able to do anything. The idea was that the art world only offered "candidates for appreciation." In that limited sense, it could not fail, though no one might in fact actually appreciate what was offered. The term 'work of art' was to be understood only descriptively, not evaluatively. That separation was artificial and difficult to maintain. It seemed to offer an explosion of works of art in which no one in fact had any interest. If the art world becomes too broad, it can do nothing because it lacks the institutional authority to create an audience or to practice performative conferrals. When no one appreciates some object as art, no imperative has been established and thus no institutional activity has been able to take place.

At the same time, institutional theories also tended to be too narrow because they depended on artifactuality. Art had to be something. But the history of modern aesthetics located aesthetic feeling in the audience and not exclusively in artifactual objects. As a new form of definition of 'work of art,' institutional theories have had limited success, therefore. They broaden our concept of definition to include relational as well as objective properties, but they remain committed to essentialist views of art that do not find much support in the history of artistic practice. They move much too quickly and simply from the kind of performatives and imperatives that institutions make possible to an art world that seems nebulous and ill defined.

More recently, however, the idea of institutions has been broadened to focus on the kinds of activities that are performed by cultural entities. Broadly conceived, these institutions can be thought of as providing meaning to fundamental aesthetic concepts within a culture and themselves offering a way to transcend particular cultures. For example, within a culture, a new art form such as film may gradually emerge. It will depend on a complex of film critics, studios, actors, and distribution systems to form an audience and to make production possible. Since it arises within a culture, it also draws on ways of viewing that include gender and also include psychologically formed limits – our responses to violence, for example, and our way of suppressing our own individuality in a kind of looking at something from outside. Current terms in film theory such as 'the gaze' get their meaning from the complex institutional activity of audience, film-makers, and critics. Trying to transfer a theoretical concept that is appropriate to contemporary film to Greek theater would be very questionable as a result. Within the world of film, many of the concepts do make sense. Audiences respond as the theory predicts they will because the audience for film has grown up out of the same institutions that define the terms.

At the same time, awareness of the institutional activity allows us to enter into other institutional activities that are not part of our own culture, or are so only in part. When one attends a football game, one learns the limited rules necessary to appreciate what is going on. One does not have to actually have played the game or grown up kicking balls with one's feet to appreciate the game and become part of its audience. Similarly, institutions that constitute an art world allow the possibility of learning the institutional practices sufficiently to enter into the art world as it is constituted in a particular culture. Institutions that no longer exist can continue to have a virtual existence as long as an audience can reconstruct the conditions required by the work.

Such an institutional theory is obviously limited. A difference between belonging to a creative cultural institution and one that is only virtually present cannot be denied. We change what we view. We cannot simply return to Greek or Elizabethan drama and experience them as they would have been experienced by someone for whom that art world was still productive. The institutions of the art world are imperialistic. They take over older forms in the same way that works of art assimilate older forms and turn them to new ends. A sonnet today is a different form from an Elizabethan sonnet even if it has the same fourteen-line scheme because today sonnets would have to be validated by an audience and an art world with different institutional practices. Nevertheless, it helps to be aware of the possibilities of other practices even if we can only take them over in incomplete ways.

The vagueness of institutional theories remains a more serious deficiency. To speak of an art world, even if it is acknowledged that only some things will count as functioning institutions in it, is to name what one seeks to understand. A name is not the same thing as an adequate theory. The analogies to performative and imperative language remain analogies. Cultural institutions are not as well defined as more ordered and artificial institutions. That may allow them more power in some cases, but it also makes them theoretically suspect. If they, in turn, generate the meaning for theoretical terms, then the meaning of those terms begins to be doubly vague. They depend both on undefined institutions and within those institutions on undefined uses. In film theory, a term like 'gaze' easily becomes a catchphrase for all kind of psychological assumptions. Only the users of the term know what it means, and then only if they are willing to use it. Theoretical terms like that tend to be self-defined. Only a certain group can use them, and that group is defined by the use of the terms! We can learn a great deal from attention to the institutions that make up an art world, but it is not at all clear that we have a sufficiently precise grasp of what 'institution' and 'art world' refer to.

Conclusions

An art world is a complex portion of a larger culture. In many ways, however, the art world defines the culture. It includes not only artists but also those who support and promote art and the audiences that are responsive to art and its promoters. The existence of an art world offers an alternative to theories based on an ideal audience and individual aesthetic perceptions. An art world is the product of institutions. The activities of those institutions can be explained through the analogy with performative language. Some language creates what it says. In the same way, institutions of the art world create an audience and aesthetic objects by their actions. Such activity is not unrestricted, however. Institutions must have authority, and that authority usually has to grow up within a culture. Institutions must be able to establish rules through a kind of imperative so that those who belong to the art world are constituted by obeying the institutional rules.

Attempts to turn the art world and its institutions directly to definitions are both too broad and too narrow. They let in too much, and they restricted art to artifacts at just the time when art was challenging that limitation. However, institutions can still account for the interrelation of culture and art because institutions form art which in turn changes institutions of the art world. The concept of an art world also provides historical depth. It helps to explain why some forms are productive at one time and not at another, because the appropriate institutions may not be present at all times. In addition, we are shown a way that, by imaginatively adopting cultural institutions different from our own – by playing a game by a different set of rules – we can enter into art forms that are not part of our own cultural institutions. The concepts of an art world and performative institutions thus allow a different kind of aesthetic theory from that which dominated modernist aesthetics.

References and Suggestions for Further Reading

Attitudes of the audience

Intentionality

The discussion of intentionality here is influenced by the work of Edmund Husserl, particularly as it is developed in aesthetics by Mikel Dufrenne in *The*

Phenomenology of Aesthetic Experience (Evanston, IL: Northwestern University Press, 1973) and Roman Ingarden in *The Literary Work of Art* (Evanston, IL: Northwestern University Press, 1973). See particularly Ingarden, §§20–4.

Participatory aesthetics

A participatory aesthetic is presupposed by much classical and medieval art. See Umberto Eco, *Art and Beauty in the Middle Ages* (New Haven: Yale University Press, 1986), particularly chapter 8. For the debates over reading, see Martha Woodmansee, *The Author, Art, and the Market* (New York: Columbia University Press, 1994), pp. 89–108.

Aesthetic autonomy

Aesthetic attitude theories have been widely held during the nineteenth and twentieth centuries. The rise of attitude theories is traced by Jerome Stolnitz, "Of the Origins of 'Aesthetic Disinterestedness'," *Journal of Aesthetics and Art Criticism* 20 (1961): 131–43. A typical contemporary version would be Virgil Aldrich's *Philosophy of Art* (Englewood Cliffs, NJ: Prentice-Hall, 1963), but many other examples could be cited. 'Disinterestedness' comes from Kant's *Critique of Judgment*, but it is widely adopted and variously understood. Edward Bullough's theory of distance is found in "'Psychical Distance' as a Factor in Art and an Aesthetic Principle," *British Journal of Psychology* 5 (1912): 87–118, which is freqently anthologized. The duck/rabbit example is traceable to Wittgenstein, but it has been widely adapted – see e.g. Norwood Russell Hanson, *Patterns of Discovery* (Cambridge: Cambridge University Press, 1958). In aesthetics, see Ben Tilghman, *Wittgenstein, Ethics and Aesthetics* (Albany, NY: State University of New York Press, 1991). Two excellent treatments of Wittgenstein's philosophy as it applies to aesthetics are by G. L. Hagberg: *Meaning and Interpretation: Wittgenstein, Henry James, and Literary Knowledge* (Ithaca: Cornell University Press, 1994) and *Art as Language: Wittgenstein, Meaning and Aesthetic Theory* (Ithaca: Cornell University Press, 1995). Hagberg argues that Wittgenstein's usefulness for aesthetics is not limited to the anti-essentialist arguments that he inspired or to aspect seeing. A more traditional approach to aesthetic objects as perceptual objects is argued by Monroe Beardsley in *Aesthetics: Problems in the Philosophy of Criticism* (New York: Harcourt, Brace & World, 1958; repr. Indianapolis: Hackett, 1981).

Aesthetic experience

The essentialism implicit in theories based on aesthetic experience is widely criticized, for example by Marshall Cohen, "Aesthetic Essence," in Max Black, ed., *Philosophy in America* (Ithaca: Cornell University Press, 1965): 115–33. The criticism that attitude theories are just failures to pay attention is part of George Dickie's critique in "The Myth of the Aesthetic Attitude," *American Philosophical Quarterly* 1 (1964): 56–65 and later in *Art and the Aesthetic: An Institutional Analysis* (Ithaca: Cornell University Press, 1974).

Critics and criticism

Who are art critics and what do they do?

The essays by Arnold Isenberg in *Aesthetics and the Theory of Criticism* (Chicago: University of Chicago Press, 1973) offer an excellent starting-point for discussions of aesthetics and criticism. For Hume's theory of a good critic, see his "Of the Standard of Taste" (1757), which appears in many anthologies.

What do critics know?

The characterization of aesthetics as "metacriticism" is found in Beardsley's *Aesthetics*. Two different formalist approaches to literature are Cleanth Brooks' *The Well Wrought Urn* (first publ. 1947; New York: Harcourt, Brace & World, 1963) and Northrop Frye's *Anatomy of Criticism* (Princeton: Princeton University Press, 1957). The critic as performer is considered by Plato in his dialogue *Ion*. The Lawrence Durrell example occurs in *Clea*, the third volume of his *Alexandria Quartet* (New York: E.P. Dutton, 1960). Durrell's book of criticism is *Key to Modern British Poetry* (Norman: University of Oklahoma Press, 1952). A large literature has grown up around the nature of fictions, particularly in literature. See, for example, Kendall L. Walton, *Mimesis as Make-Believe* (Cambridge, MA: Harvard University Press, 1990); David Novitz, *Knowledge, Fiction and Imagination* (Philadelphia: Temple University Press, 1987); Susan L. Feagin, *Reading with Feeling* (Ithaca: Cornell University Press, 1996); and Peter Lamarque, *Fictional Points of View* (Ithaca: Cornell University Press, 1996). Among the intentionalists who defend authorial authority is E.D. Hirsch, *Validity in Interpretation* (New Haven: Yale University Press, 1967). The problems of relativism in interpretation have recently occupied Joseph Margolis in *Interpretation Radical but not Unruly* (Berkeley: University of California Press, 1994) and *The Truth about Relativism* (Oxford: Blackwell, 1991).

Hermeneutics

For an overview of hermenutics, see R.E. Palmer, *Hermeneutics: Interpretation Theory in Schleiermacher, Dilthey, Heidegger and Gadamer* (Evanston, IL: Northwestern University Press, 1969). The classic source for much contemporary discussion of hermeneutics is Hans-Georg Gadamer, *Truth and Method* (New York: Seabury Press, 1975). The essays in Hans-Georg Gadamer, *Philosophical Hermenutics* (Berkeley: University of California Press, 1976) are also useful.

Institutions and the role of the audience

The art world

A good starting-point for defining an art world is Arthur Danto, "The Artworld," *Journal of Philosophy* 61 (1964): 571–84, which has appeared in a number of anthologies and is followed up by Danto's subsequent books. For courtly love, see C.S. Lewis, *Allegory of Love* (Oxford: Clarendon Press, 1936) and Denis de Rougemont, *Love in the Western World* (New York: Pantheon, 1956).

Institutional theories of art

The institutional theory of art is associated with George Dickie, beginning with *Art and the Aesthetic: An Institutional Analysis* (Ithaca: Cornell University Press, 1974). For the role of imperatives in an institutional analysis, see Dabney Townsend, *Aesthetic Objects and Works of Art* (Wolfesboro, NH: Longwood Academic Press, 1989).

5

The Artist and the Audience

Thus far, our aesthetic theory has included some identifiable object in an extended sense of 'object.' The object might be a physical work of art; it might be a performance; or it might be some natural object or scene. It could be a perceptual object or even an object of consciousness. Whatever it is, it provides a focus for aesthetics by being what we have aesthetic experience of. When such objects form part of aesthetic experience, we have asked how they came to be aesthetic objects (the artist and the work of art) and how they could be experienced as aesthetic objects (the audience and the work of art).

It has become clear in our investigation that a wide range of possible explanations for both relations have been explored in philosophical aesthetics. Our discussion of institutions in chapter 4 reminds us that a complex context is implied by whatever aesthetic relation holds between artist, audience, and work. We must now explore how that context is established in more detail. Who are the artists, and how are they related to their audience? Does the artist create the audience? If so, what happens when the world changes so that the context the artist created no longer exists? Does the audience create the artist? Does that help explain why some kinds of art flourish for a time and then disappear? The relation of artist and audience qualifies our explanations of the production and interpretation of works of art.

The Aesthetics of Reception

Communication

One aesthetic theory takes communication as the fundamental model for aesthetic experience. We have already explored some aspects of aesthetic communication in the discussion of the artist's intentions in chapter 3. There we noted that the relation between an artist's intentions and an aesthetic object is often thought of in terms of something that the artist wants to express by means of the object. Presumably, aesthetic communication is something that an artist says and some audience understands in extended senses of 'saying' and 'understanding.' So the primary relation is between the artist and the audience. The aesthetic object is a means to that communicative end. A subset of communications are held to be aesthetic, and how aesthetic communication is to be distinguished from non-aesthetic communication is the problem the theory has to address. For example, communication might be held to be aesthetic if it promotes oneness with the divine (Plotinus) or if it unites human beings (Tolstoy).

Aesthetic communication can be a part of both classical and modern aesthetic theories. In classical theories, it would most commonly be linked to inspiration. The artist or performer need not even understand what is communicated. In modern aesthetics, communication is linked to expression theories. The primary relation is between the mind of the artist and the minds of the audience. In idealist theories (those that take mind or ideas as the fundamental reality), the audience simply repeats in a somewhat attenuated form what the artist has already conceived. In other versions, what is expressed may come, in part, from unconscious motives that are present only symbolically. In any case, by taking the aesthetic model from communication, one makes the relation between artist and audience primary. The work of art is at best a means to further aesthetic communication.

Some more general considerations about how communication takes place, particularly in language, may be helpful in understanding how aesthetic reception takes place. Consider a normal communicative event. Someone says something to someone else and is understood. The speaker intends some outcome, and the hearer is attuned to what the speaker is saying. They share a common language (and perhaps other common conventional resources such as body language). A speaker not only speaks in that common language, he or she believes that the person to whom the utterance is addressed will understand. From the hearer's side, the hearer believes that the speaker is speaking in a way that can be understood. If these common beliefs were not in place (together with others like them), communicative speech would be impossible. So communication presumes a common language and a common bond of presumed intelligibility between speaker and hearer. If one does not believe that the noise being made is speech and is intended as speech, then even if it sounds like words and phrases, it would not communicate anything.

Imagine a computer that randomly constructed sentences for its voice synthesizer. Every sentence makes sense grammatically and even in terms of the meaning of the words. Yet nothing is communicated because there is no speaker. An intelligent machine must respond in context; speech alone is not enough. Even if someone speaks coherently, we come to understand them only when his or her speech is sufficient to establish some kind of identity for the speaker. It may not be necessary to know exactly who the speaker is, but it must be at least enough to identify the speaker as the voice of this message. We do not know who most of the writers and speakers of the Hebrew testament are. It makes a difference, however, whether we believe the true speaker to be YHWH or some fallible prophet. Every speech has a speaker.

Every speech is also addressed to someone. The addressee may be identified in such a way that a wide variety of people would qualify. By hearing and understanding, however, the person addressed becomes part of the history of what is sometimes called a speech act. Even if anyone can understand what is said, it makes a difference who is being spoken to. "Fire!" in a crowded room is addressed to everyone in the room, but it has force as an utterance only for those in the room. In the absence of an appropriate addressee, language loses its communicative force, even if it is understood. We are unmoved by the cry that was frightening when the great London or Chicago fires broke out.

We are trying to show that in ordinary language meaning and communication depend on the who and how as well as the what of a speech act. A speaker–speech relation or a hearer–speech relation is never enough. Communication is possible only when a speaker is related to a hearer as well. The situation might seem to be different in aesthetics. Either there is no speaker, or if there is, the speech act – the production of a work of art – is presumed to be timeless. Think of a novelist who breaks new ground. Henry Fielding (1707–54) wrote novels that create the successive adventures of a hero against the background of eighteenth century-society. Fielding's novels are part adventure, part satire on actual contemporary people, and part allegory. They are something essentially new in the history of literature, although they draw on earlier forms, particularly the Spanish writer Miguel Cervantes (1547–1616) and his comic adventures of Don Quixote. So Fielding is addressing a very specific historical audience. Nevertheless, as a novelist, Fielding is not limited by his own audience. He wrote "for all times" or at least for a great deal more than his immediate time. All artists do. We can read Henry Fielding's novel *Tom Jones* even though Fielding is long dead. We know little about him and he could have known nothing specific about us (though he knows a great deal about our shared humanity). One of the things that seems to distinguish aesthetic experience, we have seen, is a disinterestedness that includes its freedom from the specifics of time, place, and individual existence.

That quality is misleading, however. Fielding did not speak to everyone in some timeless manner. On the contrary, he wrote in English that is conditioned by its eighteenth-century situation. Part of the difficulty for a modern audience in reading *Tom Jones* is simply the lack of knowledge and common understandings that Fielding took for granted in his audience. Much, though not all, of that context can be recovered with work. In making that effort we shape ourselves into the kind of audience that Fielding presumed. In a real sense, an author shapes the consciousness of his or her audience by the very act of writing. I do not exactly become an eighteenth-century person by reading an eighteenth-century novel, but I do come much closer than might be imagined. If I could not, literature would be limited to its own time and place by the limits of normal communication.

What is true for language can be extended to other art forms. The audience for a Mozart chamber symphony does not exactly become the cultivated salon audience for whom Mozart wrote. I may be listening in private on my CD system that very faithfully recreates the sound of the orchestra – something Mozart could not even have imagined. However, what I hear and what Mozart wrote are so related musically that my experience is close to that of his audience. Musically, I can understand the sensibility of an eighteenth-century musical performance, even if I hear the music in a context transformed by the Beatles and heavy metal. I also share western conventions of tonality, harmony, and musical practice with Mozart's audience. The depth of shared understanding can be concealed by the extent to which it is taken for granted, but it is not limitless. One need only listen to some of the exotic sounds from other cultures to hear the difference.

Nothing mysterious is implied by these observations. They tell us only that when an artist produces some work of art, he or she also produces an audience, and the relation of the artist and the audience is a real relation that transcends the particular work of art in question. I like Mozart and Fielding because they speak to me. They do it through their works, but part of the reason I like their work is because they make it possible for me to perceive in a way that I would not otherwise be able to do. I am transformed into the kind of audience that they demanded. I can make that transition only because we share sufficient communicative foundations, however. The relation is never created in a cultural vacuum. It is built on shared conventions, expectations, and language.

This relation has a negative side. If an artist's sense of an audience is patriarchal, restrictive, illiberal, or otherwise at odds with who I am, my becoming that audience may not be neutral or disinterested. I have to decide to surrender myself to some other way of forming consciousness. That is why some films, such as Leni Riefenstahl's magnificent documentary of the 1934 Nazi Congress, *Triumph of the Will*, remain controversial. The film shows Hitler as a German messiah, but its real force comes from its spectacular visual effects of massed party members and the good-natured union of German youth. There is something dangerous in becoming the audience for a film that glorifies communal bonding on the basis of ethnic myth. Even if one's participation is only imaginary and insulated by a distance of time, one has been manipulated. That is why some aesthetics insist that a normative condition – a positive sense of humanity – is a condition of aesthetic experience. No matter how moving and involving some works of art may be, they could fail that test if their effect were to divide people into hostile groups.

There is a more serious criticism of this model for aesthetic communication, however. It is too simple. If an artist shapes an audience, an audience also shapes an artist. This can be done in many ways that we will explore in more detail. Consider here only that a novelist such as Fielding or a composer such as Mozart cannot write just anything. Each can only produce what an audience is prepared to hear. In one sense, the actual artist does not matter. The persona of the artist is a product of the work and the audience. I do not know the historical Fielding. I know only the Fielding that *Tom Jones* shows me, and that Fielding is primarily the result of a novel that was shaped to an eighteenth-century audience. If we are to use communication as a model for the artist–audience relation, we must be prepared to look at the relation from both sides.

This can also mean introducing time into the relation. I see things in Riefenstahl's film that no one at the time could see because I see the film in the light of the horrors of a war that the film helped produce. Not only are the actual people shown in the film all dead; many died as a result of just what the film glorifies. That is a part of my experience, though it could not be a part of Riefenstahl's when she made the film. When one considers the relation of artist and audience, therefore, one is considering a mutual relation that can potentially change with time and context. Aesthetic experience involves elements of a relation that is not simply between an object and its audience or its producer.

Conditions for receptivity

Our receptivity to aesthetic experience is conditioned by who we are, and that in turn is affected by how we establish our relation to an artist.

Our approach may be resistant or cooperative. In order for an audience to respond to an artist, some commonalty must be found. The choice of whose situation controls the relation is not always conscious, and it almost might be considered a contest in some cases. Who will define the relation – the artist or I? It will not always be the case that an artist succeeds in imposing his or her own situation on an audience. Sometimes the audience is in control.

With this idea of receptivity in mind, we may consider one particular relation that has special importance in aesthetics. If there is no artist, or if the artist does not control the relation, the audience may have to supply the context. One instance of this is natural beauty. Natural beauty presents an aesthetic problem. On the one hand, it is the source of much pleasure. In some ways, it is the very model of aesthetic experience. We need have no practical interest in it to enjoy it. Its appeal is immediate and requires no interpretation. And it is there for its own sake. At the same time, it does not fit the paradigms of aesthetic experience because nothing is expressed by nature, nor does the imitation of nature bring us closer to the kind of shared experience that classical aesthetics made central. Nature lacks an artist, and thus it fails to establish the conditions for us as an audience.

We remedy that by what we might call the humanization of nature. When we find aesthetic pleasure in a natural event or scene, we transform it by our own activity as an audience so that it becomes an event or scene for us. We make it ours, and in the process we assimilate it to our experience of art. We do that essentially by being an audience even though no artist is at hand. Metaphorically, we may even supply an artist – Nature itself, the muses, or God. Such projections are part of the way that we assimilate our perception to a model of aesthetic communicability. We are able to fit something that is essentially indifferent to our human values into a human world as well as a natural world. For example, recent work on chaos theory has shown us how to generate computer displays of Mandelbrot sets. In themselves, these are nothing more than mathematical formulas controlling a video display. Yet they are beautiful, and in approaching them in that light we no longer limit them to their mathematical context. We make them something that we, as humans, value. This regard transforms the displays into objects for a human world and finds their aesthetic value in that transformation. In earlier aesthetics, such humanization took the form of finding expressive qualities in nature – the joy of spring, the grace of a bird in flight. An implicit anthropomorphizing is at work in such theories: that is, natural events are viewed as important for displaying human characteristics. This aesthetic impulse is very strong.

The kind of audience–artist relation that is required by aesthetics has to be created culturally. In fact, 'culture' is a word that acquires a meaning through the interaction of artist and audience. We depend on some basic resources to create a common culture. First, there must be some symbolic commonalty. Language itself is a common symbol system that unites artist and audience. Chaucer, in the *Canterbury Tales*, and Dante, in the *Divine Comedy*, helped establish English and Italian as national languages. Each consciously chose to write in a particular language that was not the accepted literary language of the time. Chaucer's use of a particular English dialect and Dante's choice of the vernacular Italian instead of Latin created new audiences for their poetry. They, in turn, are founding poets because their choice of language is validated by the existence of an emerging national audience. Within language, more specific symbol systems provide common ground. For example, common beliefs about the gods, about the origins of a people, a state, or an ethnic group, provide symbolic unity. Heroes become symbols. Legends produce shared agreement. The relation feeds on itself. The stories of gods and men provide Homer and Hesiod with their subject-matter. Their writings in turn provide common ground for classical Greek tragedy. Milton and Spenser draw upon Christian beliefs. Their epic forms in turn give English literature its Christian, allegorical focus. Language and shared symbols make aesthetic experience possible; and, conversely, shared aesthetic experience is at the center of establishing a cultural identity. That is one reason why culture wars are so serious.

What is true of the arts that use language is also true of the more extended language of music and the visual arts. Symbols are not the property of a single work of art or of a single artist. Artists who rely on private symbol systems have to find some way of communicating their system and relating it to an audience. W.B. Yeats tried to explain his system in a separate book (*A Vision*), for example, but his deep involvement with Irish politics and mythology makes his poetry speak to an audience. T.S. Eliot insisted that every poet borrows from and depends on other poets. The same is true of painters and composers. Techniques such as perspective, symbols drawn from religion, the harmonic patterns and the folk motifs of music all indicate the extent to which artists and their audience share symbolic resources that transcend the particular works of art that embody them. They constitute a community of symbolic understandings in which audience and artist alike share. Such a shared community is not independent of the works of art that it produces and that in turn spread its influence, but it is not limited to them either.

A different resource in the artist–audience relation is found in the forms of address that are at work. Artists do not address their audience in their own persona but in that of an artist. The historical personage who creates works of art may be petty or manipulative, politically reactionary or revolutionary or both at different times. None of that necessarily dictates the persona that the artist presents to an audience. That persona, not the "real" person, creates the aesthetic possibilities. The form of address says, in effect, "I" am the author or presenter of this work. My existence is as real as the work itself. When the historical artist becomes the persona as well, as sometimes happens, the historical person as much as the artistic persona is transformed. In some art forms, it is not uncommon for the artist to be more important than the work. One thinks of some romantic poets, for example, or of someone like Oscar Wilde (1854–1900), whose public presentation was deeply influenced by what he took to be his artistic role. Wilde dressed as a dandy and called attention to himself as if he were his own work of art. The object of such personal transformations is to utilize the possibilities of artistic address to create a common ground with an audience that will support works of art. Sometimes the result is that the artist is more interesting than any particular work of art he or she produces.

One of the common features of modern aesthetics is the rise to prominence of the concept of an artist as a persona capable of creating an audience. This is seen clearly in the tendency of some artists to also become the heroes of their own work. A classical aesthetics based on participation tended to diminish the presence of the artistic persona, though an artist was still necessary. The seer, the singer, and the bard were all based on an artistic persona that transcended the actual person. However, their common understanding of that role as one that sought union with some essential otherness – a unification of the artist, audience, and object in an aesthetic experience – precluded the artist from appearing in person.

The individuality stressed by theories of aesthetic expression reverses that role. The novelist begins to appear on stage to direct the action, and gradually the very idea of being an artist becomes the subject-matter as well as the means for communication. James Joyce's *Portrait of the Artist as a Young Man* (1916) provides a clear example. Joyce transforms his own experience into that of his hero, Stephen Dedalus, and the heroic action toward which the novel moves is the transformation of Stephen into a novelist – something that is taking place before our eyes in the novel itself. That kind of reflexivity carries the creation of artist as persona to its aesthetic limits.

Much the same thing can be said about the audience, however. Audiences also have their own role to play, and by acting as audience they create a community that makes possible the presentation. Consider the existence of a theater as a center of classical drama. The theater is a civic monument (along with the stadium). It creates a common place and testifies to a coming together for a common purpose. Drama is created for that audience specifically. Greek tragedy was written for a festival competition. Elizabethan drama was written for a mixed audience, a place where the new city dweller and the aristocrat could share a space. The early movie theaters broke down class lines by providing a darkened space in which dress and social distinction disappeared from view, and the movies shown fit that audience. Outside those spaces, the members of an audience each had their own lives and personalities. Together, they constituted an audience that transcended the particular works of art shown. The recent move first to theater in the round and more recently toward forms of audience participation show the continuing possibilities of an audience projecting a persona that creates a relation with artists.

The example of the theater extends easily to other forms as well. The novel is to some extent a product of the demands of an audience that reads in a private setting. Now video is changing the forms and expectations applied to movies. The ability to reproduce music changes music. Through the technical ability to record and mix music at will, we now have music that exists only on the compact disk. Once the audience becomes a private audience, the forms change to meet that audience's expectation. The artist and performer no longer appear in a public performance. The very idea of a public performance as the standard for musical performance is changed. An aesthetic theory must account for the whole range of artist–audience relations. One limitation on both the classical aesthetics of participation and imitation and the modern aesthetic theories based on expression and creativity is that they do not take account of all of the possibilities that recent technologically influenced art forms present, nor of the extent to which an ephemeral, popular art based on the artist and performance have supplanted the timeless expectations of classical and modern art.

The dehumanization of art

Thus far we have been exploring the way in which artists and their audiences depend on common symbol systems and understandings of their roles. They share a community in which their artistic expectations can be realized. That shared community can be extended to nature by what we have called the humanization of nature. A different relation exists when artists take as their role a self-conscious separation from a shared community. Then the artist becomes the avant-garde, and we find the "dehumanization" of art.

The perceived problem is this. Aesthetic experience and true art are never ordinary. There is thus a competition between art and the impulses of human community. The community is founded on the need for stable order and demands that, within limits, everyone "fit in." Its values are the values of common life. Whatever is disruptive must be controlled, limited, or eliminated. Communication takes place on that basis. But art and aesthetic experience are not like that. They cannot be limited by rules or by the expectations and values of a pre-existing harmony. So a true artist is by nature an outsider. Artists form an advance guard that must always be disconnected from the culture and society that it precedes. When the avant-garde falls back into conformity, it loses its function. It becomes imitative, domesticated, even antithetical to true art. Since the human is the normal condition, art must be dehumanized in order to be art. Communication is less important to the avant-garde than shock. Rather than sharing a common message and understanding, the avant-garde sees itself as breaking up established communication so that art can exist in the space left behind. Such art is by nature esoteric: it appeals only to small group of like-minded people. If that implies a negative, anti-social force, so be it. It is only negative from the standpoint of the ordinary world that is being left behind.

The insistence on the otherness of art and the artist finds its expression in a form of philosophy that also perceives the external physical world as essentially non-human and thus non-caring in terms of human values. In the face of that inhumanity, people are forced into conformity and defensiveness. They create culture and society to hide the lack of meaning in the universe itself. The artist, however, cannot hide from the truth. So instead of losing himself or herself in the collective defense, the artist seizes the lack of humanity and finds in it art's possibility. For example, just those mechanical and meaningless elements of industry and language that seem most distant from art as it is popularly understood become the basis for the avant-garde art of the futurist painters and writers. The machine, war, sex, free forms and even formlessness become the only true forms of art. The impetus for this kind of movement is the paradoxical sense that only that which is neither human nor art in its domesticated sense can be truly art.

Since the dynamics of art and audience demand that some audience be found at the very time that the possibility of a real audience is being denied, avant-garde movements frequently generate byproducts in the form of manifestos, programs, and small circles of artists who take pride in their difference. They become their own audience, and anyone who begins to become too popular or commercially successful is suspect and is expelled from the group. This phenomenon can be seen in many of the movements in painting in the nineteenth and twentieth centuries and in such literary movements as futurism and surrealism. Surrealists, for example, look to dreams and random combinations of words for their artistic models just because those are the areas that do not conform to the discipline of wakeful consciousness. Surrealists then claim access to a different reality, a "surreality," that only they can appreciate. One of the interesting features of the denial of the ordinary by movements such as surrealism is that the manifestos and the artists frequently are more interesting than their art. Art as a product drops out, and talk about aesthetic experience and the interaction of the individual with a group become the ends of the movement.

The dehumanization of art in this sense is a product of increasing industrialization and an existential loss of belief in transcendent values. If God, or the One, or humanity or honor are real, then one can at least hope to find some way to understand them through art. That hope sustained both classical and modern artists. In contrast, if existence is only a rapidly shifting point in a time that is moving nowhere and there are no transcendent beings or ideas, then art is only possible on the basis of a realistic assessment of human capabilities that appears to many as despair. To those who experience this loss of cultural faith, the modern world seems to have come to an end, and we have entered a new period that can only be called postmodern. This postmodern existential angst and loss of faith has its counterparts in earlier cultures, however.

There always seems to have been a tendency for art to break the confines of the culture that it creates and to which it belongs. Classically, tragedies whose purpose is to affirm community values in the face of divine inscrutability and individual suffering are paired with satyr plays that allowed rebelliousness and disorder to erupt. If Homer (eighth century BCE) and Virgil (70–19 BCE) celebrate the founding of civilization, the explicit love poems of the lesbian Sappho (sixth century BCE) and the decadent Catullus (84–54 BCE) defy convention. As Friedrich Nietzsche pointed out in the nineteenth century, the civilizing impulses of Apollo are countered by the frenzy of Dionysus. Classical art is at once the source of divine inspiration and a threat that must be censured and subordinated to reason. Artists seem always to require an audience, but they are never allowed to simply satisfy that audience. An audience looks to artists for insight, but they are always repulsed as well as fascinated by what they come to see because artists will not be limited by their cultural restrictions. Art is a threat as well as a consolation.

Conclusions

We began this section by re-examining communication and the conditions that are necessary for an artist to communicate with an audience.

The model is linguistic communication, which presupposes shared symbols and mutually agreed attempts at understanding. The work of art is thought of as a means to connect artist and audience. The aesthetic situation is more complex than that, however. Artists try to create the kind of audience that they need, and audiences demand the work that they desire. Out of that dialectic, the conditions for art are formed.

If no artist is present, one must be invented. Nature becomes aesthetic by being humanized. Common cultural symbols make possible but also restrict what artists do and audiences understand. The actual artists are less important than the artistic persona that they create. Sometimes an artistic persona actually replaces the work of art, or the artist becomes the hero of the work. The audience too must be created, and the form of the audience dictates the form of the work of art and thus what artists can do.

In place of the communicative model, avant-garde art plays upon the tension between artist and audience. Art is potentially disruptive and threatening to the common assumptions of an audience. Art must be "dehumanized" in the sense that ordinary humanity is at odds with the kind of separate, open experience that art requires. So avant-garde artists feel that they must oppose society and shock it. They turn to small groups, their own audience, in place of the cultural audience that more traditional artists strive to address.

The relation between artist and audience is thus always tense. Critically, each contests the field for authority. If aesthetic experience is a form of pleasure, then an audience cannot be wrong. If the audience is pleased, no amount of artistic scolding can shake the immediate evidence of its pleasure. Every generation knows its music is best. But equally, artists insist on their ability to break the rules. They do not so much satisfy an audience as transform it and make it into their own image. Picasso is supposed to have replied to the objection that his portrait of Gertrude Stein did not resemble her: "But it will." No artist is prepared to surrender to the demands of an audience if they conflict with his or her vision. Euripides wrote tragedies that violated all of the rules of tragic composition. Abstract painters stood academic, realistic painting on its head by abandoning all pretense of painting beautiful scenes that could be recognized by someone. Contemporary music refuses to be tonal or even listenable to. Somewhere in the tension between the audience's demands that an artist be comprehensible and the artist's claims to be a new source of insight, a meeting takes place.

The result is not neat. The avant-garde tends to produce kitsch – the kind of pseudo-art that is of interest only to its own producers. Culture is threatened by such junk. The establishment tends to imitate itself.

Every Broadway play begins to look like every other one as success determines what gets produced. Every movie is judged by its box-office take. But art finds a way, and audiences and artists tend to emerge. That is one reason why art tends to be associated with relatively small-scale groups and movements. Art on the kind of national and international scale demanded by today's economy is very difficult. But Virginia Woolf and the other writers associated with Bloomsbury, or the school of impressionist painters that grew up in Europe, or the southern writers associated with Robert Penn Warren and Alan Tate, manage to support each other at the same time as they form a new taste and style that is gradually freed from their insularity. Any aesthetic theory must account not only for the ways in which artists and audiences depend on each other but also for the messiness and changeableness of their relation as they form and reform their relationship. We must now see how basic aesthetic theories have tried to accomplish that task.

Mythopoesis: Myth and Ritual

Imitation, expression, and imagination give us a rough categorization of aesthetic theories. Under the influence of anthropology and psychology, new ways of understanding the philosophical problems of aesthetics appeared near the beginning of the twentieth century. Anthropology probed our cultural past, and psychology uncovered the hidden past in our individual psyches. As sciences, anthropology, together with studies of folklore and history, and psychology and psychoanalytical theory showed us how the cultural artifacts that make up the art world were shaped. A school of literary studies focused on myth and ritual, and its influence spread to studies of all of the arts.

Myth and ritual

One consequence of these studies was to show us that myth is not simply wild tales about the gods or false stories that no modern person would believe. Myth has always involved ways of telling stories that had special significance. Myths change history into significant history. They tell how things were in the beginning, and thus how they *must* be now. Myths can be so old that their origins are lost in prehistory, but they can also grow up within our own history. One of the functions of myth is to select from among ordinary events those that have lasting significance beyond their specific time and place. Thus myth frees events from historical time and locates them in a time that can be revisited.

Stories, poems, plays, music, painting, and even architecture embody myth.

Likewise, ritual is not just the religious observances of a particular religion. Ritual acts out myth, shows it, so to speak. So there are ritual elements in poems and plays as well as festivals and performances. Ritual allows someone to repeat the myth in a way that appropriates its meaning. In one sense, ritual is always a repetition of a previous act, and it is related to myth because myth provides the story or instructions that make the repetition possible. In another sense, ritual is always changing. Every repetition is also a new occurrence, so ritual is a way of making the myth new and even of allowing it to change. Variations in myth and ritual do not disqualify them from remaining the one true story that they tell. In one version, the daughter of the king may be sacrificed. In another, she may be spirited away by the gods. Both stories are the same in that they retain the significance of the origin and the establishment of some pattern of events that gives meaning to ordinary existence. Myth is controlled by its significance, not by facts.

Aesthetics is interested in these elements of myth and ritual because they apply to a wide range of art forms and account for a fundamental relation between an artist and an audience. Every work of art is different. As we have seen, however, originality need not be a virtue. Difference can be regarded as a failure to grasp the essential elements. Myth and ritual hold to the center and allow different works to exhibit variations without losing that center. For aesthetic theory, theories of myth and ritual account for the elusive commonalty between different art forms. That means that individual artists are important not for their individuality but for their common grounding in the myths of a culture. The myths provide a common place that can be shared by audience and artist. Neither artist nor audience is able to exist without that common space, and with it neither is able to dominate the other. The old stories, the true stories, are already implicitly known. The function of the storyteller or the painter, the sculptor or the dramatist is to make them available at a particular time and place to a particular audience that is prepared to participate in them.

Thus aesthetic theory that understands the artist–audience relation primarily in mythic terms looks back to the classical models of participation and communal existence for its justification. It explicates aesthetic experience in terms of elements that are shared by artist and audience, so it looks for common elements in works of art as well. For example, a hero, no matter how different from other heroes, will be seen as sharing a common pattern with them. Heroes conform to a heroic model set out in the myths that a culture takes as basic. Individual heroes are recognizable by their conformity to an archetypal pattern. Jesus, Moses, and George Washington all have similar kinds of stories told about their childhood, for example. Then new figures conform to those patterns, so literature and drama are understood to present Jesus figures or a Washington type. For aesthetic theories based on myth and ritual studies, the emphasis is on common themes, and that in turn makes possible the shared understanding of an artist and an audience.

This kind of aesthetic theory is called mythopoetic because it uses theories of myth and the origins of language and poetry to account for how artists and audiences can share in something that is more meaningful and important than either. As aesthetic theory, mythopoesis fits best with classical literature, art, and sculpture. However, it is not limited to them. The origin of new art forms can be understood as mythopoetic renewal. For example, the rise of the novel in the eighteenth century gives us new forms of storytelling in the mythic tradition. Henry Fielding's *Tom Jones* is one of the most important early novels that helps to shape the new form. Its central character, Tom Jones, can easily be understood as a kind of everyman, a modern Adam. Similar examples could be drawn from painting and drama.

Mythopoetic theory need not make explicit use of concepts such as myth and ritual. Rhetorical theories that emphasize metaphor, irony, and other linguistic and symbolic possibilities share an account of the commonalty of artist and audience through language. The essential element is that neither artist nor audience is regarded as an independent agent. They are regarded as meeting and depending on some structural possibility either in the basic order of things (myth) or in language or culture. While an artist may be the specific agent responsible for a work of art, what that artist does is a product of metaphysical or linguistic or cultural forces. The significance of the work of art produced comes from its revelatory powers in respect of those forces. Audiences are defined not in relation to economic or individual desires but by their ability to participate with an artist in a common perception.

Psychological theories and their deconstruction

A number of interesting variations on structural and anthropological theories of myth have been influential as aesthetic theories. Instead of looking for the structural possibilities in myth itself or in some metaphysical version of myth and ritual, one can look inward and find the patterns in the psychology common to humans. We have, it is said, a collective unconscious that we share as a result of either our genetic make-up or our mental development. That unconscious finds expression in dreams and myths, but it also can be controlled and exploited by artists who are particularly sensitive to its possibilities. An artist exhibits for an audience that which the audience already shares by virtue of its collective unconscious. The common patterns that can be seen culturally and cross-culturally – the similarities that appear in stories that can have no real historical connection – are accounted for by the psychological factors at work in our impulse to account for our own place in the cosmos by means of our deepest psychological images. Our imagination is freed so that a work of art is almost non-essential once it has released our imaginations. Audience and artist share a deep psychological union that is more basic than any specific form of art.

The mythopoetic theories described so far all depend on structural similarities to account for how one knows an aesthetic experience and how one distinguishes some experiences as aesthetic from others. More recently, the ability to recognize those structural similarities has come to seem to many theorists a product of a particular time and culture. The logic of myth looks to origins and repetition. Mythopoetic theories of a collective unconscious or of a deep psychology depend on a concept of individual minds as thinking machines. Even the earlier idealists who viewed art as a shared thinking of creative thoughts depended on mental models that link language, thought, and mind. What, one might ask, is to decide between these competing models themselves? How is one to judge the way we think when judging itself is thinking?

A possible answer is to look to the freedom of play and to "deconstruct" theory itself by playing off one theory against another. The idea is that not even our ways of thinking can claim to be absolute, so we must find ways to let thinking itself go beyond the bounds of logic and metaphysics. For example, myth and ritual and their successors in psychoanalytic theory model their theory on speech. Philosophy itself has its origins in spoken forms, especially the dialogues based on Socrates' debates. In considering communication, our model was the spoken word. In order to uncover the hidden presuppositions in such aesthetic theory and philosophizing, it is not enough to point them out because the pointing is still bound by the model. Instead, speech must be opposed by writing. The written word has an independence of its source that opens it to other interpretations. As written language, it continues to exist after it is no longer spoken. The emphasis shifts from a fixed meaning that depends on the intention of the speaker to a fluid meaning that depends on a reader and what he or she can make of a text.

Deconstruction requires that we expose the structural presuppositions as nothing more than variations, none of which is essential. Consider, for example, the dependence of myth on stories of the origin of things.

These stories have their parallel in our individual psyches in terms of our own origins, which are exemplified in impulses as simple as our desire to know our genealogy and our celebration of our birthdays. As such, they provide cultural expression to a conservative order that is essentially unchanging. But they are stories, and stories can be varied infinitely. So we might shift the story from a patriarchal to a matriarchal form. Then we might play one story off against another so that neither can be taken as absolute or final. Such techniques of change, variation, and retelling are powerful ways to deconstruct and reconstruct myth. Examinations of gender, of logic, and of language are intended not only to uncover old structures and suggest new structures but also to show how limited any structure is. Instead of one myth replacing another, which was the traditional structuralist pattern, myth itself is modified and made flexible. The danger of traditional theory is always that, like Narcissus, we will fall in love with our own image and fail to recognize it as an image in the water that is constantly changing and lacks permanence. Deconstruction protects us from that mistake by shattering the single image into many different images, none of which is the sole correct one.

The point of this playfulness and breaking of boundaries is not unlike that of the earlier dehumanization of art by an avant-garde. It is an antitheoretical form of theory that sees its function as creating a space for art without restricting art to the intentionality of either an artist or an idealized audience. At the same time, deconstruction must be fully engaged by its subject-matter if it is not to become merely destructive games. Nero is reputed to have fiddled while Rome burned, and the futurists' love for war and the machine was swallowed up in two world wars. The techniques of deconstruction require immense learning if they are not to be equally superficial. When that learning is brought to bear on the present art world, deconstruction frees both artist and audience to meet in a new engagement. When that learning is absent, the game degenerates into a kind of linguistic exhibitionism. But even that claim must be viewed ironically.

The limits of mythopoesis

We have ranged over quite different theories, many of which are not just incompatible but even antithetical. Each paradigm sees the alternatives as an enemy to be rejected. From a standpoint within one myth, any other myths must be explained in terms of the dominant myth. Our primary forms of explanation, scientific theories, also function as if they were myths. We use them to explain the "mistakes" in the pseudo-science of mythical cultures. (Nothing in the previous sentence should be taken to mean that science is not correct to explain things as it does. That is just the point; even correctness can only be asserted from some standpoint.) What counts as explanation is dictated by the fundamental paradigm of a culture. Traditional myths gained their power from their closeness to our psychological needs. Science is such a strong explanatory system because it can appeal to observations and empirical evidence that are hard to deny.

A politics of aesthetics emerges. The deeper difficulty in all mythopoetic theories – whether they look explicitly to myth and ritual or substitute some other account of the artist–audience relation – is that they require us to accept theoretical terms that are not themselves subject to testing. Consider myth itself. Myth is at once true and false. It is false if regarded from the standpoint of either ordinary experience or science. If one objects that things did not happen that way – that George Washington did not cut down the cherry tree – one will be told that facts do not matter, that one has missed the significance of the story. Myth is true because it is about something that is not supposed to be directly accessible in the "profane" world. Only by entering the myth does one understand. But then nothing can challenge the truth-claim. In *Parables and Paradoxes*, Franz Kafka's parablist noted:

> Concerning this a man once said: Why such reluctance? If you only followed the parables you yourselves would become parables and with that rid of all your daily cares.
> Another said: I bet that is also a parable.
> The first said: You have won.
> The second said: But unfortunately only in parable.
> The first said: No, in reality: in parable you have lost.

A truth that cannot be challenged places the theory beyond testing; but that will never convince those who inhabit the myth. To satisfy the conditions imposed by reality is to lose the myth.

Psychological theories in aesthetics are equally untestable. This is a particular problem for theories that claim to be based on empirical research. The path to the unconscious is never direct. The stories, dreams, and personal accounts that make up the data of psychoanalytic aesthetics have to be interpreted, but the interpretations are either based on the stories, in which case the theories are circular, or based on models of the human mind that require independent explanation. It is often difficult to tell the psychological accounts of aesthetic phenomena from the phenomena that they purport to interpret.

Even the earlier idealist accounts that ask only that one rethink the intuitions of the author run up against the dual problem that the intuitions are only available in the forms in which they have been embodied and that they are supposed to refer to thoughts that cannot be independently observed. It is attractive to believe that as an aesthetic participant who has an experience of some work of art one is in direct contact with the artist – that the thoughts that the artist had continue to exist in the work, to be reawakened by a sympathetic audience. Yet surely a confusion invades such theories. Thoughts, whatever their status, are not the same kind of things as works of art. Because both thoughts and aesthetic objects are intentional objects (i.e. they both require that someone is conscious of them for them to be fully present), the confusion is easy to fall into. But thoughts belong to the thinker in ways that works of art do not. Unless some account can be given of how ideas can be captured by works as different as novels, paintings, musical compositions, and buildings, the theory of ideal re-presentation is little more than praise for an aesthetic mystery.

Even the playfulness and iconoclasm of deconstructionist, poststructural aesthetics fail to sustain its theoretical pretensions (which in spite of its protestations, it certainly does have). Here one is caught on the horns of a dilemma. If the anti-absolutism and playfulness succeed, then nothing of theoretical interest has been accomplished. If instead they become theory, then their own denial of theory reduces them to a kind of authoritarianism. Denying that claims can be defended in the traditional ways, one is left either with no defense at all or with a defense that becomes political and coercive. (In the seventeenth century, the rationalism of René Descartes (1596–1650) faced a similar problem. If all people are equally rational and capable of recognizing truth by the light of nature alone, then those who deny the truth can only be doing so perversely. They must be forced to acknowledge their error. The step from granting equality to everyone to claiming that everyone who differs is unenlightened is all too short.) If I am not allowed to persuade by argument, and yet must persuade in order to establish the relation between artist and audience that aesthetics requires, only one alternative is left – coercion.

Conclusions

Myth and ritual have both anthropological and psychological forms. Myth is a telling of stories that are culturally significant, and ritual allows those stories to be re-enacted and actualized. Thus they create a place in which artist and audience can meet, a shared set of symbols, and an account of the significance of aesthetic experience. Psychological theories give similar accounts of how we share symbols and significance on an individual level. These theories are based on science and structural descriptions of cultures and of individual psyches. They are most clearly applicable as part of a theory of imitation, but they can also be adapted to theories based on expression or imagination. For example, idealist theories that understand aesthetic experience as a repetition of the thoughts of an artist in the audience provide a kind of demythologized version of mythic repetition.

Mythopoetic theories depend on our ability to describe structure psychologically or anthropologically. They are in constant danger of making their own structural constructs primary, however. Deconstruction turns to play and reflective retelling to show a relativity of thought that cannot be directly described because to do so would involve making some new structure primary. Even deconstructed mythopoetic theory cannot escape the problems of mythopoesis, however. In trying to describe basic structures of reality, myth places those structures beyond criticism. They are stories, but empirical testing of them is impossible because the link between truth and significance has been broken. As myth, or as descriptions of a psychological unconscious, they are acknowledged as false or unreachable by normal, conscious standards. That is just their purpose. So one is left with no way to challenge different versions of the myth or different unconscious forces.

These criticisms point us back to a more concrete, historical kind of relation between artist and audience. However, they should not be taken as ending the debate. Mythopoesis and its more modern and postmodern successors continue to offer two theoretical advantages. They account for the significance of aesthetic phenomena in terms of the human world. By looking for the point at which artist and audience are united, we are led to understand the reasons why we care about our aesthetic worlds. They define our cultures and our humanity. At the same time, myth, language, the mind, and culture are presented as the central aesthetic terms. Surely this is at least partially correct. These are in fact the kinds of things that we must understand if an aesthetic theory is to be defended.

Institutional and Post-Institutional Aesthetics

The alternative to understanding the relation of artist and audience in mythopoetic terms is to place them in an historical setting that is conditioned by non-aesthetic forces. The initial attempts at recasting aesthetics in empiricist terms in the seventeenth and eighteenth centuries followed the models of the successful scientific empiricism of the time and the philosophical recasting of knowledge in terms of experience alone. Aesthetic phenomena were recognized primarily as feelings and emotions. The task of philosophical aesthetics as it was conceived by early empiricists was to make room for feelings and emotions in our whole scheme of experience. The final step in modernist aesthetics was to adopt psychology as the science most appropriate to aesthetics. That gave us the theories of aesthetic attitudes, psychical distance, and aesthetic perception that formed the central strands of twentieth-century aesthetics.

We have seen that, in a number of ways, that initial empiricism was too simple. The natural sciences could identify their phenomena in theory-neutral ways, at least for practical purposes. Aesthetics could not. The move to psychological models only made the situation worse because psychology itself had difficulty describing mind, consciousness, and emotion. The basic insight that aesthetic experience can only be understood in terms of theories that can withstand empirical criticism cannot be lost, however.

In particular, history provides an alternative model to the natural sciences for aesthetic explanation. History begins with a story, as does myth. The story told by history, however, must be grounded in evidence and specific events. Moreover, every historical event is unique. None is repeatable. The inability to conduct repeatable experiments in historical investigation requires a different approach from that of the natural sciences, but it is no less empirical. Aesthetics is increasingly located in specific historical contexts. That justifies considering aesthetic theory as an empirical discipline like history.

An historical art world

From the standpoint of historical experience, the relation of artist and audience is part of a life world and an art world conditioned by emergent historical conditions. These conditions can be studied historically and their influence traced in their results. They create an art world, and that art world in turn shapes the aesthetic responses of artist to audience and audience to artist. Artist and audience are related directly to each other as well as being related by their joint relation to a work of art. All of the factors that are covered by various mythopoetic theories are still operative.

Consider first the intersubjective relation in which an artist is an artist for an audience and an audience is defined by its relation to artists. In mythopoetic terms, this relation is understood primarily as a meeting of consciousness. It may be metaphysically participatory, or it may be cast in terms of psychological possibilities. Even the deconstructed openness remains essentially psychological in the way it regards meaning. The metaphysical version tells us how an artist and audience share a common sacred or special reality. The psychological version tells us how an artist and audience are able to share either a common collective unconscious, some cultural equivalent to that, or a common set of mental representations. The conditions of conscious meeting are those imposed by the ideas and mental possibilities of artist and audience, even if some of those conditions remain beneath the level of consciousness. Such a meeting does not take place in time but "out of time" or "once upon a time." Every reading, every viewing, every performance is a repetition that retains the original identity of the singular work of art. But from the standpoint of an empiricist history, every aesthetic event is unique and different. Occurring in history, no two aesthetic events can ever be precisely the same. Consciousness either is reducible to psychological behavior or is a concealed way of describing actions and beliefs that exist in historically conditioned situations. To find common elements, one must examine not the event but the causal chain of events that produced it. Sameness is provided by similar event-chains or common ancestors, not by identity of minds.

Historical similarity depends on our analysis of cause and effect. The most important of the historical conditions with respect to artists and their audience was, for a long time, patronage. Patronage defines a relation in which the patron is the primary audience and the artist responds to the patron's commission, often in ways that stretch the relationship beyond what was originally expected. The patron creates the conditions for art. For example, Pope Julius II commissioned Michelangelo to undertake the decoration of the Sistine Chapel ceiling. The patron sets the conditions for performance and makes the work possible by paying for it. Equally importantly, the patron gives a status to the work being done. To be selected is already a mark of distinction and a way of giving status to the work that will be produced. But a patron does not control the process. Frequently, as in the case of Michelangelo's Sistine Chapel paintings, the work exceeds all expectations. It changes the conditions that patronage had established.

Patronage takes many forms. In western art the church began actively promoting the arts as part of its mission of communicating dogma and enhancing its religious status in the early middle ages, but similar relations of church and artists appear in Roman and Byzantine contexts as well. Monarchs and princes were patrons of the arts for the same kinds of reasons. By commissioning works of art, the royal figure could exhibit his or her legitimacy and power. Art provided status. It exhibited the riches and reach of the patron. It also carried both an explicit and implicit message. Explicitly, it told the stories (in paintings, poems, chronicles, and songs) that placed the patron in the best light. It provided a history in which the patron was placed in relation to the past and future states. If one did not have an appropriate set of ancestors, one had to invent them. Or art taught a moral lesson, and by implication the patron became a moral exemplar. Implicitly, art exhibited the power of a patron as a source of public good and munificence. Only those who had attained a certain status could be patrons.

From the artist's side, patronage provided both economic means and an assured audience. As an artist, one knew who one was working for and what one's resources were. If the Duke of Milan wanted the largest bronze horse in the world, Leonardo da Vinci would try to find a way to make it for him. But in the process, Leonardo had a creative freedom that a more precarious existence would have denied him. If one must worry about one's next meal, then one cannot afford to fail. One must play it safe. An artist with a powerful patron could experiment as long as the patron was kept satisfied. The patronage relation between artist and audience was often mutually beneficial and conferred much more freedom than a purely autonomous artist could have enjoyed on his or her own.

Of course, the relation of patron and artist could also be limiting. Artists were kept in their place by such a system. A counterbalance could be provided by guilds and craft unions. These at least provided some common protection for artists. They also provided control and group discipline. One had to have the approval of one's peers as well as of one's patrons. There was, in effect, a body that certified that someone was an artist. That kind of authority is needed if an art world is to function. Artists could also play one patron off against another, much as athletes now depend on team or club owners but can often bargain their way to better deals.

Patronage was not limited to church and prince, however. As new economic forces came into play, new sources of patronage became available. One might look at the portraits that became important in the seventeenth and eighteenth centuries, for example. They are not all of princes and cardinals. Increasingly, a Rembrandt (1606–69) or a Joshua Reynolds (1723–92) painted prominent citizens who wanted to perpetuate their own images, exhibit their new status, and provide a family history. Reynolds' technique incorporated the self-conscious use of classical and heroic models to give his portraits increased status. Somewhat the same impulse lay behind landscape painting, which was often in effect a portrait of an estate. One of the great eighteenth-century English painters, George Stubbs (1724–1806), made his career principally by painting portraits of horses for their proud owners.

Gradually, patronage was replaced by other economic support systems. However, it continues to play a role. It can be seen at work in architecture, where corporations and public bodies play the role of patron. A corporate headquarters is not simply a utilitarian building. It is designed to exhibit just those qualities that made patronage important: power, stability, legitimacy, and the standing of the corporation in the community. Powerful collectors remain a force in establishing artistic reputations. What has changed in that respect is the idea of collection as an end in itself. Public art continues to be controversial in part because it does always have an agenda. The demand for artistic freedom at the same time as an artist accepts public support mirrors the old struggle between the expectations of a patron and the need for an artist to advance his or her own artistic agenda.

Patronage is not the only way that an artist and an audience are related in historical terms. More or less at the same time as empiricism was shifting the basis for philosophy to individual experience and science was shifting from a holistic, organic approach to a mechanistic model based on chains of cause and effect, the economic basis for the relation of artist and audience was also shifting. More of the economic power was in the hands of a middle class; money replaced land in economic importance; cities replaced the country; industry replaced agriculture; religious individualism replaced a single unified church. One result of this economic upheaval was to redefine the importance of artists in relation to their audience. Where patronage was essentially personal and direct, so that the artist was effectively an extension of the patron, the alternative cast the artist in the role of a free entrepreneur with a product to sell. The consuming public made correspondingly different demands. Leisure and literacy produced time and a taste for art, particularly new forms such as the novel and popular drama, including melodrama. Painting, sculpture, and building appealed to a wider but much more nebulous audience. Music had to attract audiences by its popular appeal rather than by its courtly or ecclesiastical function. Even the relative security of church music had to appeal to a wider audience as different religious options became more widely available.

The results of this new relation included new forms of art and new forms of presentation. Art was going to be more successful if it could be widely disseminated, and this favored some forms such as the novel over other, more intimate forms such as sonnets addressed to one's beloved. Alliances and animosities between artists and critics arose as the competition for defining an audience response determined success or failure. Critics could exist as independent professionals because consumers of art sought guidance in what they should buy and how they should understand it. Artists came increasingly to be regarded as individuals. From that individuality arose a sense of the artist as an isolated, autonomous being. That artistic role redefined the audience as well. Increasingly, aesthetic experience was private rather than public. It was considered genuine only if it was based directly on contact with the artist rather than with a community of shared symbols.

Most importantly, artists operated as free agents in an aesthetic marketplace where success was determined by popular demand. In this respect, artists became like other entrepreneurs with a product to sell and an audience became a buying public. The public was always right because it could not be wrong when 'right' was defined by what the public taste approved. Aesthetic experience meant having a personal, private emotional experience; that could not be challenged. What the public approved must be good because 'good' aesthetically meant being able to produce certain kinds of feelings. The autonomy of the artist and the incorrigibility of the audience fit perfectly with an aesthetic theory built on taste, genius, and sense.

The concept of fine art arose out of these new demands. In the course of the seventeenth and eighteenth centuries, a distinction between fine art and the popular arts on the one hand and craft on the other arose to give value to the new realm of aesthetic feeling. To some extent, the distinction was implicit in many earlier aesthetic situations. It was always possible to distinguish between high and low art. Aristotle made such distinctions when he placed poetry above history because of poetry's greater universality, and when he placed tragedy above comedy because comedy dealt with "low" situations while tragedy dealt with human beings above the average. In the modern European world, however, the distinction was codified in cultural institutions and recognized as theoretically important.

The distinction of fine art from other forms of making intended for an audience fits perfectly with the aesthetic situations produced by artists as independent producers and audiences understood as passive consumers of art. In that situation, the ability to distinguish some kinds of art from others depends on the make-up and taste of the audience. A refined audience prefers poetry to popular song, symphonies to martial music, serious drama to puppet shows, mimes, and jugglers. We know that some art is "fine" because of who it appeals to, and we know who that audience is because of its economic and social status. Patrons had no need for the distinction because they commissioned the work directly. But in a competitive situation that was also subjectively diverse, some way of distinguishing good from bad in generic terms had considerable utility. Thus there was an alliance between the empiricist aesthetics that arose with modern philosophy and the way that artists and audiences redefined their mutual interdependence in economic terms.

The result was aesthetic theory that elevated some responses to the status of aesthetic experience and reduced others to the status of mere ordinary pleasure and interested self-satisfaction. Aesthetics attempted, as we have seen, to isolate and identify a kind of experience and a corresponding kind of pleasure that were qualitatively different from other experiences and pleasures. Now, we might consider the possibility that popular culture is in the process of redressing the balance. Once again, the relation of audience and artist is being redefined, and in the process aesthetic theory is being rethought. Instead of the middle-class audience that responded to individual artists and aspired to have its artistic experience in some secondary way, mass media define an audience in terms of numbers unthinkable to traditional aesthetics. Success is measured in box-office figures that rise inexorably. For example, concerts, movies, TV programs, and popular novels gain audiences in the millions. Such forms feel no need for the distinction of fine art because their success is palpably measurable in other terms. Their influence is felt in more traditional art world institutions as well. Increasingly, museums mount blockbuster exhibitions that draw huge crowds. New symphony halls are based on mass subscriptions. Monumental art works become public projects.

Extreme new forms emerge from this new situation as artists continue to be redefined by their audiences. Pop art – the soup cans that outrage the public – and performance art – the transient art that celebrates its own impermanence – actually appeal to the very audience that they attempt to defy and shock. Andy Warhol's paintings of ordinary objects are more statement than aesthetic object in the traditional sense. When a performance artist such as Chris Burden shoots himself, his action is supposed to be the work of art, not the anguished act of an artist, as with Vincent Van Gogh lopping off an ear. It requires no special education or culture to go to a modern museum or to participate in street art. The result may offend or disturb conventional expectations, but as art, it is addressed to an essentially popular audience. Its success or failure depends in large measure on its ability to stir a response not in the elite of the art world but in the everyday, popular audience that can make it successful. The very outrage of the would-be censors is a desirable response to popular artists. The need to continue to shock raises the stakes with each new movie or play.

All of this indicates that a turn away from the aesthetic theories based on taste and individual exaltation in significant form may have been underway for some time. The result is an aesthetic theory more attuned to the institutional and historical forms of empiricism than the earlier individualist forms of the seventeenth and eighteenth centuries. In many ways, the artist and audience conspire to make the actual work of art less and less important. It is neither a timeless artifact nor a stimulus to a special experience. What is much more important is that an artist has succeeded in attracting attention to a kind of performance, and in the process that the various audiences that constitute the art world have begun to pay attention. In that context, it matters less and less that the actual product is mundane, transient, and relatively uninteresting in it-self. One does not look at soup cans or buildings wrapped in plastic because they provide some unique kind of experience. They don't. One looks at them because they fly in the face of the older expectations and, in effect, shout "look at me." So we look, and in the process of looking we allow the artist to single out a bit of the world in a different way from before. It is not beautiful, and it is not significant. But it is direct and present in a way that its utilitarian analogues are not. Perhaps that is all that art can produce in the present context and thus all that aesthetics can demand.

The role of theory

Attending to the examples provided by patronage, entrepreneurial art, and popular culture should not cause us to lose sight of our philosophical goals, however. Aesthetic theory can explain after the fact what is going on, but its task is not to predict or direct the practices of the art world. A scientific model for aesthetic theory needed such predictive confirmation. An historical model does not. History is always limited to what has been. It helps us to explain and understand our present by tracing the influences and events that brought us to that point. On an empirical, historical model, the job for aesthetic theory also is to explain and help us to understand. But aesthetic theory is not simply history. Its object is to give an account of what aesthetic phenomena are and how they are known.

As philosophers, we are concerned less with the details of aesthetic history than with the shape of aesthetics itself. Patronage, entrepreneurial support for the arts, and popular culture are not exclusive alternatives. At any time, all three could be found represented. Greek tragedy was balanced by Roman circuses. Shakespeare was a popular dramatist. All of the ways of being an artist and an audience coexist and represent different relational possibilities. At different times, the realities of economics, politics, social order, and natural resources conspire to give one or the other prominence. In different contexts, different theories for a time seem fully adequate. Just as Euclid and Ptolemy produced theories that fit for a time, only to be supplanted by Newton and Galileo, and then by Einstein and Heisenberg, so aesthetic theories that capture part of the picture may for a time seem more adequate than they are. We learn from them all. We do the best we can. But just as scientists know that their theories will eventually be replaced by better accounts, so in aesthetics better accounts will subsume older theories. And even that observation is part of an historical, empiricist view.

From the standpoint of aesthetic theory, the existence of both patronage and the kind of expectations that it created, and entrepreneurial artists and their production of an art market, is significant for what they tell us about the nature of the artist–audience relation itself. First, that relation is not simply productive. That is, it is not solely about the production of specific works of art. It is also about what kind of works can be produced, how they will be received, and even directly about what will count as works of art and who will be acknowledged as an artist at a particular time. Works of art exist in a context that is defined by the relation of producer and consumer. Aesthetic subjectivity is qualified by the existence of an art world. Now we are in a position to see how that art world is created.

Second, since more is at work than simply perceiving works of art, aesthetics is not limited to the subjective feelings that gave rise to the term 'aesthetics' in the eighteenth century or to individual forms of aesthetic experience characterized by disinterestedness. While it may be the case that many aesthetic effects are essentially emotional responses to specific works and natural objects, the situations in which aesthetic response takes place and the production of the works themselves are historical occurrences. The realities of the art world are prior to both the participatory aesthetics of classical theories and the subjective autonomy of modern theories. Aesthetic response is response to a demand that exists prior to its fulfillment and that determines who will be recognized as an artist and what will be produced to meet the demand.

Consider what happens to two key aesthetic concepts – style and taste – in the light of the facts of patronage as a factor in the construction of an art world. We think of style as a property of a work of art or, secondarily, as a characteristic of a movement or individual artist. Thus, we might say that Mozart's *Requiem* has a particular style, or that the mannerist style in painting is characterized by elaboration, or even that Vermeer has a distinctive style all his own. Style then leads us to look for the formal properties that distinguish one style from another and for the characteristic content that belongs to a particular style. In other words, we treat style as a property of works and by extension of the artists who produce the works. It is not a singular property like color. It is more like the representational properties that make something a picture of a cat or a dog depending on how the lines, shapes, and colors are arranged. We sometimes call such properties gestalt properties because they have to be seen as a whole pattern.

When we begin to think of the conditions such as patronage that set the context for production, a different aspect of style emerges, however. If I, as an artist, am to satisfy the demands of my audience, which is providing patronage, I must do at least two things. First, I must work in such a way that I actually meet the demands and can be understood to have met them. If the commission was for a painting of the last supper, it will not do to provide an abstract color panel and call it "Last Supper." However, if the commission is to decorate a room, a color panel called "Last Supper" might not only look good but also provide a status that would enhance its appeal. Second, I must not simply provide a product. Any copyist or hack could do that. What I produce must be distinctive and distinctively mine. I would especially like it to carry my mark. Together, these conditions are met by style. Even anonymous artists can be identified by their style. At one extreme, style slides back into anonymity – it becomes "the school of." At the other extreme, style becomes eccentric. It is so singular that no one knows what to make of it. In between, style pushes the limits without losing contact with the demands of the situation. Paolo Veronese (1528–88) pushed those limits when his painting of the last supper drew the attention of the Inquisition because it introduced too many secular figures into a religious painting. Jacopo Pontormo (1494–1557) lost contact with them altogether in a fresco that his contemporary, the art historian Vasari (1511–74), describes as incomprehensible.[1] Style, in this sense, is not simply a property of the work or the artist. It is a complex technical response to a problem of how artist and audience are related.

Once a style has been established, it can be commercialized. That is, it can be reproduced. The very ability to make reproductions changed the history of art and of aesthetics as well. Engravings, printing, photography, recordings, multiple prints of the same movie all allow the dissemination of a style to a wider audience. In the process, however, a style loses its relation to the situation that produced it. That is one reason why 'imitation' changes in meaning from a positive to a negative description in the course of the history of aesthetics. Style that is repeated tries to satisfy many different patrons with the same work. It loses both its distinctiveness and its audience.

1 See the appendix at the end of the book.

The history of taste follows a similar path. We think of taste as a distinctive ability of some audiences or audience members. Those who can appreciate the aesthetic characteristics of something have taste. Others lack it. Good taste is a judgment that is at once elitist and destined to be admired. Above all, taste is individual judgment and pleasure. It can be criticized, but it cannot be right or wrong because it is not about the object but about the response of the audience. So taste is to style as the audience's relation to a work is to the artist's relation to a work. Taste is the subjective side of aesthetic experience. Theories based on taste understand it as a sense or quasi-sense, perhaps qualified by an ability to be formed by experience and training. Taste is describable only in terms of the individual psychology of the perceiver. It is a mysterious "I know not what," the "it" that some people have and others do not.

Yet the kind of situations that patronage shows us change taste into a much more manageable kind of description. A patron does not depend on some private, eccentric judgment. That would never allow art to do the jobs that patronage assigns to it. Rather, a patron exhibits a taste that is on public display and is subject to public approval or scorn. What would be the point in commissioning a portrait that was so eccentric that it could not be recognized? If Picasso was to paint Gertrude Stein in a cubist style, it could only be because some prestige was attached to Picasso and cubism that made that portrait a thing worth having. Tastes change, but they do not change randomly or without reason. When a taste for novels emerged in the eighteenth century, that taste was not some whim. It was the product of a class of people who had leisure to read privately. The lovely devotional illuminations produced during the middle ages responded to a taste that was formed by the reliance of laity and clergy alike on religious consolation in a precarious existence. Taste cannot be understood as individual judgment alone. It is a way of knowing what will satisfy a particular aesthetic need.

The point of these observations is that the art world that is created by artists and audiences within specific historical situations provides a different theoretical way to understand what makes something art or some experience aesthetic. Instead of looking for characteristics of the object and its maker (imitation theories) or of the experience itself (aesthetic attitude theories, for example), one looks for the particular ways in which artists are being defined by audiences and the particular strategies that artists use to meet those expectations. Then, what one finds is a complex history of successful and unsuccessful attempts to satisfy a unique kind of relation – an aesthetic relation.

The relation is aesthetic because of the directness of its productive needs. All that is required is imagination, perception, or form. Thinking is enough to make it so. But thinking is not enough to make some actual object satisfy the demands of this aesthetic relation. That takes much more – skill, knowledge, and fitting opportunity to means. Not every attempt at art succeeds. Most probably fail. Not every patron is satisfied. Most are probably disappointed, or, if they are not, they settle for something less than the aesthetic relation called for. But sometimes artist and audience conspire to produce art, and then the relation is transcended by the work of art produced.

Post-institutional aesthetics

Many of the lessons for aesthetics that we learn from earlier theories are captured by what is sometimes called a postmodern view of subjectivity. Modern subjectivity was defined by individual minds potentially isolated from each other and the world. Its problems were how the mind could know itself, how it could be certain that there was an external world at all, and what foundations subjective ideas could provide for true theories about the world. Postmodern subjectivity does not so much deny those problems as find them misconceived in the light of our historical situation. We have neither the stable identities nor the atomic ideas that modern subjectivity held to (or perhaps inherited from earlier theories of substance and identity). Instead, our subjective identities are constantly shifting as we move through time in relation to others. Thinking is a constant play of shifting identities. The appearance of stability is not an illusion compared to some unattainable correct answer but our practical (pragmatic) resolution of our own instability. Mathematics shows us that not all equations produce a predictable set of solutions. Some are "chaotic" in that solutions are interactive. Stable patterns are local conditions that cannot be extended. Postmodern aesthetic theory is like that.

Neither audience nor artist is understood as a stable identity in this way of thinking. Each is constantly changing. We should not think of Shakespeare as simply an Elizabethan dramatist, fixed for all time by his birth, death, and English, male, western thought patterns. Shakespeare is also the dramatist who appears now with nearly four hundred years of shifting interpretations as additions to his identity. We, as audience, cannot simply transport ourselves back to the end of the sixteenth century and see Shakespeare's plays as they were seen then. Time does not allow that kind of timelessness. We are defined by the plays and their interpretations, and we add to them. Gone is any possibility of a single, correct interpretation.

Two results follow from this increased awareness of our own subjective instability. Artist and audience are even more involved in a competition.

We are reflected in the work, and that means that the artist seeks a kind of control over a future that he or she could not physically be a part of. In place of the timeless immortality of the gods or the permanent adulation of the classics, artists seek to inject themselves into a future that they cannot know. Conversely, an audience insists on its own visions. It has no reason to subordinate itself to some artist. So the artifactuality of the work is replaced by an evolving history of production and performance. Performance applies as much to reading and viewing as to listening or attending. The center is wherever the audience finds it. It is not located at some fixed point in space and time. The result is a kind of creative chaos that to the older theories looks disordered but to postmodern theory is the only way that art can continue.

In effect, everything is reduced to the level of "text." Traditionally, a text was the physical object, the poem, novel, or, by extension, the score or painting. That text was sacred, in a sense. One could get no more authentic starting-point for art. Now, however, the text is defined by the interpretation – it is whatever appears in the interpretation as the object to be interpreted. It has a changeableness that defies fixed authority. That means that whatever is interpreted is text, and text is whatever is interpreted. The only way to find an identity in that situation and avoid a vicious circularity is to follow the history of production and add to it with one's own interpretations.

This approach may seem hopelessly confused, and in one sense it is. It substitutes play for truth, independence for authority. In the process, it loses seriousness and the claims that serious interpretation imposed. One of the fundamental principles of modern aesthetics was that aesthetic judgments have the form of universals – they are not simply "for me" but implicitly "for everyone" – even if that universality is based on subjective feeling. The idea was that some subjective feeling is so basic that it escapes the personality of the one who feels it. Now postmodern aesthetics holds that aesthetic judgments are just those that, like play, are never subject to universals. They are always in the process of being changed and reformed. In effect, aesthetics becomes the celebration of subjectivity in a world that must pretend to a stability that it cannot justify.

Thus far, one might applaud the attempts of a postmodern subjectivity to reassert the aesthetic as a kind of mirror image of its modern counterpart. The problem, of course, is that while one might applaud it, one cannot assert it, and the whole enterprise tends to become a political contest to see whose interpretation will be voiced. The result is somewhat like everyone speaking and no one listening. (Deconstructionists, of course, would take issue with the implicit basis of this analogy in speaking rather than writing.) What has been forgotten in this approach to subjectivity are the conditions of communication with which we began. Speakers are defined by listeners, and that applies to artists and audiences and to writers and readers. If we are not to revert to modern theories of aesthetic experience, or go even further back to the mythical union of speaker and hearer in an organic whole, we must have some way of acknowledging that an audience is implicitly in the position of listener.

One way to accomplish that is to hold not to a single historical author who is probably not accessible (and not even "real"), but to an historical world in which identity is a product of causal relations and institutions get their authority from their ability to understand as well as from their ability to speak. The first condition suggests that an artist is defined not just by the present but by his or her entire history. That history has a beginning, and its beginning is a necessary condition for its being a history with an identity. We do not know who Shakespeare was. He could even turn out to have been Christopher Marlowe or the Earl of Oxford, though the arguments are weak. But we do know the point at which Shakespeare entered the stream of our history. The accuracy of that knowledge determines the accuracy of the whole historical chain. If I am wrong and think that Shakespeare only began to write in the eighteenth century, I lose more than just an important context. I lose the correctives that his earlier history can potentially supply.

Facts matter not because they are timeless truths but because they limit and correct what comes afterwards. They supply the boundary conditions without which even chaotic systems cannot have solutions. Thus, for example, not all interpretations of Shakespeare's plays are equally successful or equally acceptable. Recently, performances with radically modern settings have been in vogue. Richard III is a Nazi; Hamlet is a modern adolescent who appears most of the time in his pajamas. What is wrong with such interpretations is that they create an historical dislocation that threatens to lose contact with the play. Embedded in the language of a Shakespearean play are Elizabethan allusions that are not just interpreted but lost or made into nonsense by the contemporary overlay. In effect, the director and actors demand to be heard in their own voices rather than as new receptions of the play. No absolute authority should be assigned to one interpretation or even to one period's reading of the plays, but that does not mean that anything goes or that all interpretations are equally good. Some are based on a reception by an audience – a genuine transformation and reinterpretation. Others virtually replace the artist altogether with the voice of the performance. In those cases, whatever is produced is no longer part of the historical chain that justifies calling this a performance of Shakespeare.

The second condition is that institutions must gain their authority from something. The entire crowd may shout "Out!" at a baseball game, but only the umpire's voice counts. Unfortunately, that may not be because he is right is some absolute sense. The replay on television may show that the runner arrived before the ball. The umpire's decision counts because he is the umpire. He speaks for the game in that situation. The audience speaks for the game only when the audience is the source of institutional authority. In the art world, that means that an audience must be perceptive, committed to understanding, and willing to be defined by a text rather than to insist on shaping the text to itself.

We recognize an implicit difference between an interpretation and a non-interpretation of some work of art, some text. The interpretation is about something and the non-interpretation is about the one who gives it. That ability to say something that is about something else implies that one has made the effort to understand first. From that move toward understanding comes the authority to speak and thus the authority to act as some part of an art world institution. Not all interpretations are equally interesting. None is absolute, final, the truth. But some at least stand as responses. They have the relation that an audience must have if communication is to even be a possibility. That is enough to distinguish them from the self-serving utterances of pseudo-critics.

Artist and audience are thus implicitly defined by each other. Each is a necessary condition for there even being an aesthetic relation. From that aesthetic relation comes the possibility of understanding, and from the possibilities of understanding come works of art. One gets then an interlocked system in which neither art, nor artist, nor audience is independent. I call this a post-institutional aesthetic because while it adopts the institutional insight that aesthetic theory is relational and depends on the ability of some institutions to sanction conferrals of status on artists and aesthetic objects, it recognizes that postmodern subjectivity changes the nature of theory and that the art world is always an historical institution that is changing. The art world can only be described by an empirical history informed by an aesthetic theory that acknowledges the contingency of its own judgments.

Conclusions

We are led to replace the modern scientific model for aesthetics that was based on physics and then on psychology with an historical model. When we approach aesthetic phenomena in that way, we recognize the shifting influences of patronage, an entrepreneurial relation between artist and audience, and the instability of popular culture. If we focus not on the history itself but on the aesthetic theory that it makes possible, we can acknowledge the insights of a postmodern subjectivity that finds audience and artist constantly shifting their relations. But we need not despair of theory altogether, because even subjectivity relies on the conditions of listener and hearer being maintained if there is to be any artist–audience relation at all. We can then move to a version of the art world that places aesthetic theory in contact with its own history.

From the standpoint of aesthetic theory, artist and audience create an art world that is sufficient only to make possible some attempts at works of art. Those attempts may succeed or fail. The artifacts produced are not fixed points in an absolute history but the beginnings of a causal chain that continues to produce new audiences and thus new possibilities for artists and new artifacts. In that continuing history, we can choose to become part of an audience, but in doing so we cannot simply impose our own voice. To be part of an audience means to belong to a continuing art world and, as audience, to attempt to understand. When we do that, we validate our place in the art world. We gain the authority to speak only by having listened.

A Conclusion in Which Nothing is Concluded

It might seem that, having worked our way up to a postmodern aesthetics and suggested how it might be developed, we have now reached the right aesthetic theory. That misunderstands how philosophical theories work, however. First of all, a theory in the required sense is a high-level generalization. Its purpose is to provide a coherent account of the explanations that apply to specific cases and to guide further explanations as new cases arise. In a sense, theories are not true or false. They are more or less well established and more or less adequate to the cases that come under them. Any theory, scientific or philosophical, must be based on specific statements that are true. Otherwise, no theory would be possible. But though every theory will account for most of the specific true statements it deals with, no theory can claim to account for everything because more remains to come. In the words of Ludwig Wittgenstein, "The world is the totality of facts, not of things," and facts continue to be added not just from more things, but from more ways of arranging the things that already exist.

Scientific and philosophical theories should not be faulted as unproven because they are subject to doubt and change. Introducing doubt and accounting for change are among their functions. Empirically, one of the things we are most certain about is that none of our present theories will last for ever. We know that because none has so far, and there is no reason to think that we have suddenly become a different kind of thinking being from our predecessors. But that is not a reason to despair. Our theories can be based on singular facts that are true and confirmed to a degree that is more than sufficient. And they can be comprehensive in a way that advances our ability to understand. In that sense, knowledge of every theory is an improvement because it allows us to understand present theory better. Otherwise, we would not have spent so much time in this book on theories that we later subjected to counter-arguments. So wherever we have gotten to, it is merely a partial understanding – a better understanding, we hope, than that with which we began, but a partial understanding nevertheless.

What is that point? For one thing, we have seen that the two major lines of aesthetic theory – the classical theories of imitation and beauty, and the modern theories of aesthetic experience, aesthetic attitudes, and aesthetic perception – provide alternative explanations of the same phenomena: the interrelation of a productive artist with something produced that we call a work of art, the interrelation of an audience that responds to something, either art or nature, in a way that we characterize as aesthetic, and finally, a direct relation between artist and audience that makes possible both production and response. Neither alternative is complete. Imitation and beauty require a metaphysics of participation that itself requires further justification, a justification that is increasingly problematic as we become clearer about the limits of our knowledge. Aesthetic experience, attitudes, and perception require identity conditions for what it is to be aesthetic that the subjectivity of their starting-point seems to preclude. So we have had recourse to a more historical approach to try to retain the empiricism of aesthetic experience while acknowledging the extent to which a complex institution, the art world, with its practitioners on both sides, the artists and their audience, can function to create a specifically aesthetic possibility. That possibility remains undefined, however. It can be glimpsed in already existing works of art, but our analysis stops short of saying what is and what is not aesthetic. We begin to understand just how tenuous our grasp is when we see the diversity of things that popular culture has begun to include in the art world.

Perhaps we have only opened the door to confusion. Certainly sometimes postmodern subjectivity seems to allow anything at all into the art world. If that is the case, then art will collapse into itself because without a distinction between art and non-art there can be no art world distinct from the rest of the world. To some, that seems already to have happened. I am not among them. The complex of art and artists, audience and artists, and audience and art as they already exist seem to me still to be sufficient to determine, not absolutely, but functionally, that there are lines to be drawn. I may not be sure where the lines are to be drawn, and even if I am sure, I may be proven wrong by what comes next. The attempt is itself part of belonging to the art world, however. The existence of a culture demands it, and our knowledge of things in themselves, apart from their uses, supports that demand. But perhaps that is only an illusion. If so, the game is still fun to play, and part of playing it is making aesthetic judgments. Welcome to the art world.

References and Suggestions for Further Reading

The aesthetics of reception

Communication

The idea of an aesthetics of reception is prominent in the work of Hans Robert Jauss, particularly *Toward an Aesthetic of Reception* (Minneapolis: University of Minnesota Press, 1982). The presentation here does not follow Jauss explicitly, however. My analysis of communication owes something to H.P. Grice, *Studies in the Way of Words* (Cambridge, MA: Harvard University Press, 1991). The concept of speech acts is too widely used to require a specific reference, but students might begin with J.L. Austin, *How to Do Things With Words* (Cambridge, MA: Harvard University Press, 1963) and John Searle, *Speech Acts* (Cambridge: Cambridge University Press, 1969).

Conditions for receptivity

W. B. Yeats' mythology is explained in *A Vision* (New York: Macmillan, 1957), which purports to be the result of dictation by tutelary spirits. T.S. Eliot argues for a common poetic heritage in "Tradition and the Individual Talent," in *Selected Essays, 1917–1932* (London: Faber, 1932). The influence of the ability to reproduce art is the subject of Walter Benjamin's "Art in the Age of Mechanical Reproduction," in *Illuminations* (New York: Harcourt, Brace & World, 1968).

The dehumanization of art

"The dehumanization of art" and the concept of the avant-garde discussed here is based on the essay by Jose Ortega y Gassett, *The Dehumanization of Art* (New York: Doubleday, 1956). Alienation from transcendent values is the theme of Albert Camus, *The Rebel* (New York: Vintage, 1956). For the futurist manifestos, see Umberto Boccioni, "Technical Manifesto of Futurist Sculpture," and F.T. Marinetti, "Futurist Painting: Technical Manifesto, April 11, 1910," in Herschel B. Chipp, ed., *Theories of Modern Art* (Berkeley: University of California

Press, 1968). For surrealism, see André Breton, *What is Surrealism?* (London: Faber, 1936). The contrast between Apollo and Dionysus comes from Friedrich Nietzsche, *The Birth of Tragedy and the Genealogy of Morals* (Garden City, NY: Doubleday, Dell, 1956). The effects of the avant-garde on culture are the subject of Clement Greenberg's "Avant-Garde and Kitsch," in *Collected Essays* (Chicago: University of Chicago Press, 1986).

Mythopoesis: myth and ritual

Myth and ritual

The view of myth explicated here owes most to Mircea Eliade, particularly *The Myth of the Eternal Return* (Princeton: Princeton University Press, 1954). It points back to Jane Ellen Harrison's *Ancient Art and Ritual* (London: Thornton Butterworth, 1918).

Psychological theories and their deconstruction

The development of a rhetoric for literary criticism based on myth is found in Northrop Frye, *Anatomy of Criticism* (Princeton: Princeton University Press, 1957). The psychological version of myth and the idea of a collective unconscious come from the work of C.G. Jung. A specific application is found in Joseph Campbell, *The Masks of God* (New York: Viking, 1959). The move to a poststructuralist aesthetic goes back at least to Jacques Derrida's "White Mythology," *New Literary History* 6 (1974): 7–74. For deconstruction, see Jonathan Culler, *On Deconstruction: Theory and Criticism after Structuralism* (Ithaca: Cornell University Press, 1982); Christopher Norris, *Deconstruction: Theory and Practice* (London: Routledge, 1982) and *The Deconstructive Turn* (London: Methuen, 1983).

The limits of mythopoesis

For thinking about the relation of scientific explanation to culture, the obvious starting-point is Thomas Kuhn, *The Structure of Scientific Revolutions*, 2nd edn (Chicago: University of Chicago Press, 1970). For the way scientific explanation relates to religion and myth, see Ian Barbour, "Paradigms in Science and Religion," in Gary Gutting, ed., *Paradigms and Revolutions* (South Bend, IN: University of Notre Dame Press, 1980). The quotation from Kafka is from *Parables and Paradoxes* (New York: Schocken, 1970).

Institutional and post-institutional aesthetics

An historical art world

George Dickie provides an historically sensitive approach to an institutional theory of aesthetics; see George Dickie, *Art and the Aesthetic: An Institutional*

Analysis (Ithaca: Cornell University Press, 1974), *The Art Circle* (New York: Haven, 1984), *Evaluating Art* (Philadelphia: Temple University Press, 1988), and particularly *The Century of Taste* (Oxford: Oxford University Press, 1996). In a very different vein, Arthur Danto explores the interaction of theory and practice in *The Transfiguration of the Commonplace* (Cambridge, MA: Harvard University Press, 1981) and *The Philosophical Disenfranchisement of Art* (New York: Columbia University Press, 1986). The eighteenth-century background is discussed by David Spadafora, *The Idea of Progress in Eighteenth-Century Britain* (New Haven: Yale University Press, 1990) and Martha Woodmansee, *The Author, Art, and the Market* (New York: Columbia University Press, 1994). For patronage at court, see Michael Levy, *Painting at Court* (New York: New York University Press, 1971). For a provocative although somewhat superficial look at the current art world, see Tom Wolfe, *The Painted Word* (New York: Bantam, 1976).

The role of theory

For the interaction of history and style, see David Carrier, *Principles of Art History Writing* (University Park: Pennsylvania State University Press, 1991) and Berel Lang, *The Anatomy of Philosophical Style* (Oxford: Blackwell, 1990). The appearance of Veronese before the Inquisition is found in Paolo Veronese, "Trial Before the Holy Tribunal," in Elizabeth Gilmore Holt, ed., *Literary Sources of Art History* (Princeton: Princeton University Press, 1947).

Post-institutional aesthetics

Among the many books that claim the term postmodernism, one might consider Fredric Jameson, *Postmodernism, or, the Cultural Logic of Late Capitalism* (Durham, NC: Duke University Press, 1991); Charles Jencks, *What is Post-Modernism?* (London: Academy Editions, 1986); and Jean-François Lyotard, *The Postmodern Condition: A Report on Knowledge* (Minneapolis: University of Minnesota Press, 1984). A useful anthology that covers the historical development and different approaches is Lawrence E. Cahoone, ed., *From Modernism to Postmodernism* (Oxford: Blackwell, 1996). A virtual definition of modernism in aesthetics can be found in §§6–8 and §22 of Immanuel Kant, *Critique of Judgment* (Indianapolis: Hackett, 1987), where subjectivity and universality are combined in a single form of judgment. In postmodern aesthetics, a useful anthology is Hugh J. Silverman, ed., *Postmodernism: Philosophy and the Arts* (New York: Routledge, 1990); see also Peter J. McCormick, *Modernity, Aesthetics, and the Bounds of Art* (Ithaca: Cornell University Press, 1990). For textuality, see William V. Spanos, Paul A. Bove, and Daniel O'Hara, eds, *The Question of Textuality* (Bloomington: Indiana University Press, 1982), and Susan R. Suleiman and Inge Crosman, eds, *The Reader in the Text* (Princeton: Princeton University Press, 1980). Among the works that explore other alternatives to traditional modernist aesthetics see David Novitz, *Knowledge, Fiction and Imagination* (Philadelphia: Temple University Press, 1987); Peg Brand and Carolyn Korsmeyer, eds, *Feminism and Tradition in*

214 The Artist and the Audience

Aesthetics (State College, PA: Pennsylvania University Press, 1995); and Hilde Hein and Carolyn Korsmeyer, eds, *Aesthetics in Feminist Perspective* (Bloomington: Indiana University Press, 1993).

A conclusion in which nothing is concluded

"The world is the totality of facts, not of things" quotes Ludwig Wittgenstein from the *Tractatus-Logico-Philosophicus* (London: Routledge, Kegan Paul, 1961).

Appendix

This appendix contains some texts that are referred to in the preceding chapters. They may prove useful as examples for further analysis.

Sir Thomas Wyatt (1503–42), "Who So List to Hunt"

Who so list to hunt, I know where is an hind,
But as for me, alas, I may no more;
The vain travail hath wearied me so sore,
I am of them that farthest cometh behind.
Yet may I by no means my wearied mind
Draw from the deer; but as she fleeth afore,
Fainting I follow. I leave off therefore,
Since in a net I seek to hold the wind.
Who list her hunt, I put him out of doubt,
As well as I may spend his time in vain;
And, graven with diamonds, in letters plain
There is written her fair neck round about:
"*Noli me tangere*, for Caesar's I am;
And wild for to hold, though I seem tame."

Giorgio Vasari (1511–74), on Jacopo Pontormo

But that which most displeased other men in him was that he would not work save when and for whom he pleased, and after his own fancy; wherefore on many occasions, being sought out by noblemen who desired to have some of his work, and once in particular by the Magnificent Ottaviano de' Medici, he wouldnot serve them; and then he would set himself to do anything in the world for some low and common fellow, at a miserable price . . . For the whole work [a fresco in San Lorenzo, now lost] is full of nude figures with an order, design, invention, composition, coloring, and painting contrived after his own fashion, and with such uneasiness and so little satisfaction for him who beholds the work, that I am determined, since I myself do not understand it, although I am a painter, to leave all who may see it to form their own judgment, for the reason that I believe that I would drive myself mad with it and would lose myself, even as it appears to me that Jacopo in the period of eleven years that he spent upon it sought to lose himself and all who might see the painting, among all those extraordinary figures. (From Robert Klein and Henri Zerner, eds, *Italian Art, 1500–1600: Sources and Documents* (Englewood Cliffs, NJ: Prentice-Hall, 1966): 80, 83.)

Christopher Marlowe (1564–93), *Tamburlaine the Great*

Nature, that framed us of four elements
Warring within our breasts for regiment,
Doth teach us all to have aspiring minds.
Our soul, whose faculties can comprehend
The wondrous architecture of the world
And measure every wandering planet's course,
Still climbing after knowledge infinite,
And always moving as the restless spheres,
Wills us to wear ourselves and never rest
Until we reach the ripest fruit of all,
That perfect bliss and sole felicity,
The sweet fruition of an earthly crown.
(Part One, Act 2, Scene 7, ll. 18–29)

William Shakespeare (1564–1616), *Hamlet*

Hamlet: I have of late – but wherefore I know not – lost all my mirth, forgone all custom of exercises; and indeed it goes so heavily with my disposition, that this goodly frame the earth seems to me a sterile promontory, this most excellent canopy the air, look you, this brave o'er-hanging firmament, this majestical roof fretted with golden fire, why it appeareth nothing to me but a foul and pestilent congregation of vapors. What a piece of work is man, how noble in reason, how infinite in faculties, in form and moving, how express and admirable in action, how like an angel in apprehension, how like a god: the beauty of the world, the paragon of animals. And yet to me, what is this quintessence of dust? Man delights not me, nor woman neither, though by your smiling you seem to say so. [*The punctuation of this passage is disputed. An alternative is:* What a piece of work is man, how noble in reason, how infinite in faculties, in form and moving how express and admirable, in action how like an angel, in apprehension how like a god: the beauty of the world, the paragon of animals. And yet to me, what is this quintessence of dust? Man delights not me, nor woman neither, though by your smiling you seem to say so.] (Act 2, Scene 2, ll. 278–89)

Henry Fielding (1707–54), *Tom Jones*

Mr. Jones having spent three hours in reading and kissing the aforesaid letter [from Sophia Western], and being, at last, in a state of good spirits, from the last mentioned considerations, he agreed to carry an appointment which he had before made, into execution. This was to attend Mrs. Miller, and her younger daughter, into the gallery at the playhouse, and to admit Mr. Partridge as one of the company. For as Jones had really that taste for humour which many affect, he expected to enjoy much entertainment in the criticisms of Partridge; from whom he expected the simple dictates of nature, unimproved indeed, but likewise unadulterated by art.

In the first row then of the first gallery did Mr. Jones, Mrs. Miller, her youngest daughter, and Partridge, take their places. Partridge immediately declared, it was the finest place he had ever been in. When the first musick was played, he said, "It was a wonder how so many fidlers could play at one time, without putting one another out." While the fellow was lighting the upper candles, he cried out to Mrs. Miller, "Look, look, madam, the very picture of the man in the end of the Common-Prayer Book, before the Gunpowder-Treason service." Nor could he help observing, with a sigh, when all the candles were lighted, "That here were candles enough burnt in one night, to keep an honest poor family for a whole twelve-month".

As soon as the play, which was *Hamlet Prince of Denmark*, began, Partridge was all attention, nor did he break silence till the entrance of the ghost; upon which he asked Jones, "What man that was in the strange dress; something," said he, "like what I have seen in a picture. Sure it is not armour, is it?" Jones answered, "That is the ghost". To which Partridge replied with a smile, "Persuade me to that, Sir, if you can. Though I can't say I ever actually saw a ghost in my life, yet I am certain I should know one, if I saw him, better than that comes to. No, no, Sir, ghosts don't appear in such dresses as that, neither". In this mistake, which caused much laughter in the neighbourhood of Partridge, he was suffered to continue, 'till the scene between the ghost and Hamlet, when Partridge gave that credit to Mr. Garrick, which he had denied to Jones, and fell into so violent a trembling, that his knees knocked against each other. Jones asked him what was the matter, and whether he was afraid of the warrior upon the stage? "O la! sir," said he, "I perceive now it is what you told me. I am not afraid of anything; for I know it is but a play: and if it was really a ghost, it could do no harm at such a distance, and in so much company; and yet if I was frightened, I am not the only person". "Why, who", cries Jones, "dost thou take to be such a coward here besides thyself?" "Nay, you may call me coward if you will; but if that little man there upon the stage is not frightened, I never saw any man frightened in my life. Ay, ay; go along with you! Ay, to be sure! Who's fool then? Will you? Lud have mercy upon such fool-hardiness! – Whatever happens it is good enough for you. – *Follow you*? I'd follow the devil as soon. Nay, perhaps, it is the devil – for they say he can put on what likeness he pleases. – Oh! here he is again. – *No farther!* No, you have gone far enough already; farther than I'd have gone for all the King's dominions". Jones offered to speak, but Partridge cried, "Hush, hush, dear sir, don't you hear him!" And during the whole speech of the ghost, he sat with his eyes fixed partly on the ghost, and partly on Hamlet, and with his mouth open; the same passions which succeeded each other in Hamlet, succeeding likewise in him.

When the scene was over, Jones said, "Why, Partridge, you exceed my expectations. You enjoy the play more than I conceived possible". "Nay, sir", answered Partridge, "if you are not afraid of the devil, I can't help it; but to be sure it is natural to be surprized at such things, though I know there is nothing in them: not that it was the ghost that surprized me neither; for I should have known that to have been only a man in a strange dress: but when I saw the little man so frightened himself, it was that which took hold of me". "And dost thou imagine then, Partridge", cries Jones, "that he was really frightened?" "Nay, sir", said Partridge, "did not you yourself observe afterwards, when he found out it was his own father's spirit, and how he was murdered in the garden, how his fear forsook him by degrees, and he was struck dumb with sorrow, as it were, just as I should have been, had it been my own case. – But hush! O la! What noise is that? There he is again. – Well, to be certain, though I know there is nothing at all in it, I am glad I am not down yonder, where those men are". Then turning his eyes again upon Hamlet, "Ay, you may draw your sword; what signifies a sword against the power of the devil?"

During the second act, Partridge made very few remarks. He greatly admired the fineness of the dresses; nor could he help observing upon the king's countenance. "Well", said he, "how people may be deceived by faces? *Nulla fides fronti* is, I find, a true saying. Who would think, by looking in the king's face, that he had ever committed a murder?" He then enquired after the ghost; but Jones, who intended he should be surprised, gave him no other satisfaction, than "that he might possibly see him again soon, and in a flash of fire".

Partridge sat in fearful expectation of this; and now, when the ghost made his next appearance, Partridge cried out, "There, sir, now; what say you now? Is he frightened now or no? As much frightened as you think me, and, to be sure, nobody can help some fears, I would not be in so bad a condition as what's his name, Squire Hamlet, is there, for all the world. Bless me! What's become of the spirit? As I am a living soul, I thought I saw him sink into the earth". "Indeed, you saw right", answered Jones. "Well, well", cries Partridge, "I know it is only a play; and besides, if there was anything in all this, Madame Miller would not laugh so: for as to you, sir, you would not be afraid, I believe, if the devil was here in person. – There, there – Ay, no wonder you are in such a passion; shake the vile wicked wretch to pieces. If she was my own mother I should serve her so. To be sure, all duty to a mother is forfeited by such wicked doings. – Ay, go about your business: I hate the sight of you".

Our critic was now pretty silent till the play, which Hamlet introduces before the king. This he did not at first understand, 'till

Jones explained it to him; but he no sooner entered into the spirit of it, than he began to bless himself that he had never committed murder. Then turning to Mrs. Miller, he asked her, "If she did not imagine the king looked as if he was touched; though he is", said he, "a good actor, and doth all he can to hide it. Well, I would not have so much to answer for, as that wicked man there hath, to sit upon a much higher chair than he sits upon. – No wonder he run away; for your sake I'll never trust an innocent face again".

The grave-digging scene next engaged the attention of Partridge, who expressed much surprize at the number of skulls thrown upon the stage. To which Jones answered, "That it was one of the most famous burial-places about town". "No wonder then", cries Partridge, "that the place is haunted. But I never saw in my life a worse grave-digger. I had a sexton, when I was clerk, that should have dug three graves while he is digging one. The fellow handles a spade as if it was the first time he had ever had one in his hand. Ay, ay, you may sing. You had rather sing than work, I believe". – Upon Hamlet's taking up the skull, he cried out, "Well, it is strange to see how fearless some men are: I never could bring myself to touch anything belonging to a dead man on any account. – He seemed frightened enough too at the ghost I thought. *Nemo omnibus horis sapit*".

Little more worth remembering occurred during the play; at the end of which Jones asked him, "which of the players he had liked best?" To this he answered, with some appearance of indignation at the question. "The king without doubt". – "Indeed, Mr. Partridge", says Mrs. Miller, "you are not of the same opinion with the town; for they are all agreed, that Hamlet is acted by the best player who was ever on the stage". "He the best player!" cries Partridge, with a contemptuous sneer, "Why I could act as well as he myself. I am sure if I had seen a ghost, I should have looked in the very same manner, and done just as he did. And then, to be sure, in that scene, as you called it, between him and his mother, where you told me he acted so fine, why, Lord help me, any man, that is, any good man, that had had such a mother, would have done exactly the same. I know you are only joking with me; but, indeed, madam, though I was never at a play in London, yet I have seen acting before in the country; and the king for my money; he speaks all his words distinctly, half as loud again as the other. – Anybody may see he is an actor".

While Mrs. Miller was thus engaged in conversation with Partridge, a lady came up to Mr. Jones, whom he immediately knew to be Mrs. Fitzpatrick. She said, she had seen him from the other part of the gallery, and had taken that opportunity of speaking to him, as she had something to say, which might be of great service to himself. She then acquainted him with her lodgings, and made him an appointment the next day in the morning; which, upon recollection, she presently changed to the afternoon; at which time Jones promised to attend her.

Thus ended the adventure at the playhouse; where Partridge had afforded great mirth, not only to Jones and Mrs. Miller, but to all who sat within hearing, who were more attentive to what he said, than to anything that passed on the stage.

He durst not go to bed all that night, for fear of the ghost; and for many nights after, sweated two or three hours before he went to sleep, with the same apprehensions, and waked several times in great horrors, crying out, "Lord have mercy upon us! there it is". (Book 16, Chapter 5, "In which Jones receives a Letter from Sophia, and goes to a Play with Mrs. Miller and Partridge")

Glossary

The terms in this glossary are all used in the text. This glossary is not a substitute for a dictionary. It does not try to give complete definitions or accounts of the terms listed, nor is it a substitute for the contextual definition that comes from reading. One should not expect difficult, complex philosophical concepts to be reducible to two or three sentences. It is intended to provide some additional assistance to students in understanding some technical terms and the special sense of some common words as they are used in philosophy.

abstract expressionism   In art, the movement that abandons completely the notion of a picture as a representation of something else and seeks to present directly the expressionist characteristics of color and form. The movement emerged in the 1940s in New York. Prominent painters who belonged to the movement included Jackson Pollock, Willem de Kooning, and Robert Motherwell.

ad hoc   An explanation or theory that is designed to fit a specific case. Ad hoc explanations are limited to the case that they cover and are thus not useful as more general theories.

aesthetic attitude   The approach to aesthetic experience that depends on the viewer or reader adopting, usually voluntarily, a special way of looking or reading. An aesthetic attitude is sometimes described as an impressionistic way of seeing because it focuses on the immediate impression that the object makes.

aesthetic experience   The experience of aesthetic objects. If it is characterized independently of its objects, aesthetic experience is taken to be a kind of experience that is free of both theoretical concepts and practical ends. It is sometimes characterized as a form of contemplation or as a singular form of experience that does not look beyond its own immediate content.

aesthetic feeling   The emotion that is raised in a viewer or reader by art or aesthetic objects. Because aesthetics is about the subjective appropriation of an object, feeling or emotion is the central form that aesthetics takes.

aesthetic intuition   The basis for all theories of aesthetics that claim that aesthetic experience is itself a way of knowing something. Many theorists insist that aesthetics is a form of direct knowing. Instead of explaining what is known in terms of some other form of perception or sense data, they make use of a special form of aesthetic perception that they call aesthetic intuition.

aesthetic object   The object that is singled out as what an aesthetic experience is about. An aesthetic object is the content of some perception or the cause of some feeling or intuition. It may be understood in terms of aesthetic experience as the object of that experience, or it may be characterized independently as the object that appears directly in perception. At its simplest, an aesthetic object is either a work of art or some natural object that is sufficiently like a work of art to be classified in the same way.

aesthetic pleasure   The pleasure that is associated with art and beauty. Art and beauty, when they are experienced, are thought to produce a pleasant feeling or emotion. Sometimes aesthetic pleasure is understood as a special form of pleasure different from other pleasant feelings in some way.

aesthetic predicates   In aesthetic judgments, the words used to describe art or beautiful things. Aesthetic predicates may be adjectives such as 'graceful' used metaphorically or they may be understood as directly descriptive words.

aesthetics   The discipline within philosophy that deals with art, beauty, and the feelings and emotions associated with them. In the arts, 'aesthetics' also refers directly to the modes of feeling and response associated with the arts.

affective state   A mental or emotional response to something. An affective state is distinguished from the physical state that corresponds to it and from the causes of it.

allegorical   A method of representation in the arts where multiple levels of meaning are associated with one thing. Allegory was especially prominent in classical and medieval literature and in biblical interpretation, where a theory of allegorical interpretation was carefully developed.

alliteration   In literature, particularly poetry, the repetition of sounds at the beginning of words. Alliteration links words by their beginning sound.

anthropology   The discipline devoted to the study of human origins and cultural structures.

apocalyptic events   The events that accompany a catastrophic end to the world. The apocalypse is the destruction of the world expected in myth so that a new creation can take place.

archaic   In anthropology and the study of myth, the common structure of cultures that depend on myth and ritual, rather than history, to explain events. 'Archaic' is used as a descriptive adjective; it does not imply a negative judgment.

art world   The complex of people and institutions that are associated with the creation, dissemination, and criticism of art. The term has become common as a way of referring to anyone or anything that is closely related to art.

artifact   A physical object that carries some cultural or artistic significance. Artifacts are things made by someone for some purpose.

association of ideas   In the eighteenth century, the explanation for how ideas could give rise to other ideas, particularly in moving from simple to more complex ideas.

auteur **theory**   In film theory, the claim that a director's entire body of work constitutes a single whole that shows the director's artistic intent and purpose. *Auteur* theory should be distinguished from the simple claim that the director is the author of a single film.

avant-garde   Literally, the advance party before an army; hence, those artists who are ahead of their time culturally. The avant-garde in art is self-consciously opposed to the received tradition.

beauty   In aesthetics, the property of objects that produces a special aesthetic pleasure. In classical theories, beauty is closely related to harmony and proportion and to an intelligible quality that transcends a particular thing.

Bloomsbury group   The group of writers, artists, and intellectuals centered in London's Bloomsbury Square in the early part of the twentieth century and known for their aestheticism, intellectualism, and disdain for Edwardian conventions. The group included Virginia and Leonard Woolf, Clive and Vanessa Bell, Lytton Strachey, and John Maynard Keynes.

canon   In criticism, particularly literary criticism, the idea that a body of work is culturally central. What constitutes the canon for a culture is usually a matter of broad critical agreement but specific disputes over details.

catharsis   In dramatic theory, the point in a tragedy where the plot is resolved so that the emotional significance is transformed. Catharsis is understood as an effect both on the protagonist in the plot and on the audience.

chaos   Mythologically, the state prior to the imposition of order. Chaos represents the lack of all order; its opposite is an organized world, a cosmos.

chaos theory   In recent mathematics, the theory of a kind of equation whose solutions are sensitive to initial conditions in a special way. Unlike linear equations, where a small change in initial conditions produces only a small change in the outcome, in chaotic systems a small change in initial conditions can produce large changes in outcome. The solutions to chaotic equations produce the appearance of order over a limited range, but that order breaks down over a wider range. There may be a number of limited centers of order. Chaos theory has been extended to aesthetics and literary theory to account for the appearance of a limited order that does not apply absolutely.

circularity   In philosophy, the form of an argument where the conclusion merely restates some part of the premises. Circular arguments are "vicious" if the restatement is so close that nothing illuminating has been shown.

collective unconscious   In psychology, particularly the psychology influenced by Carl Jung, the theory that individual humans share a common psychological structure that includes symbols and images. The collective unconscious is supposed to become conscious through literature, dreams, and psychoanalytic investigation.

concept   In philosophy, concepts are the ideas or ideational structures that give order to thought. A particular concept is the content of a thought. Concepts can be understood as ideal, psychological, or neural states.

content   In philosophy and the theory of language, that part of a sentence, belief, or thought that carries the meaning. Content is distinguished from form, which is understood as the means for making the meaning known.

cosmological   Anything having to do with the universe or ordered world as a whole. Cosmology attempts to describe the universal conditions in which we exist.

cosmos   In mythology, the ordered existence in which both gods and humans live. Cosmos is opposed to chaos as order to disorder on the highest level.

counter-examples   In philosophy, a way of arguing by showing that some argument leads to cases or claims that are clearly unacceptable. If an argument can be made to result in such a claim, then the claim is a counter-example to the argument.

critical formalism   In criticism and theory, the approach that bases its claims solely on the formal elements that a work exhibits. Critical formalism does not use historical, biographical, or psychological information to explain the meaning of a work.

deconstruction   The movement that opposes structuralism and rejects its claims to be able to show the significance of some object, cultural artifact, or cultural practice from the construction of it. Deconstruction attempts to undermine claims to methodological independence by show-ing how methods can always be used to produce more than one result. The movement is associated most closely with the work of the French philosopher and critic Jacques Derrida.

deus ex machina   In dramatic theory, the introduction of some super-natural being that has not appeared earlier to bring about the ending of the plot. By extension, in philosophy, any unexplained outside force used to resolve difficulties.

dialectic   In medieval philosophy, the method of working by logical opposition, and by extension, any argument that depended on reason and logic rather than authority. More generally, dialectic is the use of opposition to argue for some third position. Dialectic can also refer to an opposition of things or positions themselves.

didactic   Having to do with teaching. Particularly in literature, didactic works have as their purpose teaching something.

dilemma   A logical form that presents two options, one of which must be the case, or two opposed claims that lead to the same conclusion. The form of a dilemma most generally goes: "If A, then B" and "If C, then D"; "either A or B"; therefore, "either C or D". It frequently takes the form "If A then B" and "If C then B"; "either A or C"; therefore "B".

disinterested   In aesthetics, the approach to a work of art that assures that non-aesthetic considerations do not affect one's response. A dis-interested response is free of prejudice, prior expectations and, in some theories, from any theoretical or practical considerations, or even any concern for the existence of the object.

empiricism   The philosophical stance that limits the evidence for know-ing to data available from experience. Empiricism is opposed to ration-alism and to earlier theories that depended on authority, revelation, or innate ideas.

entropy   A term borrowed from the physics of heat where systems move from states with temperature differentials to a state of uniform heat dispersal. Entropy is the tendency of any physical system to arrange itself in a uniform state without differentiation, hence from order (which depends on difference) to disorder (which has no difference from one point to the next).

epic poetry   An extended poetic form that tells a story, usually in terms of the most important myths of a culture, and gives an account of central cultural events.

epistemology   In philosophy, the attempt to give an account of what we know and how we can know it, including what counts as evidence and what, if anything, can be known with certainty.

esoteric   Appealing to, or accessible to, a small, select group. In particular, cults and intellectual groups often claim an esoteric knowledge that cannot be understood by outsiders.

ethics   In philosophy, an attempt to give an account of right actions and the basis for values in human affairs. Ethics includes theories of what kind of values are possible in human action, the meaning of ethical terms such as 'good' and 'evil,' and theories of how to determine what one ought to do.

exemplar   An object or instance of something that shows the nature of a more general category. An exemplar teaches something or gives us a way to know something by showing an instance of it rather than telling us something about it.

expression   In aesthetics, the theory that the mind grasps reality primarily by a process of ordering data, including its own powers.

extension   In philosophy, a list or catalogue of things that correspond to a term. The extension of a term is all of the things that that term names.

form   The basic order of anything, referred to independently of the specific application. The form of something is common to all instances of it, while other aspects apply only in a limited way. In aesthetics, both form and content may be unique to a work of art, however.

futurism   The movement, primarily in Italy before World War I, that sought aesthetic value in the manifestations of the modern, industrial world. Futurism valued the machine, speed, and even war.

genius   In aesthetics, specifically that aspect of a creative artist that is not subject to rules or generalizable explanations and is productive of new work or insights.

gestalt perception   In psychology, the ability to see patterns as a whole.

gestalt properties   Those properties of an object or a representation of an object that only emerge when the whole is perceived. Gestalt properties appear as more than the sum of their parts.

harmony   In philosophy and aesthetics, a pattern, usually expressible mathematically, that links the parts of something into a whole. Harmony is borrowed from music where it specifically refers to the relation between the auditory frequency of tones.

hermeneutics   The theory and method of interpretation. Hermeneutics began as the theory of interpretation of scripture and has come to include the interpretation of any text (even non-verbal texts) that involves the interplay of both the producer and the respondent in an historically changing context.

iambic pentameter   In poetry, the pattern of a line with five stressed syllables arranged in the order of unstressed, stressed [⁻ ´]. An iamb is a single unstressed, stressed unit, and pentameter is five units in a line.

idealism   The philosophical theory that finds mental phenomena to be basic and attempts to account for all knowledge ultimately in terms of mental forms. Philosophical idealism should not be confused with high-mindedness.

identity   In logic, the sameness of two symbols. Strictly, identity requires that there be no significant difference between two things or between what two terms refer to. Identity also characterizes those properties that make something what it is and not something else.

identity criteria   The conditions that allow one to pick out something from other things. In particular, identity criteria allow the assignment of a term or name to all and only those things to which it should apply.

imagination   The power, faculty, or ability to conceive of objects independently of their existence. Imagination is variously regarded in the history of thought, particularly as either an assembling of ideas that do not occur together naturally or the creation of new objects and concepts.

imitation   In aesthetics, making something as a dependent version of something else.

imitation theories Those theories of art that understand the productive process as imposing form on some material that does not possess it naturally.

imperative The linguistic form used to issue commands and instructions.

intentional fallacy The error, in the opinion of some critics, of relying on the biography, psychology, or external statements of the author to determine the meaning of a literary work.

intentional object The object of conscious attention on the part of some individual. The intentional object is the "what" of a specific thought regardless of whether what is thought exists independently of the thinker or not.

intentionality The characteristic of thought as having an object. The intentionality of thought refers to the fact that every conscious thought is about something.

internal sense In aesthetics and ethics, the ability to perceive aesthetic objects and the rightness or wrongness of acts. Originally, internal sense was the power of the mind to unite different sense perceptions into a single perception of an object. Later, it became a kind of sixth sense, a sense without an organ of perception.

ironic Term used of something spoken or written in such a way that its meaning is to be taken in the opposite sense to its literal meaning. Irony is a way of conveying ideas that are easier to state negatively than positively.

je ne sais quoi Literally, "I don't know what." In aesthetics, it is used to explain the cause of an aesthetic quality that can only be experienced, not described or produced according to rules.

metacriticism In aesthetics, the theory that takes critical language as its object and tries to explain aesthetic properties as the application of such language.

metaphor A comparison produced by means of a literal assertion of identity: A is B. "Metaphor" is also used to characterize the basis of all figurative language and as a way of accounting for changes in the meaning of words as they acquire new applications.

metaphysics   That part of philosophy that deals with what there is and how it exists. Metaphysics seeks to describe the fundamental constituents of reality just as physics seeks to describe the fundamental constituents of physical reality and their relations.

modernist   The historical period and way of thinking characterized by appeal to individual reason and individual autonomy. The modernist period begins roughly with the renaissance and may or may not still be with us.

myth   Stories or accounts of the way things came to be "in the beginning" and of their origins, particularly of divine origins. Myth encompasses accounts of the sacred (as opposed to the profane) in all of its manifestations.

mythological drama   Any dramatic portrayal of the mythic beginnings, even if it appears in disguised or allegorical forms.

mythopoesis   The complex of thought and symbolic depiction based on a mythological view of reality. Mythopoesis can be either literal telling of myths or a disguised psychological form of thought that carries mythic meaning.

Narcissus   The Greek boy who refused all love including that of a goddess; as a punishment, he was made to fall in love with his own image in a pool of water, the one image that he could not possess. In some versions of the myth, he pines away and is turned into the flower known by his name (hence the origin of the name of the flower); in other versions, he is drawn to his own image and drowns in the pool.

necessary condition   In logic and philosophy, a condition that every instance of a term must satisfy. If "all A is B," then B is a necessary condition for A. Simply because A is B, however does not imply that being a B is sufficient for being an A, so a condition can be necessary without being sufficient.

neo-classical   The period, particularly in literature and art history, that consciously tried to revive and apply what were taken to be classical rules and values in art. Neo-classical art and literature are characterized by a formality of style and a subject-matter that draws on myth and classical legend, either directly or indirectly.

neo-Platonism   The school and style of philosophy based on the work of Plotinus (204–70). Neo-Platonism conceives of reality as arranged in related, dependent levels from the highest, which is undifferentiated unity and reality, to the lowest, which is matter and lacks all being.

open terms   Those words whose reference is determined by their use in such a way that they do not have sharply defined boundaries. An open term clearly applies to central cases, but at the limits of its application does not allow a definite "yes" or "no."

originality   In aesthetics, the property of some works of art that makes them new and independent of what has appeared before. Originality only becomes a positive value if newness itself is valued.

paradigm   A model or central case that can be used to define or describe a larger set of cases. A paradigm defines by providing an example.

perceptual object   The object that appears in the act of perceiving, just as it is perceived. A perceptual object is distinguished from both the external object that causes the perception and the mode of perception. Thus, a perceptual object is the same whether it is real or imagined.

performance art   The contemporary art form that makes use of improvisation and the immediacy of an actual event. Performance art breaks with the tradition that art is supposed to be the production of some permanent object.

performative language   Language that both says something and at the same time makes what it says the case. For example, an umpire who says "Out!" both tells us that the player is out and makes the player out at the same time.

persona   The hypothetical speaker or producer of a work of art. The authorial persona is presented by the work and need not have the same characteristics as the actual author.

phenomenal   Appearing directly to perception. A phenomenal appearance is limited to what is immediately available to perception.

phenomenon   Whatever appears to perception. A phenomenon is the immediate presentational form independently of either its underlying causes or its effects.

photo-realism   The movement in recent painting that presents a picture so that it looks like a photograph. By exaggerating the ability of paint to reproduce an image, photo-realism draws attention to the fact that reproduction is actually controlled by the painter.

picturesque   The properties of a natural scene that suggest a painting. The picturesque reverses the move from object to painting by modeling nature after art.

Platonism   The philosophical movement that traces its origins to Plato. "Platonism" is applied generally to any philosophical position that asserts the existence of forms independently of the objects that have the form.

pop art   The movement in art that takes ordinary objects or trivial events and makes them the object of art. Pop art challenges the idea that some objects are more suitable for art then others.

possible world   In logic and some philosophical approaches, any arrangement of terms or objects that does not involve a logical contradiction. Possible worlds are all of the arrangements of things (or terms) that are internally coherent regardless of whether anything is actually that way. The actual world is one of many possible worlds.

postmodern   Postmodernism refers to the psychological, cultural, political, and philosophical awareness of a world that is conditioned by economic, social, and material forces and by a radical subjectivity in thought but no longer takes individual autonomy as a given basis for truth. The term is so widely used with such different connotations that one must approach it as a generic characterization of the rejection of optimistic western individualism and then try to find its specific use from context.

practice   In philosophy, those activities that are sufficient to define the meaning of terms. Attention to a practice shifts the question of what some term or set of terms means from definitions to what people who use the term do.

profane   Ordinary reality conceived as dependent on and opposed to a sacred reality that supports it. The profane can only exist because of the sacred; without the sacred, the profane would return to chaos.

psychic   Term used of that part of reality belonging to the mind.

psychical distance   Edward Bullough's term to describe the psychological states conducive to aesthetic experience. Psychical distance is a metaphor for a way of perceiving some object.

rationalists   Those philosophers, particularly followers of René Descartes, who conceive of knowledge as an orderly, logical arrangement of clear and distinct ideas. Rationalists hold that certain knowledge, on the model of mathematics, is available in all areas by reference to a set of ideas (innate ideas) that belong to the mind itself.

renaissance   The period in western cultural history, beginning roughly in the mid-fourteenth century in Italy and continuing until as late as the seventeenth century in northern Europe, that saw a rejection of medieval conceptions of knowledge based on authority and an assertion of the individual as an independent, creative actor. The renaissance thought of itself as a rebirth of classical culture, but in fact it represented a new dependence on science and individual experience.

rhetoric   In classical and medieval education, one element, along with logic and grammar, of the basic division of knowledge. Rhetoric deals with the presentational forms of language, and in recent thought it has become a discipline that considers all elements of language-dependent thought.

ritual   The acting out of myth in a religious performance according to carefully prescribed conditions. Ritual is a way of making a religiously significant story present and effective.

romanticism   The movement in literature and related cultural forms that asserts the autonomy and importance of art as a creative, original expression of human powers. Romanticism begins in the late eighteenth or early nineteenth century and attempts to reassert the powers of myth and poetry as creative forces.

scientific revolution   The break with the classical science based on Aristotle's work and the assertion of the importance of empirical evidence rather than deductive reasoning. The scientific revolution begins in the sixteenth century or earlier with thinkers such as Galileo who insist on the priority of their own observations over what "must" be there according to some logical or theological requirements.

simile   An explicit comparison, centrally of the form "A is like B." A simile links two terms and focuses on some relation between them.

sonnet   A verse form of fourteen lines on a single subject, often divided into an eight-line beginning and a six-line conclusion. A sonnet may have one of several different rhyme schemes.

speech act   In the philosophy of language, the approach to language centered on recognition that saying something is always also an act of some kind. A speech act may have a number of different forms, ranging from assertion to evocation, in addition to expressing some thought.

sublime   In aesthetics, the effect produced by large, great, or grand subjects and presentations. The sublime was taken to be a different kind of aesthetic experience from that produced by beauty. The sublime is characterized by awe approaching fear and pain.

substance   In philosophy, that aspect of anything that supports its existence and properties. Substance is distinguished from accidents, which are properties that can change without changing the identity of the object.

sufficient condition   In logic and philosophy, those conditions or properties that serve to locate anything having the property in some class or set. To know a sufficient condition is to be able to say of an object that has that property that it belongs to a class or set, but not that every object of that class has that particular property. For example, having the set of properties that makes some animal a beagle is sufficient to make that animal a dog, but not all dogs are beagles.

surrealism   The movement in twentieth-century painting and poetry that sought by means of symbols drawn from dreams and the unconscious to depict a different kind or level of reality. Prominent surrealists included André Breton and Salvador Dali.

taste   In aesthetics and criticism, the name for a sensory ability like the physical sense of taste associated with the tongue that enables someone to perceive the aesthetic properties of things and guides judgment to choose between good aesthetic experiences and experiences that fail aesthetically.

theory   In philosophy and science, high-level explanatory statements that systematize what is known and guide further observation. Theories are confirmed or rejected on the basis of their ability to explain particular observations that are true or false and to avoid contradictions, inconsistency, and predictions that are not accurate.

tragedy   The dramatic form that shows a person better than most who, as a result of some irreconcilable set of moral, religious, or civic demands, suffers in such a way that some greater good is affirmed. Tragedy is exemplified by sets of plays from classical Athens and Elizabethan England.

trompe l'oeil   A kind of painting intended to fool the eye in an illusionistic way. The most common *trompe l'oeil* paintings give the illusion of three-dimensional architectural features.

type/token distinction   A common distinction used in philosophy to refer to a single entity by means of multiple instances of a symbol. A type is one thing, perhaps abstract or ideal; its tokens are multiple instances, each of which represents the same type. For example, there are two tokens of the letter "y" in the previous sentence.

Index